DAVID KINDON

Climbing
the
Silver
Pyramid

novum ◢ pro

This book is also available as e-book.

www.novum-publishing.co.uk

© 2022 novum publishing

ISBN 978-3-99107-639-1
Editing: Hugo Chandler, BA
Cover photos: Victoria Porkhun, Chunni4691 | Dreamstime.com; David Kindon
Cover design, layout & typesetting: novum publishing
Internal illustrations: David Kindon

The images provided by the author have been printed in the highest possible quality.

www.novum-publishing.co.uk

*I DEDICATE THIS BOOK TO THE SUPPORTERS, STAFF
AND PLAYERS OF TAUNTON TOWN FOOTBALL CLUB*

*May the glorious claret and blue plumage
of The Peacocks never lose a feather,
Dave.*

ACKNOWLEDGEMENTS

Sincere and heartfelt thanks to the following people for their invaluable contribution to this project and for giving me a deeper insight into the Beautiful Game.

Greg Coulson	Chairman	Westbury United FC
Sean Rothwell	Referee	Football Association
Andy Power	Secretary	Taunton Town FC
Matt Wright	Captain	Taunton Town FC
Rob Wenham	Head Steward	Taunton Town FC
Dan Carter	Mascot	Taunton Town FC
Keith Tuckwell	Supporter	Billericay Town FC
John Croot	Director	Chesterfield FC
Neil Shipperley	Ex Player	Crystal Palace FC
Trevor Higgins	Manager	Elburton Villa FC
Richard Walker	Head of Media	Watford FC
Gary Cotterill	Reporter	Sky Sports News

Barry Silkman	Agent	Professional Football
Tom Sampson	County Rep	Devon FA
John Martindale	Rival	Subbuteo

"Football is undoubtably the oldest of all English national sports. For at least six centuries, the people have loved the rush and struggle of the rude and manly game ... and Kings with their edicts ... divines with their sermons ... scholars with their cultured scorn ... and wits with their ridicule, have failed to keep the people away from the pastime they enjoy."

SIR MONTAGUE SHEARMAN
(English Judge and Athlete)
Late 19th century

FROM KIMBERLEY TO WEMBLEY

10) MONEY MAKES THE BALL GO ROUND
Crystal Palace v Tottenham

11) ROY AT THE ROVERS
Doncaster v Crystal Palace

12) THE EAGLES ARE LANDED
Watford v Crystal Palace

13) THE RETURN OF MAGIC MIKE
Watford v Wolves

14) BLACK DOG AND A BLUE MOON
Manchester City v Watford

A RIDE WITH ME

A long time ago in a stadium, far, far away …

I blame a footballer called Kevin Keegan for not only my love of the FA Cup, but of football itself.

May the fourth is celebrated by fans of ancient galactic religions, wizardry and space pirates, but for me, that date in 1974 is as momentous to this fifty-three year old Englishman as Wembley Stadium stands as an iconic symbol to generations of football fans brought up kicking, screaming and falling in love, watching the greatest sporting competition in the world.

A few years before Luke Skywalker destroyed the Death Star and Han Solo blasted his way onto the silver screen, it was the green hallowed turf of our national stadium on which Keegan and his team mate Steve Heighway blasted three goals between them and destroyed Newcastle United's hopes of returning to their north east base with the famous silver trophy.

The future captain of England replaced musician Bryan Ferry and, before him, my dad as a hero, and as far as my immediate family was concerned, I was lost. The boy who was still young enough to dream grew into a troubled teenager with a chip on his shoulder, a 'rebel without a clue'.

Time took away the magic of Christmas and birthdays became just a number, but the FA Cup final was always there, keeping me on the good side of the law. Non-scripted but dramatic. No musical lyrics, yet poetic. And it was real.

The idea for this book was simple but took on a life of its own. Starting with the Cup's preliminary rounds I watched Saltash United, geographically the nearest team to my doorstep who had a home tie in mid-August. I followed them until their elimination and then their victors until they lost and so on ...

Nine months later, having travelled over five and a half thousand miles, I completed an epic journey through all fourteen stages of the competition. An adventure which started in Cornwall took me to Wiltshire, Gloucestershire, Somerset, Essex, Derbyshire, Surrey, Yorkshire, Hertfordshire and ended at Wembley in north London.

There are fourteen chapters in 'Climbing the Silver Pyramid' representing each round of the 2018-19 FA Cup, and each one includes interviews with football folk involved in all aspects of the game, a match report and a nostalgic nod back to the notable Cup finals of the competition's glorious past.

But what happened to the FA Cup? Why has it lost it's appeal to generations of football fans? How does the pyramid in English football work?

Money it seems has replaced the magic.

This journey was just as much about investigating the reasons why as much as it was about the glory. Coming out of depression in January 2017, I decided to give myself a long-term target to ensure my personal focus steadied itself on the track known as life contentment. Thus, my life was dominated on this nine-month quest as two ticks appeared on my bucket list.

The structure of our national game is unique and in my opinion, the best on the planet. I want this book to go some way to explain why anyone born post the mid-1980's possesses more passion for The Premiership and only holds a mild sense of curiosity as to why the older generation's love of the FA Cup remains strong.

Whatever age you are, and what ever team you follow, I'm sure you'll agree that football is still and will always remain 'The Beautiful Game'.

DAVID KINDON
JULY 2019

"Lose your dreams and you may lose your mind."
MICK JAGGER

Chapter One

DASHES TO ASHES

If looks could kill! The Cornishman says nothing at first, but his eyes say it all. His glare bores into my confused look. What have I done to deserve such a warm welcome in the most westerly county in England? Then it dawns on me. I've had the nerve to park outside his house. What was I thinking? Stupidly taking for granted that I could park a taxed car on a public highway! Ah, but that's not the point is it. Not only is it his house; but it's his pavement, his road, his empire. Not content with having a driveway, this local resident of east Cornwall wants the whole damn street to himself and probably the playing fields that separates his castle and Kimberly Stadium, home of Saltash United Football Club.

"You're one of those aren't you!". It's more of an accusation than a question.

"One of what?" I needlessly ask because I know which angle he's coming from.

"That lot!". He points eastward in the direction of the Tamar Bridge which spans the river between Devon and Cornwall. And he's right, I am one of that lot. I'm English, I'm the devil!

Cornish folklore has it that when Isambard Kingdom Brunel designed the railway bridge which joins Plymouth to the county the locals call 'Kernow', he was in fact giving the Devil a route directly into God's Country. Since the mid-nineteenth century a certain amount of resentment has built up in this Duchy towards the rest of the English race. Politically and professionally Cornwall may be a part of the UK, but from an emotional point of view Plymouth the 'City of Pilgrims' may as well be the natural Land's End.

Today Cornwall may as well be another country. The self-appointed traffic enforcement officer of Warfelton Crescent sees me as a foreigner, but I haven't got time for this territorial shit. I'm going to miss the kick-off between Saltash, known as 'The Ashes' and their opponents today, Odd Down from Bath. This is the first game of fourteen in this season's FA Cup which signifies not only the start of a great adventure for me but also fulfils a promise I made to myself years ago. The start of a nine-month journey and starts are the one thing I hate to miss. So, biting my lip I literally move the car ten yards further up the street just to appease him. Possibly coming back to a scratched company car would be ultimately costly and inconvenient for me, but for the eighteen stone brave warrior it would mean a symbolic and justly strike against the invading enemy. I'm only here to watch a football match for Christ's sake!

Just a few minutes to spare as I cross the playing field and into the ground where it costs a fiver to get in. The reason I've chosen this game as my first is twofold. Firstly, Saltash are geographically the nearest team from my doorstep who have a home tie in this FA Cup preliminary round. The idea is simple. Follow a team in this knockout competition until they are eliminated and then follow their victors. The second reason I've chosen The Ashes is that they have a player called Callum Martindale whose father is a lifelong friend of mine.

Ah, my old mate John Martindale! Both hailing from a place called Efford in Plymouth, we've known each other since primary school. As kids we were keen rivals on the Subbuteo pitch and as young men, bitter rivals when it came to the fairer but at times, crueller sex. But in the words of Frank Sinatra …

'I've loved, I've laughed and cried, I've had my fill, my share of losing. And now, as tears subside, I find it all so amusing.'

Saltash United is only eleven miles away from where I live and easy to get to via the A38 Devon Expressway. It's a 3pm kick off on a Saturday so why am I nearly late, especially when I sacrificed a Friday nights works do when all the booze and food was free? It's because twenty four hours earlier I'd volunteered to meet a customer at 7.30am today for an emergency call out. Ideal for me. It meant I could take the company car home and drive it not only to work early on Saturday but also use it for the rest of the weekend, including this game. Trouble was, I had nothing else to do but catch up on some sleep in bed. Waking up at 2.15pm, oh shit! Jumping into the shower, jumping into the car and negotiating heavy traffic heading west. And it's typical August weather, pissing down. This obviously made driving that little bit more hazardous as I weaved in and out of more sensible slower drivers treating the A38 like an American highway. Basically, anything goes. The Devil crossing the River Tamar? I'm driving like him!

And even from the weather's point of view, Cornwall really could be a different country on this day. As soon as I enter God's Country the sun breaks through. A rainbow appears in the direction I'm driving, which makes me dream about the pot of gold that could be waiting for me on this quest. No pot of gold waiting near the ground though; only an overweight tosser who would be better off spending his time at a Weightwatcher's meeting rather than imitating a demented and bitterly failed traffic warden.

The town of Saltash has a football team they can be proud of, due to their success ever since being founded just after the war; three times Western League champions all achieved in the 1980's and various other silverware dotted around the decades. They currently play in the South West Peninsula which stands at level ten in the English football pyramid; the structure of our national game. They are one of no less than seven hundred and thirty six teams that have entered this season's Cup, the holy grail of every football club in England, untouched by money and built on dreams. The FA Cup works like this ...

It's a knockout competition comprising of fourteen rounds (six qualifying and eight proper).

The seventh stage and therefore the first proper one introduces the professional League teams and it's here where the magic begins.

It's where full-time footballers are challenged by electricians, plumbers, builders and welders. Another two rounds take place and then the best teams in the country join the party. So, in theory, Saltash United could take on Manchester United in a small stadium situated in a small town. There's nothing like it in the rest of the world which makes it unique, special, magical, envied and widely regarded as the most famous of all sporting competitions on the planet. David leaps out of a biblical fairy tale to take on Goliath.

Although the teams are not seeded (they are represented by a numbered ball in a free-for-all draw administered by a machine noisier than a faulty boiler), there is a format of 'byes' which ensures that the higher ranked teams are entered in the later rounds, and thus giving the so-called smaller teams huge incentives to battle through and achieve heroic status.

Today's game sees a team from level ten of the football pyramid taking on a team from level nine. What sort of standard is that? There are roughly fifteen levels in the pyramid and at the bottom of that structure is possibly your next-door neighbour or the local pub drunk who's forever telling everyone that he was once scored the winning goal for some team or other and once played alongside someone who nearly made it as a professional and could have played for England.

Saltash United play at level ten in the pyramid so therefore their status just qualifies them to play in the FA Cup as shown in this table …

ROUND	PYRAMID LEVEL INTRODUCED	TEAMS PLAYING
Extra Preliminary	9 & 10	368
Preliminary	8	320
First Qualifying Round	7	232
Second Qualifying Round	6	160
Third Qualifying Round		80
Fourth Qualifying Round	5	64
First Round Proper	3 & 4	80
Second Round Proper		40
Third Round Proper	1 & 2	64
Fourth Round Proper		32
Fifth Round Proper		16
Quarter Finals		8
Semi Finals		4
Final		2

It's at this preliminary stage that you'll see working class players take each other on. Plasterers versus estate agents, gardeners versus drivers, factory workers versus the unemployed.

Pele once called football 'The Beautiful Game'. It's beautiful because dreams can come true. Imagine playing alongside your mates in the latter stages of the Cup against a professional team in a big stadium. That's where a number of future stars are spotted. The twenty-three-man England squad in the 2018 World Cup for example had seven players who started out at non-league clubs further down the pyramid.

After spoiling myself and splashing out an extra quid for a match programme, I'm pleasantly surprised to see that the Ashes' secretary is Scott Cooksley, son of another lifelong friend Steve. If John Martindale and I loved playing Subbuteo as kids, it was Steve Cooksley who pioneered it in our area, by forming a league at the wide-eyed age of eight years old.

FA CUP EXTRA PRELIMINARY ROUND
SATURDAY 11TH AUGUST
KIMBERLEY STADIUM
ATTENDANCE – 92

SALTASH UNITED 1 ODD DOWN AFC 0

In a crowd of less than a hundred, it's not hard to spot John. It takes a few seconds for him to recognise me as I haven't shaved for two weeks and am wearing a beanie. He grins, gets to his feet and shakes my hand. Then he motions me to sit down next to him on a damp wooden bench; damp because it had rained earlier you understand and not because he's that pleased to see me! He has no idea I was going to be there or why;so he points out Callum playing in Saltash's home colours of red and white stripes. Very smart,but looks too much like Exeter City for my liking.

So, this is it then! The first of fourteen rounds to attend. Starting here at Kimberley Stadium and ending at Wembley Stadium.

"When a father gives to his son, both laugh;
when a son gives to his father, both cry."
WILLIAM SHAKESPEARE

John is rightfully proud of Callum. At first glance Martindale junior shows an effortless ability to do the basics well. He moves into space to receive the ball, controls it, then gives it to a team-mate before gliding into another space.

Closer examination of his game however shows so much more. An intelligent mind enables him to always be in a position to receive the ball. A deceptive turn or burst of pace beats opponents with ease. His left foot tells the ball exactly what to do and the fact that he plays out wide on the left-hand side of the pitch makes his game all the more impressive. Where there is hardly any or no space, he creates it. As far as I can see, if he was given carte blanche in a more central attacking role, he would be a constant threat to the opposition.

But it's two things that show that Callum Martindale is no prima donna. He works hard. Off the ball, he covers large areas of the pitch with a casual style of running which is both effective and economical, always ready to retrieve the ball and launch an attack. He also possesses a controlled aggression; not afraid to put his foot in and stare down the recipient who takes exception. At one point he says something to an Odd Down player who can't seem to grasp the fact that being strongly but fairly tackled is actually permitted in the laws of the game. I look at Martindale senior and smile, but he's wearing the same look as his boy; like father, like son.

Concentrating on Callum's performance, I almost forget that there's an FA Cup game taking place. And it's not a bad one. Saltash look the better team in the early stages. Odd Down from the Bath area, look leggy in comparison and off the pace. Later, Ashes' assistant manager Dane Bunney tweeted that in his opinion, the visitors only turned up to waste time and ruin the game. I didn't agree. Only once did I see anything untoward the spirit of the game when an Odd Down player was fouled, and made a meal of it by rolling around in mock agony right in front of the main stand. Although there's a small crowd this isn't the smartest part of the pitch to employ this tactic, and makes him about as popular as a fart in an elevator.

But it's not any of the visiting players that frustrate the home supporters. The referee starts to make some bizarre decisions which all too often interrupts the flow of the game and helps Odd Down grab some much needed respite.

The biggest criticism of referees is their lack of consistency. One official's view on breaking the laws of the game can differ from another's. This referee however is inconsistent in the same game; penalising and cautioning one player but then not even blowing his whistle a few minutes later when another player does exactly the same thing. It's the same for both teams today, so in a strange way you could call it a fair contest. It's driving the Saltash faithful mad though.

Respect is a word that often pops up regarding the man in the middle. But respect is a two-way street which has to be earned. This referee is not only stopping the game for no apparent reason, he's also failing to explain to the players why. In Rugby, the whole attendance can hear the referee explain his decisions so there is no doubt and no dissent. In football, most referees fail to communicate properly to the most important people in the game, the players. No interaction with footballers equals no respect.

Even as a Sunday footballer, the referee would communicate with me, even if it was in a negative way. I've never forgotten some of the things said or shouted at me. The best referees gave as good as they got …

-"Hey ref! Where's your fucking glasses?"
-"At home with my fucking hearing aid!"

Or their little quips that made me smile in the heat of a game. After misplacing a pass I'd mutter, "Oh bollocks!"

"Wasn't even that good player!" came the in-depth tactical analysis as he jogged on by. Instant respect, he made me laugh. There was the other side to the villainous man in black though that could wind me up and only provoke my wonderful lowest form of wit known as sarcasm.

On one occasion in my … ahem, illustrious career as a hungover parks player, I was on the receiving end of a nasty blow from an opponent where, on the Sunday League stage, such actions frequently went unpunished.

Chasing a long pass from the opposing team which was over-hit to such an extent that it wouldn't have looked out of place on a golf course, I ran shoulder to shoulder with an opposing attacker. Knowing he wasn't going to reach the ball first, he decided to take his frustration out on my Adam's Apple by administering a spiteful right elbow, which left me on all fours gasping for oxygen. There was no referee's whistle. On recovering, which basically meant your manager running at you with a bucket of ice-cold water and a sponge, I felt a little hard done by.

However, that little word called respect came into my head, so I thought I'd give the visually impaired official some helpful advice. As soon as he was in earshot I casually mentioned that Boots opticians were currently running a two-for-one sale and if he was lucky, may even qualify for a better deal, given his age. Thankfully, there was nothing wrong with his hearing as well as his eyesight and brandished a yellow card in my direction – just one of the many reasons I love the game. An assault on my throat followed by a fine of £8. Such ingratitude for looking out for his welfare!

By the way, did you know that referees in Scotland are sponsored by Specsavers? Oh, the McIrony!

But the best piece of man-management by a referee I ever saw and heard was so good it earned him a spontaneous round of applause from both teams, and it involved me directly.

A bit worse for wear one Sunday morning after a stag night (happily not mine), I turned up to play at a place called Victoria Park in Plymouth for a Cup match. Despite it's regal name, Victoria

Park was a mugger's paradise by night and a dog walker's heaven in daylight. In fact, there was so much dog mess you could have mistaken the place for the film set of 101 Dalmations.

My manager, Neil Penhallurick, in his wisdom decided to play me at right back. This meant chasing a younger, quicker and more skilful left winger all morning. Just what you want when nursing a hangover! One saving grace however on this autumnal morning was the state of the pitch. A mixture of sticky mud and wet grass made it ideal for slide tackling and therefore giving a one paced defender such as myself a couple of yards advantage over an attacking player who would prefer to stay on his feet and maintain balance.

The game was in it's early stages when, once again, a long pass was hit down my side of the pitch and keenly chased by the aforementioned young, quick and skilful winger. I read the flight of the ball and moved to engage him just as he accelerated. Damn! He's quicker than my half-drunk brain anticipated! There was no other choice but to go to ground and slide. It wasn't reckless. It was a controlled challenge with my right leg extended towards the path of the ball and my left leg trailing behind me.

Now if I'm being honest, I'm not sure if I made contact with the ball first or his complete lower body. What I do know is that both ball and players went flying over the touchline and unbelievably avoided tons of dogshit. As I got up, butter wouldn't melt in my mouth, and I jogged back to a position to defend the throw-in which the referee awarded. It was a brilliant performance worthy of an Oscar nomination, which convinced the official that nothing had been done by yours truly to break any law, or leg for that matter.

'Ladies and Gentlemen, the winner of this year's Academy Award for Best Supporting Actor goes to David Kindon for his performance in YOU DIRTY BASTARD'

Cue a standing ovation from a handful of dogwalkers as I step forward for my acceptance speech.

Had the referee given a free kick and even cautioned me, I wouldn't have complained. But he didn't and the winger was incensed. He was pointing at me, making accusations of trying to hospitalise him and shouting at the referee to send me off. At least he wasn't covered in shit! I just outstretched my arms to the side of my body in that 'what have I done wrong' classic posture that all footballers, professional or not, have mastered over the years.

The game continued, but the wronged winger still demanded justice. In fact, he moaned for so long that even I wanted him to get a free kick just so he would shut up. Eventually Paddy the ref blew his whistle and stopped the game. Standing in the centre of the pitch he invited the winger over for a friendly chat.

-"Yes please number eleven, over here. Yes, you, number eleven!"

As number eleven walked toward him, Paddy reached for his top pocket. We all thought he was going to book him. But no! Instead of producing a yellow card, he pulled out a baby's dummy.

-"Here you go player, suck on that and you'll feel a lot better"

Laughter and applause all around the pitch. Having to save face in front of his mates, the winger decided to go with the advice and literally didn't spit his dummy out. A few seconds later he returned it, and a football match broke out. Brilliant man-management.

Now I'm not suggesting that officials working at the the top level of the game should pop into Mothercare to replenish their equipment on the way to a game, but what I am saying is that communication is an essential part of a referee's kit.

That day, Paddy earned respect by disarming the dissenting player by his own means of communication. As players, we're always told that referees are only human and make mistakes. Well, it's the same for footballers. They want a little respect as well.

Talking of referees, time to get back to Saltash versus Odd Down. This ref stops the game yet again but this time for good reason. One of the visiting players is injured on the far side of the pitch and receiving treatment. The Ashes' supporters are sympathetic to his plight.

-"The bridge is that way mate! Piss off home!"

There are two incidents in the game I recall more than any other. Callum Martindale had a chance to score. Having once more found space, the ball came his way. He was fifteen yards from goal but didn't make a clean contact with his weaker foot and their goalkeeper saved it easily. I was so disappointed. How appropriate would it have been if Callum had scored the first goal of this cup run! After all, he was the reason I chose this game to start my path of destiny.

Strangely enough though it was the other Callum in the team who broke the deadlock to score the only goal of the game. Defender Callum O'Brien stepped forward for a succession of corner kicks and finally headed the ball towards goal. Somehow the ball landed in the back of the net via the goalkeeper's legs, and red and white striped shirts joyfully converged on the un-likely goalscorer as mad celebrations took place by the corner flag. At first, I thought it was the captain and number nine Ryan Richards who'd scored but I only realised it was O'Brien's goal when he ran back over the halfway line wearing a smile as wide as the River Tamar.

I'd left my glasses in the car so a lot of things on the pitch were a little blurred. It was obvious that I needed to wear glasses a few years before when after making an appointment with Specsavers, I walked into the wrong branch for the eye test!

The goal woke Odd Down from their lethargy and prompted them at last to attack. They create half chances for the remainder of the game, which was more than they had done in the previous seventy minutes. The game ended. Thanks to the Football Association doubling its prize money this season, Saltash received £2250. They needed it too. The pitch wasn't the best and the whole ground needed more than a lick of paint. Odd Down received £750 just for turning up.

The Martindales hug. I shook Callum's hand and told him "well played". Previously, he'd played at a higher level for Taunton Town and at this standard, he positively shone.

The Father

Immediately after the game, John Martindale walks away from the ground and points out the state of the pitch I'd walked across earlier. Although it's August and has hardly been used this season, the stage on which Saltash United's junior team play is in poor condition. Owned by the local council, the grass is uncut, puddles gather in uneven goalmouths and the whole scene looks generally neglected. He tells me that this is a common theme in grass roots football and rather than some of the obscene amount of money generated at the top of the pyramid funding this level, youth teams are feeding on scraps.

A while later, John and I caught up over a couple of beers. He works for the Wrigleys factory in Plymouth and told me their social and sporting facilities are much better than anything you'd see at Kimberley Stadium. Wrigleys have enough employees to field football teams, but they know that if they pick up any injuries even while representing their employer, it might affect their staff bonus. However, their factory pitch is good enough to reduce any risk of injury as it's regularly maintained.

You can't point the finger at Saltash United FC for the state of these pitches as they're struggling financially with the season-to-season costs of running a football club. If they're averaging just under a hundred spectators every home game, then the fiver I paid to get in isn't going to go far. Welcome to Planet Non-League. The further down the pyramid you go, the wider it gets, and the funding is drip fed amongst the immense number of amateur football clubs making up the foundations of the national game. The top of the pyramid represents a multi-billion hyped up global product existing through self-interest and pure greed; but it's not illegal. It's called business, and like any other industry, the small companies can only hope for huge windfalls which the FA Cup can bring.

When his two younger lads were picked to play for Plymouth Schoolboys, it was John and his wife Beverley who had to fund any trip they undertook. And what if they couldn't come up with the money? Would that mean young talent being denied a chance to make it in a fast-growing pastime which we're told is the best thing to keep kids off the street and stay on the right side of the law?

Sitting next to John was a chap called Darren Raven who was watching the game with his son Owen, currently on the books at Plymouth Argyle. Not for long though it seems. Apparently, Argyle haven't got the set up or the investment required to sow seeds and reap the rewards from an academy system. Ridiculous when you think that they are the biggest football club in four counties, a large catchment area.

John told me about Brentford Football Club based in west London. It's smaller than Plymouth Argyle historically, but are planning on moving to a bigger ground thanks to a thriving youth academy. It wasn't the first time that I would hear praise about Brentford on my journey up the pyramid. As I found out later, they do things right there; a football club who realises that you can't have a top without a bottom; but try telling that to The Football Association Premier League Ltd run by it's twenty share-holders (i.e. the executives and directors of the Premiership clubs).

John, Bev and their sons Harvey & Brennan are holidaying abroad as from the next day, so they will miss Callum's next Cup match in a fortnight. I promise I'll keep him posted through the game.

And the father walks away, a very proud one.

As I approach the company car across the neglected pitch I see my favourite traffic warden is still patrolling his side of the street. He doesn't say anything, just wears a smug fat look. I get into the driver's seat, fasten the seatbelt and turn on the ignition. As I've now got more time for a bit of banter I decide that I should congratulate him on his country's victory today over an English county. Down goes the electric window and I inform him that Cornwall have beaten England 1-0. He can't hear me above the engine so I reckon sign language will be more appropriate. I give him the thumbs up and then gesture the final score. ONE (I ex-tend the middle finger of one hand), NIL (I place my thumb across four folded fingers on the other hand whilst shuffling it to and fro near my mouth, moving using my tongue against the inside of my cheek in harmony with my hand, for a clearer message).

For some strange reason he looks angry, and being the brave invading warrior that I am, I pull away just as he's waddling out of his precious driveway.

As I drive back into Devon across the Tamar Bridge (this time adhering to the Highway Code), I think about Plymouth Argyle and the lack of foresight they possess. To me it only makes sense that there should be a youth academy for so many reasons. For a start, they could recruit a whole generation of young talent from Cornwall, Devon, Dorset and Somerset. Seasoned professionals on the whole are reluctant to join Argyle for two reasons. Firstly, they like to mingle with players from other teams, but the nearest club is Exeter City forty miles away. Secondly, players hate travelling long distances for away games and Argyle cover more mileage than any other team in the country. Playing Bristol Rovers is a case in point. It's one hundred and twenty miles away but still classed as a westcountry derby! Yet if Rovers travelled to the midlands to play Walsall for example, you'd never call that a local clash, but Walsall are much closer to Bristol than Plymouth is.

All the more reason to invest in youth. Local pride. According to the 'Green Army' every other supporter in England is a northern bastard, something to boast about apparently. Apart from being the most southerly and westerly professional team, another fact about Plymouth is that it's the largest city in the United Kingdom never to have played in a top-flight division; and a big reason for that is in the previous paragraph.

Everyone in the game knows only too well the huge potential of Plymouth Argyle. But the answer doesn't lie in paying out big money for players or even loaning them short term. Think long term. Think about the untapped talent in this huge area and invest in a scouting/coaching project. The proven talent will naturally follow later when it's seen that the club is ambitious and going places. Don't believe me? Then ask someone like Ian Holloway who left Argyle to manage Leicester City only to regret it for the rest of his managerial career.

1970 WINNERS – CHELSEA

John Martindale's second favourite team is Chelsea. If you're from Plymouth, chances are that you will follow a team from the top flight, simply because Argyle have never been there.

Chelsea from London's West End have always been the glamour boys, even if their ground was falling to bits during the seventies. Flamboyant on and off the pitch, they rubbed shoulders with the likes of Hollywood beauty Raquel Welch.

In 1970, the FA Cup final was billed as glamour versus grit. Chelsea took on an uncompromising side from Yorkshire whose ruthless professionalism had struck fear into many an opponent and seemed to relish the fact they were hated. Leeds United took no prisoners. This wasn't just a football match contested between two of England's best teams of the day, this was a clash of cultures and style.

The name 'Dirty Leeds' which has stuck for decades has never done their talents justice. They could be nasty, yes. But they could play good football, and on their day they were brilliant. A deadly melting pot of physicality, cynicism, artistry and skill; a mixture of industry and invention. But for all their title challenges and Cup final appearances, they finished up as runners up more times than lifting silverware, which never mirrored the brilliance of their international players; possibly due to a manager who seemed more paranoid than charismatic. The phrase 'always the bridesmaid never the bride' could have been invented for Don Revie and his football family. A family looked upon as a Yorkshire mafia.

Leeds had their followers in Plymouth; a close friend of mine Steve Marshall for example. Four years older than me, he was one of an estimated twenty-eight million viewers to witness an epic Cup final in the three-channel era of BBC1, BBC2 and ITV. "The best team lost" he always tells me. I believe like so many other friends of my generation that when Steve saw his first final that year, he fell in love.

A close and mutual friend of ours is Sean Scott, another Chelsea fan. Born in 1968 he would be too young to watch this final, but being born and bred in Plymouth, once he was old enough to see a top team on TV he too was hooked. Your first team is always your favourite team, and there's no going back.

For his fiftieth birthday, I bought Sean a replica 1970 Chelsea FA Cup winners retro shirt. On the morning of his half-century he texted me a message from Dubai where he was celebrating and simply said, 'Awesome!' I've never seen him wear it though!

Chelsea beat Leeds and lifted the Cup for the first time in their illustrious history after the first game at Wembley was drawn two goals each. The replay was held at Old Trafford in Manchester and this time 'The Blues' triumphed two goals to one in a bruising encounter. Striker Peter Osgood is still the last player to score in every round of the FA Cup after the introduction of level one clubs in the third round.

The state of the Wembley pitch for the first game was absolutely disgraceful. Back in the day, the Football Association didn't own the stadium so they would hire it from the local council to stage not only its flagship game but also England internationals. A week before the final, the iconic twin towers of Wembley oversaw 'The Horse of the Year' show which left the place with hardly a blade of grass and a surface dominated by mud and sand. It made Victoria Park in Plymouth look like a bowling green in comparison and meant that the ball itself would act unpredictably. Skidding instead of bouncing just added to the drama. The ground beneath the players' feet was constantly moving as they struggled to keep balance and poise. A magician of a footballer was Eddie Gray of Leeds who could make opponents disappear. He tortured the Chelsea defence that day with pacey and mesmerising runs on a surface that didn't seem to bother him. It was football's equivalent of walking on water in a show stealing performance. He didn't deserve a loser's medal.

And it wasn't just the pitch that showed the ugly side of the game. Referees in this age would usually let the game flow as much as they could, enabling the hard men of the period to take advantage and kick lumps out of their opposite number. Most teams had at least one player who had attended the 'if it moves then kick it' school, and these two teams graduated with flying colours.

There was no love lost between two sides who couldn't have approached the game more differently. 'We respected them as professionals' commented the systematic Leeds players. The feeling wasn't mutual. 'Hate. Pure fucking hate. There's no other word for it' the Blues corner stated.

Almost three decades later, an experienced referee was asked to review the 1970 final on video. His damning verdict was twenty yellow cards and six red. Compare that to just one booking on the day itself!

The most serious crimes witnessed from the Royal Box included punching, head butting and the odd Kung Fu kick. The good old days eh?

The day after Saltash eliminated Odd Down, I checked the FA website to see where the next leg of my adventure would take me. This is where the fun begins. Where Saltash United go, I will follow. To my surprise, the draw has been pre-determined as the competition is still in the preliminary stage and … I'm on my way to Westbury in Wiltshire. Conveniently a no change direct journey from Plymouth Train Station. So, late one afternoon as I was in the city centre, I decided to buy a ticket there and then. The lady behind the glass partition looked tired, no doubt from carrying out her tedious duties all day long.

- "I'd like a return ticket please"

- "Where to?" she sighs.

- "Back here of course!"

It seems the old jokes aren't the best ones, as her bored rolling eyes suggest.

Chapter Two

TALES OF THE WHITE HORSE

What have the town of Westbury and Wembley Stadium got in common? Both places were built on legends of a white horse.

If you've ever headed east on a train journey from Somerset and into Wiltshire, the first stop is Westbury. On leaving the station take a look at the rolling hills of Salisbury Plain on your right and you'll see a magnificent chalked white horse carved into the countryside. It's not known for sure of either its origins or age, but there are plenty of theories why the Anglo-Saxon town is represented by this iconic symbol.

Overlooking one corner of the ground that is home to Westbury United Football Club the 'Westbury White Horse' to give it its official title is both loved and worshipped in this green and pleasant part of England.

During the country's notable 2018 World Cup run, two large red ribbons were placed overnight both vertically and horizontally onto the heraldic landmark, depicting the St George Cross measuring the proud and patriotic feeling sweeping the nation. The locals were obviously amused but the town elders reacted angrily. Incensed by what they saw as an act of vandalism and not just a mischievous bit of fun, the police were summoned to seek out the perpetrators but gladly to no avail.

The horse is symbolic of battles past (apart from playing Croatia in a semi-final) when it was believed that if your enemy spotted a white one in the midst of a battle, death would certainly follow.

Westbury United are therefore known as the 'White Horse Men', playing at level nine in the pyramid and slight favourites against Saltash in the next preliminary round of the Cup. At this infant stage, all games are regional which saves on travelling costs for the away team and boosts local interest and therefore generates a sizeable attendance. That's the theory anyway.

A week before the game, I leave a message on the club's answering machine requesting an interview with a member of staff or player for the purposes of this book. I receive a call from a chap called Greg Coulson, chairman of Westbury United who doubles up as secretary to save costs. It's a similar picture when running a local parks team at the base of the pyramid, where sponsorship is the name of the game for the working-class player and money isn't the be all and end all. He kindly agrees to give me a few minutes of his busy schedule before the game, which I'm grateful for.

On the same weekend Manchester City lay down a marker for this season's domestic domination by thrashing Huddersfield Town six goals to one. The result triggers something in my mind's eye. 6-1 against Huddersfield in August brings back sweet memories of an era when watching Plymouth Argyle was the one constant in life; singing, chanting and celebrating in the Lyndhurst Road End at Home Park after the few obligatory pints. And in the eighties there was plenty to cheer about.

Some of us enjoyed Saturday lunchtime in the Noah's Ark pub, sinking lager and then rushing to get into the ground with minutes to spare. The Lyndhurst stand ran the length of the pitch opposite the player's tunnel and the team would be greeted with an explosion of green and white as they entered our back garden. In an era before you were forced to sit in plastic seats on a cold day, you were part of a choir that harmonized in 'janner' tones, swaying and jumping to the beat of The Pilgrim's attack. At times it felt as if we were winning before the game had even started, and who stood with me in this raucous green church? John Martindale! Along with Mark Ross and Steve Vaughan, the four of us became virtually inseparable for a while, the pre match drink was just a dress rehearsal for Saturday night's main event.

There were pockets of estate lads on that side of the ground, each group proud of the area he lived in and even prouder of the City he hailed from; Efford over here, Eggbuckland just over there, Devonport on our right and Honicknowle at the back. The four of us got to know the faces of the Eggbuckland lads who drank in a pub called The Mermaid, just a few years after the older generations of our neighbouring pissing grounds would have been at each other's throats. In these heady days of competing (and winning) in level two of our national structure however we all got along as we verbally took on the so-called bigger clubs of Leeds, Sunderland and Birmingham. Singing as one, the crowd you were part of became the much clichéd twelfth man, forerunners of the now famous Green Army which today travels the length and breadth of the Football League in their thousands.

To this day, someone I would never have met if it wasn't for Argyle such as Kev Wheeler from The Mermaid will still shake hands wherever and whenever I bump into him. The bond is still there after celebrating and sometimes suffering in an alcohol fuelled haze with the rest of the Lyndhurst lads.

On this particular day, we were definitely celebrating. I'd seen Argyle smash six goals past the opposition before and a few more followed, but this game sticks out more because of an impromptu free gig we gave the rest of the ground including a coachload of Huddersfield supporters.

Argyle were cruising towards victory when a Mermaid regular called Andy Collins decided to start singing non-football songs. He was the sort of bloke who on entering a pub would at first ignore the bar and instead head straight for the jukebox. Didn't matter if it was U2, UB40 or Ultravox, Andy had a love for a broad range of music.

For some reason, his opening number was 'I'm Still Waiting' by Diana Ross but this didn't quite catch on despite our mellow and merry state. His second choice though 'Bohemian Rhapsody' produced a brilliant vocal performance by our choir which in this day and age would have even left Simon Cowell impressed.

'Is this the real life? Is this just fantasy?
Caught in a landslide, no escape from reality ...'

The most impressive thing of this version of Queen's classic isn't how a load of half pissed football fans stayed in tune, but actually remembering all of the operatic lyrics.

'Mama, just killed a man. Put a gun against his head.
Pulled my trigger now he's dead ...'

And then one of the deadliest goalscorers in English football pulled his trigger to kill off Huddersfield. Tommy Tynan, assassin extraordinaire, scored a shedload of goals for Argyle, but none as good as this one. Controlling the ball on his chest from a long clearance he was all alone near the halfway line. Quickly engaged by two defenders he turned with the ball and dribbled past the first before sidestepping the second. Thirty-five yards from goal and intelligent enough to realise his average pace couldn't outrun the recovering defence (the one reason he couldn't get a regular place in Liverpool's great side where he learned his trade), he struck the ball powerfully into the roof of Huddersfield's goal. Spectacular doesn't even come close to describing this awesome shot. Both arms typically raised in the air triumphantly, he ran towards us in the Lyndhurst milking the astonishment and sheer joy his amazing goal had made us feel.

It was almost an act of defiance. 'Bored are you lads? Singing pop songs from years ago are we? Okay, I'll just go and score one of the best goals of my career just to get your mind back on the game'.

A few minutes later the football crowd's cheers die down and the choir continues its gig.

'I see a little silhouette of a man. Scaramouch,
Scaramouch will you do the Fandango. Thunderbolt and
Lightning very, very frightening me ...'

Argyle score another almost immediately. It's a rout.

'Galileo, Galileo, Galileo, Galileo, Galileo, Figaro, magnifico...'

And how can you possibly have a medley without including The Beatles?

*'Weeee all live in a yelluh submareeeeen,
yelluh submareeeeen, yelluh submareeeeen ...'*

Of course, it's much easier to sing when you're winning, and when you're standing. Two years before the Hillsborough tragedy claimed 96 innocent lives, most football supporters stood to watch a game and did so safely. It's become official now of the sheer injustice that happened before, during and especially after that awful event. But all those years ago, all football fans up and down the country knew the truth. We weren't listening to the lying police or reading what the shithouses printed in The Sun newspaper. We didn't need enquiry after enquiry and the people of Merseyside shouldn't have had to wait thirty years for a Government apology. We knew what had happened. We trusted the system but the system despised us.

Hillsborough was a result of authorities treating us like cattle, herding us from pen to pen. We were tarred with the same brush ever since the 1960's when football hooliganism first reared its ugly pathetic head. Nothing was ever done to stamp out the violence, simply because the law and the courts which represent it are too soft on crime, so the footballing bodies and football clubs had just one option open to them. They fenced us in. That tragedy was waiting to happen. There were near fatalities in the previous two decades but no one took any notice. We had no voice. We were sub-human. The Prime Minister at the time, Margaret Thatcher, voiced her concern that Her Majesty's finest would shoulder the blame and whether she ordered a cover up or not isn't really known. What we do know because it came to light years later, is that the officers on duty that day falsified their notes, and guess who got the blame? We did. We were drunken violent louts who got what we deserved. Welcome to Planet Power Abuse.

1923 WINNERS – BOLTON WANDERERS

Also known as 'The White Horse Final' 1923 was the first year that the newly built Wembley Stadium hosted the Cup final. It's also become the first nostalgic look back of so many footballing folklores in the World's most famous sporting venue, but it almost became the first spectator disaster that would have eclipsed the Hillsborough tragedy.

In a stadium designed to hold one hundred thousand people the Football Association decided it was a waste of time making it an all-ticket affair as they estimated only half of that number turning up; but they reckoned without the fascination and national pride. The Empire Stadium at Wembley was the latest and grandest structure to be built as part of The Great British Exhibition, which celebrated the country's glorious industrial achievements at a time when we owned a quarter of the globe.

In the event, a crowd of nearly three times the official capacity descended onto Wembley Way and swamped the ground to such an extent that not a single blade of grass could be seen. Thankfully, there were no fences trapping spectators on the terraces and therefore instead of being crushed to death, they simply made their way onto the pitch. But another big difference was that this was a time of no social unrest. The United Kingdom was a triumphant nation full of pride represented by good humoured and friendly football fans. Even the fact that the vast majority of the crowd hadn't paid to gain entrance didn't bother the few that had; and this game only went ahead due to one unlikely hero.

Step forward PC George Scorey astride his white horse Billy. With both two legged and four legged saviours of the day, the level headed partners headed towards one of the goalposts gently nudging spectators aside as they went. Once there, he asked everyone to hold hands and slowly walk backwards. When they reached the white perimeter lines of the pitch, he asked them to sit down before repeating the trick all over the hallowed turf so that when the teams came out to play, there was in effect a human touchline.

Bolton, nicknamed 'The Trotters' beat West Ham United 2-0 with the first ever FA Cup final goal scored at Wembley by David Jack, an ex-Plymouth Argyle player. It was the police officer and his trusty steed that really won the day though.

The next day, aerial shots of the stadium dominated the front pages of the national newspapers. Grainy black and white images recalled the desperation and near fatalities of a huge bowl filled with human beings vying for position to witness an historic match. And in every picture there was Billy clear as day. With a calm temperament and good nature this creature would never realise that he was Wembley's first ever hero. He was in fact a grey horse, but looked white in the distant photograph taken from an airship.

For many years after George Scorey would be offered free tickets for the final which he always declined. Apparently, he hated football.

It's a twenty-minute walk to the ground from Westbury Train Station. Westbury United FC play their home games at Meadow Lane. Meadow Lane? Make that memory lane. Waiting to greet me are Steve Cooksley, a lifelong friend whose son Scott as I mentioned in the previous chapter is secretary at Saltash United, and ex-colleague John Nickson who now lives in Swindon, just up the road. The connection between us lies in our Sunday League football team. John and I were the two managers in it's seven-year existence, while Steve was the original captain. Between us, we barely made double figures in the art of goalscoring. John in fact only ever scored once, which was one more than me. They're waiting in the clubhouse when I rock up. Steve is dressed in pumps, three quarter trousers, a casual zip top and a baseball cap which he sports back to front. 'Where's your skateboard?' are the first three words I say to him in the last three years. A dedicated marathon runner, Steve actually looks a lot fitter now than when he played for us a quarter of a century ago.

The Westbury mascot walks through the bar. He's wearing Westbury's first strip and a huge horse's head, white of course. Why the long face mate? He walks out, rather than canters, totally unnoticed by everyone inside. Did you see that? A horse with a human body just went by! Am I the only one who can see this?!!! I haven't even had my first pint yet! Shoulders are merely shrugged.

I then meet Greg Coulson and true to his word, he grants me a few minutes as kick off approaches.

The Chairman

Westbury United play in the Western League and proudly own their own ground. It's a tidy venue with decent facilities and prettily flanked on one side of the pitch with trees. It's appropriate that they play in green because that's the prominent colour of the attractive surrounding area.

Greg Coulson has been chairman for just under a year. He's a busy man. Getting up earlier this morning to clean the changing rooms and mark out the pitch. This is the working-class side of English football all right. It's all hands on at this level; living the dream by competing in the FA Cup, watched by spectators who can only dream about playing when working full time.

He's hoping for a sizeable attendance of about one hundred fans. In FA Cup rules, the entrance money is split 50/50 between the two clubs. The winners of today's game will also receive £2890 in prize money. I paid a fiver to get in so what happens to the

£2.50 share which Westbury get? it's invested into maintaining and improving the ground as much as possible. "You could offer a player £100 a week to sign for you" Greg tells me, "But you can't attract a good player if you've got a crap pitch."

This makes sense. Players will move on but your home ground stays forever. And if you want to compete at a higher level further up the pyramid, your ground has to meet a certain League criteria.

To help enable this, there is an organisation that provides funds for lower-level clubs called the FSIF (Football Stadia Improvement Fund), which has awarded over fifty million pounds to non-League clubs since the millennium. Their contribution to Westbury resulted in a new drainage system, fencing and walling which had to be brought up to standard. The FSIF in turn, is helped out financially by the FA's Premier League. This slightly contradicts what I've heard earlier with regards to funding the bottom of the pyramid. I'd like to know what percentage of the pyramid's top level obscene money eventually trickles it's way down the structure.

Greg is hoping this season that the White Horse Men can emulate the team from 1936 and reach the first round proper of the Cup. I can picture it. Westbury versus Sunderland, This is the sort of tie dreams are made of for a family club such as this; but being a family club could work against them today. The father and son management team of Neil and Joe Kirkpatrick will be missing the game due to their attendance at a family wedding!

Greg has to go and carry out his duties for the day as chairman, but leaves me with his motto … 'Everyone must work hard to a standard which the chairman sets.'

Damn right! I mean, nobody hands you cups on a plate do they?

FA CUP PRELIMINARY ROUND
SATURDAY 25TH AUGUST
MEADOW LANE
ATTENDANCE – 55

WESTBURY UNITED 3 SALTASH UNITED 0

*'Genius is one per cent inspiration and
ninety-nine per cent perspiration.'*
THOMAS EDISON

And working hard is exactly the one thing Westbury are made to do. Saltash settled into the game immediately with vigour and invention; forcing goalkeeper Ed Baldy into two early saves, one brilliant which denied Ryan Richards from scoring;not to be confused with Ryan Rickard who made a save at the other end once the home team got a foothold.

Baldy, Man of the Match in the previous round had carried on where he left off and later in the first half produced two more good saves from shots by Henry Wilson and Callum Martindale. These Ashes were on fire! How did they not win?

John, Steve and myself stood about fifteen yards from the corner flag on the touchline when Callum jogged over to our side to take a free kick. Steve was also in the same primary school class as John Martindale and commented on how much the son resembled the father. Phew! No need for a DNA test then John me ol' mate!

With his left foot, Callum whipped in the free kick fiercely struck with pace and swerve but was left holding his head in near anguish as Ed Baldy got a vital hand to it. Two minutes later, my iPhone vibrated. It was Martindale senior requesting the latest score from abroad where he was sunning it up with Bev and his other two lads Harvey and Brennan. I almost couldn't believe what I messaged back… '1-0 down!'

Westbury had taken the lead just before the half time whistle when Dan Kovacs converted a half chance from close range. At that point I was thinking… 'how can the Ashes' management duo of Matt Cusack and Dane Bunney lift their team who had been playing superbly but are losing'. To use a boxing analogy, after six rounds, the team in the green corner had been outpunched, out manoeuvred and were almost out on their feet, but just before the bell, they hit back with a sucker punch which floored their more skilful opponent.

They must have been sitting in their changing room feeling virtually invincible, saying to each other…'look lads, they can't beat you! You're cut and bruised but you've got the killer punch. Hit them again!' That goal changed the whole game. The White Horse Men came out for the second half with their bushy tails up and took the attack to Saltash. It's a fickle game. Sir Alex Ferguson was strongly rumoured to be just one more defeat from getting the sack at Manchester United in 1990 but he managed a 1-0 victory in the FA Cup to save his job. He went on to win the final; bringing home his first piece of silverware to Old Trafford. When he left The Red Devils twenty-three years later 'Fergie' had won more League titles and Cup finals than any other manager in English footballing history.

About ten minutes into the second half the score was 2-0. A scrappy goal was scored which was nowhere near the best I would witness in the coming months but it was definitely the best celebration. And the entertainment was supplied by another Ferguson, first name Josh, who amazed the three of us by launching himself into an acrobatic backflip before landing gracefully on his feet. All the more remarkable when you take into consideration that this was his first game since returning from a back injury.

Goalscorer in the first game, Callum O'Brien nearly put Saltash back in the game but was denied by yet another bloody good save from Ed Baldy. Steve Cooksley blamed himself. He reckoned he'd jinxed it. Every time he watched the Ashes, they failed to score. His son Scott, so he believed, would ban him from attending future games.

In between attacks and counter-attacks the three amigos commented on burning issues such as Brexit, the environment and the badly designed layout of the men's toilets at Portsmouth Football Club. Then, with less than ten minutes of the game left, the tie was killed off once and for all as Francois Allen made it 3-0, with a skilful individual goal. To add to Saltash's hard luck, they put the ball into the back of the net only for it to be ruled out via the offside rule. Smiles were wiped from the faces of would be goalscorer Lee Phillips and the secretary's dad.

The referee blows the full-time whistle. Ashes to Ashes, win or bust.

There was time for one more lager in the clubhouse before John gave me a lift back towards the train station. Steve quickly introduced me to his son Scott who basically shared the same view as everybody else who had travelled up. Saltash were unlucky. Ed Baldy take a bow.

No kidding, John's car is the best and meanest I've ever sat in. Cue the brilliant and vastly underrated Indie band Feeder ...

'He's got a brand new car, looks like a Jaguar,
it's got leather seats, it's got a CD player, player, player...'

Jaguar John drops me off at a pub nearest Westbury Train Station imaginatively named The Railway Inn. There's hardly anyone in there but they're showing Liverpool play Brighton on Sky Sports which keeps me company.

I'm leaning against the bar when a young woman approaches me and with her thumb jabbing back over her shoulder towards the pool table, asks me how much it is to play snooker. Uh? I tell her I'm not a regular so I wouldn't know. I then scan the virtually empty pub and add that I don't think this particular pub has any regulars. She laughs, which doesn't impress her boyfriend. He's sat down facing me, giving a brilliantly visual impression of Skeletor, with gaunt pale features. 'I have to go now,' she says, 'my boyfriend gets paranoid when I talk to other men.'

Turning my attention back to the Football, Liverpool are winning 1-0 after Egyptian talisman Mo Salah scores what proved to be the only goal of the game. Coming from Egypt, it's obvious he would settle into our own pyramid (sorry), and he seems a nice 'Giza' (sorry again). He's come a Pharoah way (last one I promise), to come and play for the Reds but it's two other acquisitions made by charismatic manager Jurgen Klopp that will make the difference this season.

Just as Manchester City have given the rest of the Premier League something to think about by smashing in goals for fun, so Liverpool have shown their intent by not conceding any goals; something that seems against their nature. But the signings of goalkeeper Alisson Becker, combined with the coveted signature of defender Virgil Van Dijk a few months ago has totally changed the dynamic in a team now taken far more seriously to win the title when year after year, the red half of Merseyside claims that this is going to be their year.

I leave the pub for the short walk to the station and hanging around outside is Skeletor, holding a joint. The air is thick with weed which goes a long way to explain his paranoia. Stepping onto the train, it suddenly occurs to me that it will only be 8.30pm when I arrive at Plymouth and I've made no plans tonight. I've been single for three and a half years, and in the words of Mo Salah's lookalike Cat Stevens ...

'Another Saturday night and I ain't got nobody...'

Bottle of wine and a takeaway is the order of the evening in that case.

So, Westbury United are through to the next round. Where will I be going next? I think I might just be falling back in love with the FA Cup just as the country fell back in love with the England team during the recent World Cup. It's Monday lunchtime in work and I'm constantly refreshing the FA's website main page to see if the draw has been made yet. Eventually it is. Where am I going? Westbury again, or elsewhere in the Westcountry?

I'm going to Bitton. Bitton! Where's Bitton?

A quick check on Google maps and I see it's virtually half-way between Bristol and Bath in South Gloucestershire. Bitton AFC are also at level nine of the pyramid, as are Westbury and Odd Down.

I'm always making references and team comparisons with re-gards to the English football pyramid, but as the top five levels are single divisions and doesn't split into regional areas until level six, it resembles more of a wigwam, with a flagpole sticking out the top of it. At the top of the flagpole is a big colourful flag flutter-ing with the words 'FA PREMIERSHIP' emblazoned upon it.

And just below that flag is another. But this one is smaller and in tatters. Across it are words barely recognisable after years of neglect; the fa cup.

How could the fathers of football do that to their own baby?

Chapter Three

MEN IN BLACK

As FA Cup fixtures take precedence over League matches, Westbury and Bitton are both obliged to postpone their respective games against …each other! So, Bitton versus Westbury will now take place instead of Westbury versus Bitton.

The bread and butter League encounter which rewards the victor with just three points in the Western League division has now been replaced with a sudden death, winner takes all football match which will reward the victors with six grand. A sum not to be sneezed at on level nine of the pyramid.

I check to see where Bitton is exactly. Halfway between Bath and Bristol on the A4, easy to drive to. A quick check of my bank balance online to hire a car and budget for fuel shows that my mum has deposited her weekly tenner hoping that I can win her some money at the weekend on Skybet's website. So far between the pair of us we've won the princely sum of bugger all but that will change soon I tell her on a regular basis, usually on a Friday evening, halfway down a bottle of white wine.

Actually it's only a fiver she 'invests'. The other £5 is paid by her fiancé Bryan. They've been together for over thirty years and have only just announced their engagement. The wedding is due in three years time and as her father passed away in 1969, yours truly has been informed that I'll be giving her away. She'll be eighty-three years old on the big day and her groom will have just turned eighty. What a cougar!

Bryan has given his blessing for them to tie the knot in church even though like me, he's an atheist. This means we don't be-lieve in just the one God; rather than hundreds of other Gods followed by those who belong to a particular religion, believing that their one is the only one that exists, and that everyone else is going to hell.

My mum became a born-again christian in her early forties and I once asked her why. She told me it was when she was working voluntarily at the local youth club and as she did on numerous occasions, organised an evening of musical entertainment. This consisted of boys and girls, men and women singing those all-time-classics from the big movies that she was a big fan of. I never attended any of them, so I don't really know how well they went but I've always had this mental picture of the Efford Boot Boys sitting at the back of the hall in utter shocked silence as Michelle Smith belted out 'Oom-Pah-Pah' from Oliver.

Back to the sermon: the night before her very first opening show, she lay in bed when suddenly was overcome by panic and fear, a common occurrence which can consume anyone on the eve of walking (or dancing) into the unknown. It's only natural to rehearse self-doubt and focus on how disastrous the whole thing could go after all.

She then said that she felt something positive. All the anxiety disappeared when an inner voice told her everything would be all right. This was followed by a warm glow. It was, she believes, a sign from up above. I've never had the heart to tell her I'd just switched on the central heating.

I criticise all religions but I think church is a good thing. My mum attends every Sunday morning and has made friends galore there. This has led to an active social life which is the biggest antidote to the disease which destroys the elderly; in a word, loneliness. It makes me laugh when she tells me that her friends think I'm an attractive man. How many have good eyesight or even their own teeth?

For some strange reason, my mum has always thought that I'm cheeky.

My attempts to contact someone from Bitton AFC in the hope of interviewing him/her for this book proved fruitless, so I decided to leave early on the Saturday morning to get to the ground in good time and hopefully meet a member of staff or better still, a player. The title for this chapter would have been 'Good Morning Bitton' but thanks to several speed restrictions on the M5 motorway I didn't reach the ground until 1pm

It's easy to find the Recreation Ground though. In fact it's on the main road. I park in a garden centre opposite the club and as I walk across the road, I see three immaculately dressed guys walking towards the entrance. It's the match officials who have also driven up from Plymouth. They're wearing smart black suits and navy-blue Football Association ties; not an ounce of fat on them. Even at this level, the referee and his two assistants have to be in good shape. The referee's name is Sean Rothwell and he kindly agrees to a post-match chat at approximately 6pm

Happy with this quick resolution I walk back across the road to the garden centre for a cup of coffee and a piece of cake. Not my usual style but I'm driving, and as they say, 'when in Rome'… or in this case 'when near Bath' which is a Roman town. Over a reasonably priced cappuccino I start to think about the game. I'm really looking forward to this one as I feel that this is now where my own personal journey begins. In the previous two ties I'd watched them with friends John Martindale, John Nickson and Steve Cooksley. Now I'm on my own and furthermore this is a genuine qualifying round and not a preliminary. This is where the fun begins.

Am I falling in love again? 'Bitton By The Cup Bug' could have been an alternative title for this chapter. Compare the way I'm feeling now about the Cup to see this venture through to when I watched the 2013 final on my own, laid out on a sofa. On that day, underdogs Wigan beat the mega rich Manchester City with a goal dramatically scored in the last few minutes. In another era, Ben Watson would have gone down in history as the unlikely hero who laid waste a team full of brilliant talent but in this day of saturated television coverage, this was just another big game to watch.

At the time, I was so disillusioned with the FA I just laid there, not bothering to communicate with anyone or look at my mobile phone. Devoid of all emotion. The only Cup final I have ever watched on my own. I would normally be in at a mate's house or have them at mine. Failing that, then a group of us would be in publand necking beer after beer, backing a team emotionally or financially, whilst taking the piss out of each other. For some reason though on Cup Final Day in 2013, I just couldn't get in the mood for it. Even the winning goal as surprising as it was, failed to raise me from my slumber.

I feel sorry for the generation of Premiership fans who have never seen or felt the magic of Cup Final Day. Bigger than Christmas a couple of decades ago, the flagship of our governing body was struck by a radical torpedo by it's own admirals, who had been secretly building a ship more powerful than the world of football had ever seen, the SS Premiership.

The reason for this superstructure to exist in the first place was because the FA wanted an elite league that would aid the England team in regards to improving the coaching in this country and therefore produce a national team bursting with quality footballers which could then win major international tournaments. Nice idea. Except the FA didn't reckon on the chairmen of what was then called Football League Division One. Basically, they couldn't give a shit about football outside their own club. Self-interest led to a bigger share of the Sky TV money pot which in turn, led to ridiculous player's salaries that rocketed into the stratosphere. Wanting to protect their investments, the managers of clubs would then try and prevent their players from playing for their respective countries, which in turn, led to a club versus country divide. This in turn hindered not helped the England team.

A good example of this occurred in 2000 when the FA decided that for the first time, the England manager would come from foreign shores. The outstanding choice was Arsene Wenger who had achieved remarkable success with Arsenal by fusing technical ability with an exciting brand of attacking but intelligent football. Trouble was, his boss David Dein was on the FA Select Committee to appoint the new England supremo and blocked any approach for his manager. He resigned soon after.

Welcome to Planet Betrayal.

And if this wasn't bad enough for a football mad country who had been starved of success since 1966, the viewing public then had to pay through the nose via monthly subscriptions to a satellite TV company owned by a megalomaniac Australian who for decades had virtually brainwashed the British public into voting for various Prime Ministers via the disturbed media of tabloid journalism.

And did he care about the England football team?

That's why the modern football fan dreams about reaching the promised land of the Premiership, rather than seeing their team play in a Cup final at Wembley. The FA Cup flagship may not have sunk but it's slipping into the murky depths, deeper with every passing year despite the hype of the terrestrial TV channels.

Yet strangely, something wonderful has happened in the Premiership era. Despite our top League being hijacked by other parties and not because of it, the England team has improved technically due to overseas players being lured here with promises of wealth and all the social benefits this country has to offer. Take David Beckham (yes I know a lot of ladies would) for example. He started out as a promising young player and developed into a brilliant international footballer, and that's down to a foreign player, Eric Cantona. Beckham was inspired by the French maestro watching him put in extra hours of training and then perfected his own skills driven by dedication and sheer hard work. England supporters are grateful for that.

And the other influence in Beckham's life was his wife as she encouraged him to virtually become a brand in his own right by advertising after shave and modelling in underwear. Women are grateful for that! There's a belief growing stronger through the years that there are too many foreigners playing in English domestic football and that promising young home-grown talent doesn't get a chance to blossom. The confusion stems from understanding the difference between a foreign player and an overseas one.

As far as the England team is concerned, the Scottish, the Welsh and the Irish are foreigners simply because they aren't eligible for selection. There's no difference in the number of quality players available for the England team now than there were fifty years ago. The difference is that back in the day, League football in this country was a BRITISH game as opposed to the GLOBAL product it is now. Think back to all the League and Cup winning teams down the years. How many players were English?

For the purposes of this book, I researched and compared two England sides fifty-two years apart. I took note of the number of games they played for their clubs and how good those teams were.

This is the team that won the 1966 World Cup final ...

Player	Club	Appearances	League position
		(out of 42)	(out of 22)
GORDON BANKS	LEICESTER CITY	32	7TH
GEORGE COHEN	FULHAM	39	20TH
RAY WILSON	EVERTON	35	11TH
JACK CHARLTON	LEEDS UNITED	40	2ND
BOBBY MOORE	WEST HAM UNITED	37	12TH
NOBBY STILES	MANCHESTER UNITED	39	4TH
MARTIN PETERS	WEST HAM UNITED	40	12TH
ALAN BALL	BLACKPOOL	41	13TH
BOBBY CHARLTON	MANCHESTER UNITED	38	4TH
ROGER HUNT	LIVERPOOL	37	1ST
GEOFF HURST	WEST HAM UNITED	39	12TH

Out of a possible total 462 league games available to the World Cup winners, 417 were played in – an impressive 90% appearance rate.

However, in a 22 team league, the average position any player's team finished in was 9th. Defender George Cohen in fact was fighting a relegation battle and only four players played for a top club.

Now here are the players that started in the 2018 World Cup semi-final…

Player	Club	Appearances	League position
		(out of 38)	(out of 20)
JORDAN PICKFORD	EVERTON	38	8TH
KIERAN TRIPPIER	TOTTENHAM HOTSPUR	24	3RD
ASHLEY YOUNG	MANCHESTER UNITED	30	2ND
KYLE WALKER	MANCHESTER CITY	32	1ST
JOHN STONES	MANCHESTER CITY	18	1ST
HARRY MAGUIRE	LEICESTER CITY	38	9TH
JORDAN HENDERSON	LIVERPOOL	27	4TH
JESSE LINGARD	MANCHESTER UNITED	33	2ND
DELE ALLI	TOTTENHAM HOTSPUR	36	3RD
RAHEEM STERLING	MANCHESTER CITY	33	1ST
HARRY KANE	TOTTENHAM HOTSPUR	37	3RD

Out of a possible total of 418 league games available, 346 were played in. That's 83%, seven percent below the '66 side.

But look at the standard of teams they played for, an average finishing position of 3rd, six higher.

Only two players didn't play for a top club in Pickford and Maguire; yet out of all twenty-two players from both eras, these two were the only ones who were ever present. Not one player from the 2018 side appeared for a club in the bottom half of the League.

As for top teams not giving young players from the lower levels the opportunity to showcase their talents in the best league in the world, I also researched all of these players to see where they started their careers.

Goalkeeper Gordon Banks was the only member of the 1966 team that started his career in a level three side (Chesterfield) while two players from 2018, Harry Maguire and Dele Alli (Sheffield United and Milton Keynes Dons, respectively) started out from there. Six players from both eras started their careers in the top League.

Conclusion? Well you may draw your own, but as far as the England team selection goes, has the number of foreign players really damaged our national game? I don't think so. They've raised the bar and influenced English young players with regardings to discipline, diet and technique. By investment not only in club's facilities but also in a national centre of excellence, the players, the conditions and the coaching has improved vastly.

But what about the rest of the British Isles? Scotland, Wales and the two Irish teams have weakened through the decades as their respective Football Associations have allowed the game to decay to such an extent that it's seen as a major achievement if any of them qualifies for a big tournament these days. Countries who have produced brilliant international players in history have stagnated and been overtaken by European states that didn't even exist before 1990.

So, as an Englishman, I'm naturally happy at the way things have gone as I've never considered myself British. When my country is eliminated from either the World Cup or European Championship tournaments, the other four countries cheer. It's the only thing they've got to smile about; but just think of what it's like to live as a football fan, only existing to watch your enemy fail.

1986 WINNERS – LIVERPOOL

During my time as a small boy to a young man, Liverpool dominated not only the domestic scene but also the European stage. For eighteen seasons inclusive they were League champions eleven times, won seven Cup finals and despite being banned for five seasons, captured six European trophies.

The Red Army were a footballing superpower and it's creator was Bill Shankly. He was passionate about the game, a man of the people, a brilliant motivator and orator, charismatic, honest and would deliver a speech that thousands of politicians could only dream of. He was also a socialist and by treating everybody the same who played under him, he made the game simple by installing rules and disciplines that were virtually impossible to break. He was a father figure to the whole squad.

His secret was to sign players shrewdly from lower League sides. Once you signed for Shankly you quickly learned the Liverpool way. Win the ball, pass the ball and then move into space to receive the ball again. The very first thing you mastered was the 'block' tackle, one foot behind the ball supported by your whole bodyweight, then find a team-mate. Allied to hard work he transformed Liverpool teams into relentless machines and brought astonishing success.

Loved by all fans, players and staff, Bill Shankly was a figurehead and everyone in the game who met him revered him while at the same time fell in love with his personality and enthusiasm. The brains behind the brilliance lay in 'The Boot Room' which was situated just a few yards inside the player's tunnel by the side of the pitch. Away from the directors of the club, here he would hold court with his backroom staff after training, over a cup of tea. Bob Paisley, Joe Fagan, Ronnie Moran and Roy Evans would all take over the reins at some point in their career and Paisley especially, reaped even more success than Shankly, but the seeds were sown inside the mind of the master. Shankly's way was the Liverpool way.

But for all their domination, only once did they achieve the coveted double of winning the League Championship and FA Cup in the same season. The 1986 side was a multi-national line up under player/manager Kenny Dalglish. The goalkeeper hailed from Zimbabwe, while the ten outfield players consisted of four Scotsmen, one Welshman, one Australian, a Dane and three Irish internationals. When someone tells me there are far too many foreigners in the game nowadays, this is the team I always use as an example to show that it's often been the case in history too.

Their opponents on the day came from the blue half of Merseyside. Everton had six Englishmen playing for them and it was one of those who opened the scoring. Gary Lineker using his pace to outrun the Liverpool defence and showing just a taster of what would follow in the World Cup later in the summer when he was the tournament's top goalscorer. This day however er belonged to Ian Rush of Wales who replied with two goals either side of Aussie Craig Johnston's netting.

Shankly's never-say-die spirit lived on in this performance five years after his death. A psychologist who made things simple and loved to tell his players things such as "there are two great teams on Merseyside. Liverpool and Liverpool Reserves!" When you played for him, you believed in him and he laid down the blueprint for all managers who succeeded him.

That night I met John Martindale and Mark Ross, a Liverpool fan, for a typical Saturday night pub crawl. The whole town it seemed was full of Liverpool fans and no doubt there were celebrations all over the country too. For the best part of two decades, Liverpool Football Club ruled English and European football as generations of fans took them to their hearts and tormented the hell out of both Evertonians and Mancunians alike.

For me, it's crazy to think that the Reds haven't won the League title in thirty long years. It's in their blood. It's the one trophy which Shankly labelled the most important one, the one they must win. The one piece of silverware that has eluded them since 1990 was once part of the furniture at Anfield brought back time and time again by Shankly himself, Paisley, Fagan and Dalglish.

Kenny Dalglish in his first season as player/manager had achieved a remarkable double and almost emulated it in 1988 and again a year later. In 1991, without warning, he resigned which sent shockwaves throughout the world of football. Liverpool at the time were top of the League and defending champions when he stepped away from the club he loved citing pressure, mental fatigue and an everlasting sadness of the Hillsborough tragedy. His successor Graeme Souness, himself a former captain during their glorious period, stormed in like a hurricane and destroyed the Anfield legacy by changing the philosophy of the club too quickly. The boot room principles were destroyed with it, and the club was never the same. Years of smooth transitions between managers had been torn apart and by the time the board had acted by relieving Souness of his duties, it was too late. Ex-boot room boy Roy Evans took over at the helm, but by then Liverpool's hated rivals Manchester United were now Kings of England. A bitter blow for passionate fans whose eternal optimism is matched only by their fantastic humour.

Bitton AFC have very good facilities. The three pitches at the Recreation Ground, two football and one cricket, are in excellent condition. It's a picturesque set up but I spend so much time admiring it that by the time I'm paying my entrance fee, all the match programmes have sold out. Richard the programme seller is the friendliest face there and gives me his copy after the game.

The White Horse Men of Westbury appropriately wear an all-white strip today as per FA rules when there is a colour clash. This can give the home team a psychological edge, given their familiar kit and surroundings; but I really want Westbury to win after the approachability of Greg Coulson they had allowed me in the previous game.

BITTON AFC 3 WESTBURY UNITED 0

As in any significant game there are three teams out on the pitch today. The home team, the away team and the trio of officials. The referee and his two assistants aren't expecting a nasty game as both teams have won all of their respective seven games this season by scoring a hatful of goals.

Their pre-match team talk proves as accurate as the precision passing I'm witnessing in the first few minutes. Both sides are already attacking each other's defences and not a dirty challenge in sight. It is however, a refereeing decision which leads to a goal after just ten minutes and it's a beauty. A free kick is awarded to the hosts in a dangerous position which results in Bitton player Josh Egan curling a brilliant effort into the top right-hand corner of the net. Let's face it, only a stunning goal like that could beat goalkeeper Ed Baldy who has just conceded his first Cup goal of the season. Previously he'd been unbeaten for three hours and ten minutes.

Bitton supporters don't have to wait long for the second goal. A goalmouth scramble ends in Josh Egan yet again finding the Westbury net. 2-0 already and the fact that Bitton haven't conceded any goals since last season means that the visitors just don't have a mountain to climb, they have a whole range of them to conquer. And just when I'm thinking that things can't get any tougher for Westbury, they're reduced to ten men.

Will Stead is shown the red card for an incident on the far side of the pitch that I struggle to see. Disappointed and downhearted as his team-mates are, they show little dissent. It's a pity for Westbury. From a football perspective they've created good chances to get back in the game before the sending off but first a goal line clearance followed by a glorious save from Sam Burgess in the Bitton goal frustrates the White Horse Men and signals armageddon.

Half-time comes quickly because it's an enjoyable game. I spot chairman Greg in the clubhouse and he merely shrugs his shoulders. He's realistic enough to know it's probably the end but his team will fight to the death.

As it happens Plymouth Argyle are playing just a few miles down the road at Bristol Rovers. The police, in their wisdom, have ordered that this powder keg of a local derby (240 mile round trip) should kick off at lunchtime instead of the traditional 3pm. Her Majesty's finest it seems, still haven't worked out that in this age of twenty-four-hour binge drinking, pissheads at a football match couldn't give a toss about the time of day when it comes to having a go at their 'local' rivals.

Two blokes on my right are Rovers fans and are listening to developments on local radio. There can't have been many because the game ends 0-0. Any point for Argyle away from home is a point won in my opinion and on hearing the final score I shout "yes!" and throw my right fist upwards in semi-triumph. They both look at me. Thinking quickly, I point towards the Westbury goal and comment, "another corner for the lads! Playing well aren't they!" I'm relieved when these guys only seem to take a passive interest in this game. This means they're not masterminds when it comes to the subject on the history of Bitton AFC and therefore won't ask me any tricky questions which would only reveal my false allegiance and in that sort of quiz, there's no option to 'pass', just an offer of a facelift, free of charge, obviously.

During the second half, I decide to turn my attention onto the performances of the three officials. A penalty shout for Bitton is turned down with a shake of the head and a smile. Nice man-management.

Westbury to their credit never give up but are leaving themselves open to counter-attacks. Then, on my side of the pitch, I see and hear an unsavoury incident. One of the Bitton defenders verbally assaults the referee's assistant simply because he's had the audacity to award Westbury a throw-in. Yelling at him to go forth and multiply, as well as implying that the young lad plays with himself is both unjustified and ugly. A mistake is a mistake, but the end result of this one is only a throw-in. His team is two goals up against ten men so it's hardly a frustrating situation for him is it? Such a trivial outcome doesn't warrant pure nastiness.

Swearing at a referee out of frustration in the heat of the moment is understandable and even accepted in the arena of sport even if it is against the laws of the game, but not verbal assault. That's a different issue. Surely a red card offence which had he done this in a public bar would probably lead to him tasting his own blood. The referee's young assistant ignores it though. Maybe he's already used to it.

The daft thing is that just a few minutes later, the gobshite actually applauds one of his team-mates who also makes an honest mistake by momentarily taking his eye off the ball and giving Westbury possession. "Unlucky!" is his biased appraisal. He obviously hasn't read the official statement by the very club he represents in the match programme regarding objectional behaviour. On page four it states that foul or abusive language will not be tolerated. Initially aimed at spectators it then addresses the staff and players of Bitton AFC:

'TEAM MANAGERS AND PLAYERS ARE ENCOURAGED TO LEAD THE WAY IN RIDDING THE GAME OF AN UNNECESSARY EVIL AND SET AN EXAMPLE BOTH ON AND OFF THE FIELD OF PLAY'.

I wonder, had he been sent off, would his club have appealed against the decision?

Now another possible title for this chapter crosses my mind. 'The Prattle Of Bitton'. And then guess what! Gobshite (I won't use his real name just yet) scores a header in the last five minutes to make it 3-0. And it is a very good header. He's had an impressive game at right back, marauding down the right-hand side of the pitch time and time again, resembling a winger more than a full back. A constant thorn in the left-hand side of the pitch for

Westbury. Such a shame his verbal skills aren't the same standard of his footballing ones.

The Referee

"The trouble with referees is that they know the rules, but they don't know the game."
BILL SHANKLY

Sean Rothwell pops his head around the bar in the clubhouse and motions for me to join him in the Bitton AFC Official's lounge. He introduces me to his two assistants, Nick Eckland and Brandon Hawkins. Thoughtfully they've ordered a bowl of pasta for me. That's four friendly faces at the Recreation Ground today.

Who'd be a referee? Why would they want to do it? I mean, every single time they blow their whistle they're disappointing at least eleven people! Sean took it up for two reasons. Firstly, his dad was a referee and secondly, when Sean himself realised he wasn't good enough to play at a high level, he wanted to stay involved in the game, so he hung up his boots and picked up the rule book.

In my eyes, he's doing it for the right reasons. As a player I would always scrutinise a referee and quickly work out whether he was a Neil Midgeley or a David Ellery. The difference in attitude between these two top-flight referees is an almighty chasm. Midgeley once said on TV that it was the attitude of the players that should determine the attitude of the referee. In other words, if you wanted to play football, he would let the game flow and hardly be noticed. But if you wanted to kick each other and act stupidly then he would distribute cards quicker than a Casino croupier dealer.

Ellery to me, on the other hand seemed to thrive on his power and authority. A schoolmaster at Harrow, he treated players as he would his pupils and talk to them as such. No adult male worth his salt will stand for that. I once saw him on a documentary admit after one game that he blew the whistle a few times because he felt it was getting too boring in the second half. Someone, somewhere forgot to tell him on his way up the official's ladder, that although he was an important part of the game, he was only a part of the game and not the star.

I'm happy to be in the company of a referee who has taken the Midgeley view into that side of the game and mainly turns up for the love of it; and these days they can love it longer as there is no official retirement age, which ensures a better and more experienced performance all the way up the pyramid. Gone are the days when referees were fast tracked at a young age and as Bill Shankly's quote resonates with almost everyone who has played football at any level, they were thrown into match situations they never seemed to understand. They never had time to play it, only to learn it. Theory is one thing but putting it into practice and taking charge of twenty-two people? Well, you'd have to take part as a player to grasp what the game is all about. "You need people that aren't that good at football but still know the game," Sean echoes.

Talking to these three guys it's clear that today's game was in good hands. It's a testament to their performance as a team that the big decision which proved the main turning point isn't discussed or debated amongst the Westbury fans or officials. As a trio, this was their first game together, but the communication was good between them. Very good actually when you take into account the temperamental behaviour of the buzzers they were wearing on their wrists.

And what about that sending off? The altercation between two opponents was dealt with swiftly. Not often do you see a dismissal so early in the game, but Sean shows a matter-of-fact attitude towards the two yellow cards given to the same player in a short space of time therefore resulting in a red. "You do what you have to do." he simply states. He calls it game management; a term football fans usually hear accredited to managers. The three of them didn't expected an incident like that today, given the quality on offer, but it's easier to accept a player being sent off when the officials have the right attitude. Communication and man-management makes the job easier. The remaining players on the pitch respected it and got on with the game.

But what about the Bitton player who had a go at Brandon? Before the young assistant can answer, Sean interrupts and says that in their official capacity they cannot commit to giving an opinion. It's a grey area. The rule in the referee's handbook (LAW 12 – FOULS AND MISCONDUCT) states that: 'offensive, insulting or abusive language and/or other verbal offences is guilty of dissent and therefore a caution' (yellow card). But further down the paragraph it states that 'offensive, insulting or abusive language is a sending off offence' (red card).

No wonder qualified referees cannot commit to an answer, it's as clear as mud! Surely it's time the footballing authorities made the laws of foul and abusive language simpler...

Dissent or Foul Language – yellow card
Abusive Language – red card

How do Sean and his two assistants feel about the newly introduced VAR (Video Assistant Referee), a system that sets out to correct 'clear and obvious errors' and 'serious missed incidents'?

"It's here to stay," he concedes. "It's meant to help but puts more pressure on us to get it right." As a football fan I'm all for video assistance to correct errors. It's long overdue and should improve the game by doing what it's supposed to do, but unfortunately the way it's implemented is actually intimidating referees. Rather than helping them to remain consistent, they feel as if they are personally judged by another official who's nowhere near the ground.

I've learned recently that it was David Ellery who came up with this system. A non-sensical approach which does actually now make more sense to me now that I have found out it's the brainchild of someone who would see video technology as a threat to his power and ego.

My solution is that both managers and captains should be allowed to challenge a referee's decision just once per half. If upheld, they would be allowed another challenge in the same half. If overturned, they would have no more opportunities to do so in that half. Once challenged, the referee on the pitch would have access to a video of the incident played to them by a fourth official who would be situated at the entrance to the player's tunnel. It would be resolved quickly and the referee's decision would be both final and accurate, as a result of not being placed under pressure by one of his peers.

The problem with VAR as it stands is that referees are made to feel they have to change their minds because another official is watching, but if challenged by either a manager or captain there's no such pressure. The referee retains their authority. I understand Sean Rothwell's almost fearful acceptance of this radical change to the game.

What is his ambition? "To go as far as possible," he answers. From what I've seen today, he can easily handle a game at a higher level. He learnt his trade in a referee's academy that ran alongside Plymouth Argyle's coaching academy. Being coached in a professional environment seems a logical blueprint for understanding the football culture. His fitness is regularly assessed and his performances are observed fifty per cent of the time by an assessor in the ground. They are marked out of ten. Just as the better football teams get promoted up the pyramid and just as the better players can progress to a higher level, so it is that the better referees are rewarded in the same way. Refereeing well and consistently is a great incentive.

I speed back to Plymouth. I'm due to meet a woman for only our second date. She says she understands when I text her to say I'm running late due to my post-match chat with the match officials. Being the romantic so and so that I am, I've arranged to meet her in one of our local pubs to watch the second half of England versus Spain in the inaugural Euro Nations League. This is a tournament devised to replace meaningless international friendlies. She's a big football fan anyway, so I'm only thinking of her happiness, yeah?

Oh England my England! Just as I watched my first FA Cup final in 1974, so I watched my first England game two weeks later. We were beaten by Scotland 0-2, an early disappointment which would stand me in good stead for the future.

But they remain my team, my country, my passion. The highs of following them, and there haven't been many, far outweighs the highs of anyone claiming to be a supporter of a big Premiership team situated miles away from where they live or come from. I'm English, born under the St George Flag. I'm Plymothian, green blood soars through my veins. What colour runs through yours? If you can honestly answer that, then you'll always have an identity.

Listening to the first half on Talksport Radio, Spain deservedly go into a 2-1 lead. I get to the pub at half time where my date is waiting outside. In the second half England outplay the Spanish dominating them all over the pitch. Danny Welbeck scores and it's 2-2. The pub's happy and the players joyful. Hang on a minute! The referee has disallowed the goal! Why? Several replays show nothing wrong with it but nevertheless, the man in black awards Spain a free kick for foul play.

At this stage of Europe's new baby VAR isn't used which allows the travesty. If there was video assistance tonight the goal would have stood and we'd get what we deserved. Welbeck's crime as it turns out is to stand underneath the ball waiting for it to drop while both Spanish goalkeeper and defender collide with each other. The goalkeeper drops the ball on the English striker's head who reacts quickly and prods the ball into an unguarded net.

Where's Sean Rothwell when you need him!

Chapter Four

THE CURSE CONTINUES

Two days later I'm into my new fortnightly routine of monitoring the FA website to see where my adventure takes me next. Just after 1pm and with impeccable timing I receive a text message from John Martindale. It reads 'Taunton for you mate'. And then I see it online, Taunton Town versus Bitton AFC.

The Cup at this stage is still regional so no venturing as yet beyond the westcountry and Taunton, just like Westbury, is a direct train journey from Plymouth. What a pity Saltash didn't make it this far in the competition. Callum Martindale would be playing against his former team in the FA Cup.

It was about this time that a mate of mine, Dave Lloyd, messaged me through Facebook to inform me that Bitton are doomed as I've put a curse on them. So far the teams I've followed have all been drawn away from home and not only have they lost, they've also failed to score. The three previous games have finished 1-0, 3-0 & 3-0. I've already jinxed Saltash and Westbury so Bitton, he reasons, are next for elimination.

Taunton Town are fresh from winning the Western League and therefore have been promoted up to level seven of the pyramid into the Southern League, precisely halfway between the division Saltash play in and full-time professional football. Halfway to paradise if you're a fan of the round ball game. Two years ago, they reached the first-round proper and in front of a bumper home crowd entertained Barrow in front of the Match Of The Day cameras on BBC1. It was very strange catching glimpses of Callum Martindale playing live on television albeit for a few minutes as the Beeb switched quickly from one game to another, searching for a big story. I remember that particular Sunday afternoon texting John who was in Taunton's ground that day and mentioning that his eldest son was actually living the dream; the same dream we had as small lads kicking a ball about on the local green. To make it a Martindale treble, the TV cameras zoomed in onto John's other two sons, Harvey and Brennan who were with him, not realising they were getting their fifteen seconds of fame.

It's a short hour and a half journey to the heart of Somerset by train from Plymouth followed by a five-minute cab ride to the Viridor Stadium. Straight away I found the place very welcoming. Taunton Town FC are known as 'The Peacocks' and I'm 'pheasantly' surprised at how friendly everyone is. A friendly face from Bitton is in the bar. Richard the programme-seller is enjoying the local cider. I shake his hand and wish him good luck.

Everything is starting to get bigger now on this journey. This ground can hold up to two and a half thousand spectators and today's attendance will be larger than the three other games put together. As well as half of the attendance money, roughly £2250 each, the winners of this tie will receive a further nine grand in prize money. A small fortune for clubs at this level which, if Dave Lloyd's vision of doom is correct, will be going the way of Taunton.

Home advantage is everything in football, most of the time anyway. It shouldn't be. The pitch has grass on it like any other and is roughly the same size as any pitch you'll find on the planet; but half the game is psychological, and the home team will always have that proverbial twelfth man … the crowd. Getting behind their team can make the players feel like superheroes and can even subconsciously influence officials into giving incorrect decisions against the away team, through sheer intimidation.

At this level you can also drink alcohol whilst watching the game. I order a pint of Thatcher's cider (when in Rome and all that) and stand behind the goal which Taunton will be attacking in the first half. As I take the short walk from the clubhouse, I notice that the home team actually have a data analyst busy inputting the player's names into his laptop. He'll be tracking their movements, their mileage, successful pass rate etc …

He's in for a busy afternoon.

The whole set up here is virtually professional. Taunton Town have a dietician, a physiotherapist and even a sports scientist. For the first time on this Cup run I see that the home fans are wearing their team's colours, replica claret football shirts.

The weather is horrendous. Driving wind and rain, conditions both players and supporters hate. Taking shelter underneath the stand I've got a decent view. That is until Chewbacca's big brother stands directly in front of me. He's half as wide as he is tall and just as hairy! Any sunlight that would dare break through the grey skies would be totally eclipsed. I move to the back of the stand holding a cider in one hand and with the other, pull myself up so I'm hanging from a girder giving me the highest vantage point in the ground. Then I almost fall off with shock when an unseen drummer boy suddenly bursts into a virtuoso solo which Animal from The Muppets would be proud of. I astound myself by not spilling one drop of cider, and now the game kicks off under a gloomy sky.

FA CUP SECOND QUALIFYING ROUND
SATURDAY 22ND SEPTEMBER
VIRIDOR STADIUM
ATTENDANCE – 450

TAUNTON TOWN 4 BITTON AFC 0

Dave Lloyd got it right! I'd put the curse on the visitors once again. There was no sign of that happening in the first few minutes though. Both teams despite the grey weather, started brightly. Classic English soccer colours are on show. The yellow and green of Bitton against the home side's claret and blue.

Individually, Bitton look comfortable in possession but collectively are playing within themselves. It's nothing like the expansive game that tore Westbury apart two weeks ago particularly in the first twenty minutes. You can sense the doubt they hold in their team-mates. 'I'm here and ready to perform but I'm not sure you are.' The Bitton fans who have made the short trip by coach in contrast are enjoying themselves underneath the covered stand at the other end of the pitch. Some of them braving the elements and stripped to their bare (and hairy) chests singing ...

'Feeling hot, hot, hot!'

The Peacocks around me respond with a tribute to one of the Taunton natives on the pitch ...

'He's one of our own, he's one of our owwwnnnn,
Ollie Chamberlain, he's one of our own,'.

Taunton captain and centre forward Matt Wright is the focal point of the home team's attack. Winning every single header from long passes launched towards him and ably supported by a vibrant trio of Dan Sullivan, Andrew Neal and local's favourite Chamberlain. Mistiming an attempt to win the ball on the wet surface, a Bitton player gets booked for a reckless challenge and the Taunton posse howl in protest. The bigger the crowd, the louder the noise, the more a referee can be influenced. The mercury that measures the barometer of bias shoots up to near boiling point and tempers soar around me. If the Saltash fans wanted an opponent to receive a yellow card for inadvertently breaking the laws of the game then these guys want the Bitton player hung, drawn and quartered. Or failing that, skip back a few centuries and have him banished to the leper colony which formerly stood behind the ground which is now an old people's home. They tell me at Taunton that the elderly residents highlight of the week is to retrieve the footballs that stray into their communal gardens. Not today though. Taunton will be ruthless in their finishing.

The home team start to turn the screw and force corner kick after corner kick. Whilst waiting the delivery of one, a Bitton defender spits onto the floor but is facing the Taunton fans as he does so. He's just clearing his chest but this is just the excuse the more vociferous Peacocks have been waiting for in this unforgiving part of the ground and they verbally wind him up. It works a treat. His attention slips from defending a dangerous set piece and onto a 'spat' with some of the spectators no more than five yards from him. Now I'm no lip reader, but words are exchanged which I don't believe you'll find in any FA coaching manual. He looks as if he's ready to take on the whole lot of them. Brave or stupid? Not as brave and stupid as a Reading fan I once witnessed one hot summer's day in 2005.

Mid-August brings about the first day of a nine-month long League season and every football fan up and down the country looks ahead to the first fixture with hope and excitement. It's a sort of late summer celebration; and for that reason, four thousand Plymouth Argyle supporters headed for Reading's Madejski Stadium, situated just off the M4 motorway. The Green Army, as they were yet to be known, had virtually taken over one end of the ground. With just a few minutes of the game left, we were hanging on by our nervously chewed fingernails watching a 1-1 draw and wilting in the heat. Then, without any signs of it happening, the Reading fans were stunned to see their team go 2-1 behind to a lucky goal, against the run of play. A rare counter-attack by Argyle ended with a scuffed effort which agonisingly for the home goalkeeper, rolled tamely into his net. You can imagine the sympathy for the opposing fans from the green end of the ground.

'Easy! Easy! Easy!'

The chant added insult to the injured Reading contingent who couldn't believe they'd just been hit by a sucker punch hardly powerful enough to knock a toddler down. As the full-time whistle blew, we started to celebrate an unlikely win and then I saw the most courageous act of my life. A Reading supporter, in his twenties I reckon, bravely muscles his way past a young female steward and starts a one-man pitch invasion. Tearing his top off to reveal a physique of a ballerina, he walks slowly toward us. Oh my God! Everyone run for your lives! He's going to chin all four thousand of us! I'd never seen so much guts … or a skinnier ribcage for that matter. Luckily for us he's apprehended by an unarmed police officer who is as appalled as we are amused. What an escape that was! We should have sent him to Afghanistan. The Rambo of Reading would have finished the Taliban off within two months.

Meanwhile back at the Viridor, Andrew 'Rocky' Neal (notice I've cleverly thrown in two Sylvester Stallone films), fires Taunton into the lead, which rubber stamps their authority on the game. Soon after, Dan 'Sully' Sullivan (now I've thrown in a Tom Hanks film), makes it 2-0 when his attempted cross is missed by everyone and ends up in the Bitton net.

And to the tune of 'Give It Up' by KC and the Sunshine Band the Peacocks are singing…

'Rocky Neal, super Rocky Neal'

Bitton never give it up though and bust a gut to try and lift Kindon's curse, but all to no avail and the half-time whistle signifies a two-goal lead for Taunton which reflects their superiority.

For the second half, I take a seat in the stand nearest the clubhouse which runs the length of the pitch. The average age of the clientele in this part of the ground makes me feel so young I've renamed it 'The Bus Pass Terrace'. Within only a few minutes of the restart, Matt Buse finishes off a brilliant team move to make it 3-0. This is the end of Bitton's excellent start to the season and the goal itself is generously applauded by their followers who are virtually soaked.

The visitors attack with spirit and this is personified by Dan Hynes, their cavalier if foul mouthed defender from the previous round who in a shit or bust situation, leaves a space behind him gratefully filled time and time again by Matt 'Socky' Wright (can't think of any films for that nickname) who is now more than ever involved in the game. It's now resembling basketball. You attack, we attack, you attack again …

The rain is belting down but despite these difficult conditions both teams deserve the utmost credit for sticking to their footballing principles and producing some quality play. Desperate to break their deadlock, Bitton force Taunton's defence to struggle amongst goalmouth scrambles and then, attacking for fun, Taunton strike Bitton's post twice with strikes from Sullivan and Wright.

Josh Egan, who scored two goals in the previous round, is denied by Peacock's keeper Lloyd Irish while at the other end of the pitch, Bitton keeper Dan Worton is giving a decent feline impression leaping about to keep the score respectable; but in a game that is easily the best I've seen so far, Taunton's Josh Nelmes adds a fourth goal late on, which is merely a statistic in a Cup match which was decided half an hour before.

"You can't blame gravity for falling in love."
ALBERT EINSTEIN

I wasn't to know it at the time, but from this day onwards, there would be three football teams in my life.

England, Plymouth Argyle and Taunton Town. I'm Plymothian, born bred and buttered. And I'm English to the core. So why now in my early fifties have I grown fond of an 'alien' team after just one game?

Legendary football manager Sir Bobby Robson once said that just walking into a football ground for the first time could make you fall in love with the place without you knowing it or even being able to do anything about it. Taunton Town are my adopted team because I'm not a native of the area. Maybe it's the friendliness of the place. Maybe it's the claret and blue colours I've always liked. Maybe it's the passion and humour on the sidelines. Maybe it's the interaction between the team and fans. Or maybe; yeah probably, it's because the team itself resembles a Sunday morning League side.

At 3-0 up I noticed there were small disagreements between the players. Nothing bitchy or immature, just demanding more from each other. the adrenaline running as smoothly as the ball being passed around the team. Believe it or not, and unless you've never been in a team, you probably wouldn't believe this but having a go at each other with a few choice words can actually cement bonds between team-mates. After the game it's not forgotten but forgiven over a few pints and many more laughs. Add the fact that these Taunton lads are bloody good players makes me reminisce two decades ago with envy when I was lucky enough to be involved with a couple of Sunday League teams similar in spirit and endeavour.

The Secretary

Andy Power is Taunton born and bred. After the game finishes, he stewards the players from the pitch to the sanctuary of the changing rooms. Helping out with crowd control and generally hands on in most departments of this football club is yet another sign of unity at this level. My chat with him is brief as he has to rush off and compile a match report for the local media, in which Taunton Town FC usually get star billing; and of course in this day and age, a website.

He introduces me to Andrew 'Rocky' Neal as I'm curious as to why the diminutive striker got his nickname. Apparently it's because as a youngster he was a battler on the pitch and according to onlookers, had the spirit of a Rottweiler. Shouldn't that be 'Rotty' Neal then?

Andy looks down the pitch towards the far goal net and absolutely purrs over the Peacock's third goal. A brilliant team move finished with style. In these horrible conditions you'd see teams struggle to put three passes together let alone six and he reads my thoughts when commenting just how good the standard of football was on show today.

As secretary, he's not the only member of the eight-man board working beyond his recognised duties. Chairman Kev Sturmey was the public address announcer today, stepping in for Nick Rickard who is unwell right now. Everyone mucks in here at the Viridor, including several of the supporters who help out on a voluntary basis. It's a community club.

His main duties are the administration of the football club, liaising with the Football Association on a daily basis before stewarding and match reporting whenever there is a game. He'll also cross the t's and dot the i's in order to complete player's transfer deals which reminds me of a funny but true story from the 1950's ...

Tom Finney was a legend in the game. 'The Preston Plumber' as he was known was internationally viewed as a world class footballer playing in the English League, back in the days of the maximum wage. This was a financially restricting system on footballers which ensured that in this country they couldn't earn more than £20 a week, and therefore, it meant that all clubs were competing on an even playing field so to speak.

Preston North End through and through, Finney shone for his local team playing at the very top level. Yet such was the demand for repairs to households and buildings just a decade after the Second World War, that he served an apprenticeship as a plumber which when completed, supplemented his footballing wage. If Preston ever played badly, they would be described in the press as 'a plumber and ten drips'.

One of his team-mates was a young, brash but talented Scot called Tommy Docherty. 'The Doc' as everyone knew him would later become notorious for his outspoken views as a manager, including leading Chelsea and Manchester United. In order to keep Docherty at the club, the Preston hierarchy invited him upstairs to negotiate a new improved contract. He was offered the maximum of £20 a week during the football season and £12 a week during the summer break.

The confident young Scottish international turned it down and demanded £20 a week all year round just like Finney.

-"But Finney's a better player than you," he was told.

-"Not in the summer he isn't!", came the cocky reply.

So, Docherty got his all year round £20 a week.

A week after my visit to the Viridor Stadium I was walking through Plymouth city centre when on turning a corner, I was amazed to see another English footballing legend standing at a cashpoint machine … Gazza!

Paul Gascoigne had appeared at the Plymouth Guildhall the night before telling anecdotes of his career and personal life before a paying audience. It had been a sell-out, just as any football ground had been whenever and wherever he played.

It was a cold bleak morning and all Gazza had on was a tank top over a tee shirt. He looked frail and smaller than I could ever imagine and a long way off from the stocky, strong and carefree talisman who scared the hell out of foreign opponents with his unstoppable body swerve and dribbling skills.

I just stood to the side of him and said, "Gazza, fuck what the press print about you. There's a million of us who love you." Forgetting the numbers he had to press, he turned, grinned and gave me a big hug.

"Thanks mate," he said in that thick Geordie accent of his and was only happy to oblige when I asked for the inevitable selfie.

I want to get one thing straight right now. I smelt no alcohol whatsoever. He was slurring his words and, as if reading my thoughts, pointed to his head, apologised (as if he needed to!) and explained that his speech was due to prescribed medication. Before I walked away, I spoke about the England team and the World Cup which was still fresh in the mind.

"Aye." His eyes lit up, "Southgate's doing great."

My final words I said to him was that even if that picture of him drying his eyes in on an England shirt had reached iconic status, the one thing we would always remember him by would be taking the ball towards the enemy, engaging them, teasing them before destroying them. He smiled again, gave me the thumbs up and turned back to tackle the cash machine which seemed right now to be giving him a bigger challenge than any previous opponent.

And then it struck me what Paul Gascoigne's problem was. It wasn't any addiction that any snake from the tabloid press would exaggerate and tell the whole world about and what it led to. They reported the alcoholism, the cocaine, the pills, the depression. You name it, he's battled it. This national treasure has had more than his fair share of demons which half the media take great delight in reminding us and trying to break his fragile spirit at the same time (a national tabloid for example would regularly leave a bottle of gin on his doorstep).

But sadly, there is one addiction that Gazza will never beat unless English football helps him.

Adulation.

Everyone in professional football who has met the man will tell you all about his pranks, humour, humanity, warmth and unbelievable generosity; not just those inside the game either. Once on a course in the midlands, I got to know a chap called Mark who worked in my firm's Glasgow Branch. When introducing himself to us at our first session, this Scotsman told us that he was a volunteer at Glasgow Rangers FC working in hospitality on matchday. As a lifelong fan, Mark was aghast when he found out that his beloved club had just signed Paul Gascoigne. He was ready to quit his post but decided he'd see for himself what this English wanker was really like. And he found out what he was really like. He finished by saying that Gazza was 'the loveliest person I have ever met'.

It all depends on your point of view I suppose or your ignorance. Either you speak as you see things, or you let the newspapers brainwash you.

Paul Gascoigne needs football in his life. They say he's brilliant coaching kids, so why hasn't anyone offered him a position within their club's academy? Get him through his coaching badges which for his brilliant football mind would be a breeze, and you've given him a focus in life. His love for the game conquers all demons.

One of England's greatest players, Jimmy Greaves, is a great example of what I'm talking about. He is an alcoholic, but he hasn't had a drink since 1979. Those close to him and the chance that football gave him working in the media has given the man a reason to live every day, and every day the demon is beaten. It's a mental target he reaches successfully because of his love for the game and the support he receives from it.

Taunton Town players didn't even exist when Gazza was at the top of his game. For one year and one year only, Paul Gascoigne was the best footballer on Planet Earth. That should have been the case for years but for a stupid challenge in the 1991 FA Cup final, which put his career on hold and very nearly finished it for good. No one back then understood mental health issues. They just dismissed his daft actions. On the day of that Cup final, manager Terry Venables would have reeled him in. But not even Venables, himself a visionary and very clever man, understood the dark side of the most powerful organ in the human body, the mind.

I'm not saying that he was the greatest footballer this country has ever produced. That's up for debate. But if you're picking the greatest England XI to date then Gazza would be in it alongside Tom Finney, Stanley Matthews, Duncan Edwards, Gordon Banks, Bobby Charlton, Bobby Moore and Jimmy Greaves.

After my brief meeting with the footballing maverick, I told people close to me that I feared he wasn't long for this life unless football came in and saved him. If he went too early, alongside the tributes pouring in out of grief would come the vultures in the press who would be dying to pick the meat off his bones; the same horrible bastards who parked outside his house for two years solid, leaving alcohol at his front door wanting him to self-destruct. I can see the headlines now. 'Gazza the wife beater!'... 'Gazza was an alcoholic'... ''I saw Gazza take heroin' ...

They'll print what they want without any form of prosecution or regulation, but if Paul Gascoigne is anything like the monster they've portrayed him as, then they are the mad and disturbed scientists who created that monster; a genius converted to a wasted talent; and they would succeed again in their aim which is to sell a few more newspapers and destroy innocent people. It's what these moral crusaders live for.

The fair-minded football fans amongst us (and thankfully there are a lot more) will simply remember Paul Gascoigne as the man who played in two major tournaments for England and stood head and shoulders over anybody else in both. How many times could you say that for any footballer who ever lived?

1975 WINNERS – WEST HAM UNITED

Watching Taunton play in their claret and blue strip reminded me of watching West Ham. In August 1989, a few of us hired a car for the long trek to east London to watch Plymouth Argyle lose 2-3 at the Boleyn Ground, Upton Park.

Two years later I formed my own Sunday League team and West Ham colours were my choice for our first strip. That colour connection may have started years before at Plym View Primary School in Plymouth as the football team there played in West Ham's second strip which was sky blue with two claret hoops around the chest and back. I would find out later that it was close friend Steve Marshall who chose that kit to play circa 1972.

The 1975 final was my first all day Cup final experience. Building up all week, the excitement in the playground had reached fever pitch by the weekend. When the game finally started at 3pm on Saturday you felt as if you knew all twenty-two players personally. At home, we usually watched BBC1 as opposed to the simultaneous ITV coverage. Only Royal Weddings back then were held in such high esteem in the three-channel era. Cup Final Grandstand would consist of special events such as 'It's a Knockout' where singers, comedians and veterans of the two respective teams competed against each other in fun games which inevitably meant all of them getting soaked by dyed water. You backed whoever you wanted to win the final itself, so you wanted the corresponding team to win this sometimes degrading competition. Today, you were either West Ham or Fulham.

What I didn't realise at such a young age or was not old enough to appreciate would be a better way of putting it, was the significance of one player's appearance in regards to both teams and the stadium where he would play.

Ex-England World Cup winning captain Bobby Moore was leading the Fulham side out in the twilight of his career, against the very team that made him, and at the stadium where he enjoyed his finest hour. Even now for me that's still mind-blowing. What are the odds of that happening? A level two club causing surprise and upset by knocking out level one clubs on their way to Wembley. And there to meet them is the captain's old team and former colleagues waiting to rip up the last pages of the fairytale.

Sixteen years a player at West Ham, he thought the best times were behind him as first he was dropped by England and then sold to Fulham. He'd won the FA Cup with the 'Hammers' in 1964. A year later he won a major European trophy and a year later, the World Cup with England. All at Wembley and all as captain of those teams, lifting each trophy in the Royal Box after climbing those famous thirty-nine steps. No wonder they have a statue of him at the top of Wembley Way! On Cup Final Day in 1975 he must have felt like best man at his ex-wife's wedding after an amicable divorce.

West Ham won the final 2-0 with both goals scored by a young pin up called Alan Taylor in a five-minute spell. Taylor was pure gold for the papers as a romantic 'rags to riches' story after being signed from Rochdale less than six months before. The twenty-one-year-old striker started a unique scoring run in which he hit the net six times in three games. All six West Ham goals were scored by him in the quarter-final, semi-final and final against Arsenal, Ipswich and Fulham, respectively.

Resembling a glam rock star which was the musical fashion in the early to mid-seventies, he pounced on two defensive errors to settle the final and for a while, catapulted himself higher than the Bay City Rollers, kings of the pop world.

But it was the captain of West Ham who became my cult hero as a kid, Billy Bonds. Not the best player on the pitch or in the country, 'Bonzo' always caught my eye on TV for some reason. Kevin Keegan may have been my boyhood idol but Billy Bonds was someone I always identified with. Like anyone who has a cult hero it's difficult to explain why. All I know is that when I played senior football I always wanted to wear the number four shirt. 'Six foot two, eyes of blue, Billy Bonds is after you' sang punk group The Cockney Rebels when five years later, Bonzo would again lift the FA Cup at Wembley, this time after beating Arsenal. Everyone of my age had a different cult hero. Everyone a generation above me had the same one; George Best.

So, the fantasy ended as the dreamers never wanted it to. Bobby Moore with just two seasons to go before he retired never got to lift the famous trophy at Wembley against the very club he had done so eleven years previously. Football is magical sometimes, but often cruel.

There is one more significant fact about the 1975 final. It's the last time the FA Cup was won with an all-English side.

Chapter Five

IT'LL BE ALL WRIGHT ON THE NIGHT

The dream is over. My hopes of witnessing the first ever FA Cup match contested between two teams from Plymouth have been dashed. Plymouth Parkway F.C. of the Western League have lost 3-1 at Gloucester City in the second qualifying round of this season's competition. Had they lasted just two more rounds there would have been a very remote possibility of a Parkway versus Argyle local derby.

The non-League outfit are based at a ground called Bolitho Park in an area called Manadon, about a mile north of Argyle's ground Home Park. It would have been quite something to hear the Green Army taunt their poorer neighbours with the traditional time-honoured insult of …

'You dirty northern bastards! You dirty northern bastards!'

Because every opponent of Argyle is north of Plymouth, even those on the south coast.

Oh well, there's always next year.

Off the pitch, a significant match has taken place in my personal life. She who shall not be named (as we're no longer together as I write this) and myself are now involved in a relationship after thirty years of 'will they, won't they' both flirting and distancing ourselves from each other, which makes Ross and Rachel from the hit TV sitcom Friends seem like porn stars. The one thing we have in common and the one thing that went a long way to finally arranging to meet for a drink was discovering that we have a mutual admiration for a notable historical figure in

Nelson. Not Lord Horatio who led the Royal Navy to inspirational strategic victories on the high seas, but Garry Nelson who played brilliantly for Argyle in our 1985-86 promotion season.

If we had ever lived together, we would have erected a massive column in the front garden in honour of the talented winger/striker.

Apparently 'she who shall not be named' had a schoolgirl crush on me. Five years younger, she would shyly run indoors whenever she saw me at my best friend's house next door to her. 'I don't go for looks,' she casually dropped into a conversation during one of our first dates. I can't hear that enough!

Being a huge football fan, 'she who shall not be named', is just as excited as I am about this adventure I'm undertaking. Someone else taking an interest is a good mate of mine called Mike Vallis who five seasons ago went on the same journey with his son Paul. It culminated in an appropriate final between Arsenal and Hull City in 2014. Appropriate because Paul is an Arsenal fan, and Mike follows Hull as he lived there while attending university.

Mike says he'd love to watch the next game at Taunton and will drive us up for the latest qualifier which until a few days before the game, we wouldn't even know who the opponents would be. The game was supposed to take place on Saturday 6th October but due to the wonderfully named Corinthian Casuals drawing with St Albans City, that date has now been pencilled in for a replay. This means we'll be shooting up the A38 and M5 to watch the Peacocks take on the eventual winners on a Wednesday night.

1990 WINNERS – MANCHESTER UNITED

I'd just got engaged to my future ex-wife after I moved in as a lodger to Tom and Val Symons in Darwin Crescent. A close knit cul de sac when I was a kid, the couple were friends of my mum and would look after anyone in the street if they could. In their circle of trust, their generosity and kindness was legendary, so much so that I insisted that they sat at the head of the table when I got married in August 1991.

The marriage lasted just two and a half years. Whenever anyone asked me what went wrong I'd respond with, "I got engaged to a sex kitten, but married a cat". A big problem was that my ex-wife wasn't a football fan. She didn't mind that much me having the ball, but I despised the chain that came with it!

Mike Vallis was my best man on the big day, and a year before in May 1990, he came round to my lodgings with his friend Rick from university to watch an epic final. It wasn't just the final itself that was memorable. Beating Liverpool and Oldham Athletic in their respective semi-finals, Crystal Palace and Manchester United brought the total number of goals in the three games to nineteen.

Less than an hour before kick off on Cup Final Day, I received a phone call from Barry Hawkings, a lifelong Crystal Palace fan and my former partner in crime. Although Plymothian, Baz claimed to be part south London and would refer to every one of his mates as 'Geez'. Had a quick word with Val who typically said it was fine, so Baz came up to watch assisted by the Westlake brothers and a couple more, as we packed the modest size living room where the lager poured like rain.

Baz wore a Palace claret and blue hat, scarf and shirt and soon had everyone else in fits over his all too obvious bias. Val told me later that Tom loved it as he usually watched the final on his own. The game ended in a 3-3 draw with Mark Hughes of United scoring a last gasp equaliser, his second goal of the game. Earlier, he'd put his team into a 2-1 lead before Palace introduced a substitute named Ian Wright who announced himself on the big stage by scoring a brace of brilliant goals and bringing him to the attention of England's top clubs. A year later he moved to Arsenal.

Crystal Palace had one hand on the famous trophy before Hughes' late strike prised their fingers away and in effect saved United manager Alex Ferguson from the sack. It seems incredible how one goal could help shape the future of England's domestic scene for the next quarter of a century. The game went to a re-play, also at Wembley, and in a comparatively low-key affair was won by a solitary goal scored by a United defender, Lee Martin. This was the first silverware for Ferguson at Manchester United, which signalled the start of the most successful collection of trophies ever won by a manager in English League and Cups before he retired in 2013.

Fast forward twenty-six years (coincidentally the same time span between former Manchester United manager Matt Busby's last League title and Alex Ferguson's first) and Mike Vallis is driving yours truly to the 2016 FA Cup final at Wembley. It was the day of my fiftieth birthday and he'd bought me a ticket for the first final I'd ever attended. And who are the teams fighting it out on this day? Crystal Palace and Manchester United! Only twice have the two clubs met in the FA Cup Final, 1990 and 2016, and both occasions mark a first for Mike and I. Respectively, the first final we watched on TV together, and the second final was our first we watched at Wembley.

The coincidences don't stop there. Nine days after the 2016 final we were back at Wembley this time watching Plymouth Argyle in a League play-off final at level four of the pyramid. It was only the Green Army's second visit to the national stadium. Twenty years before they had reached the same play-off final and who was sitting next to me watching it on our first trip there together? I should have married Mike!

Back to this season's Cup run. My 'Wembley Wife' picks me up from work and we head seventy miles east to Cider County. St Albans have won their replay and therefore are Taunton's opponents tonight. They play at level six of the pyramid in the National League South. Half of their team have previously been registered with a professional club and are managed by ex-Arsenal footballer Ian Allinson. This will be a tough nut to crack, on paper anyway. An overpriced sandwich baguette bought at the local Sainsburys is quickly devoured and it's off to the Viridor Stadium.

The Captain

Matt Wright cuts a thoughtful figure as he gazes onto the flood-lit turf. His attention switches to his team-mates as they warm up for the biggest game of the season thus far; but as captain, he won't be leading them into battle tonight. He's been suspended after being sent off a few days before for a rash heat-of-the-moment and 'over the top' challenge against the last side you would want to do such a thing to; the Met Police.

Matt's immediate reaction was to see if his opponent was all right, possibly fearing leaving the pitch placed in handcuffs as well as seeing a referee's card. Being the honest guy he is, he tells me that his marching orders were warranted and deserved the red card, even if his manager Rob Dray disagreed with the decision on social media.

He's agreed to meet me before tonight's game for a few words and the Taunton skipper is the first footballer I have shaken hands with since Paul Gascoigne and was born in April 1991, the same month as Gazza was scoring a wonderful goal for Tottenham against Arsenal in the FA Cup semi-final. At sixteen years old Matt was released from Plymouth Argyle by Mike Pejic, an ex-England international who held the position of 'Head of Youth Coaching'. Also released from the same set up was Sean Morrison, currently captain of Cardiff City, playing in the Premiership. The only reason for his departure was that decisions had to be made at the time. Seems that Argyle have regularly made those same decisions over the years and watched from a distance as players they have nurtured found a future in the game at higher levels. Pejic himself then left to work for Ipswich Town.

Matt managed to stay on the professional circuit, including signing for Crystal Palace and Swansea City where he played and trained under successful managers such as Neil Warnock and Roberto Martinez. After finally settling at a lower level in the pyramid, his only link to the professional side to the game was when Hartlepool United expressed an interest, but never made a move for him. Now at twenty-seven years old there was a danger of Taunton losing him, along with a number of his team-mates, his previous manager and assistant manager, in a mini-exodus to Truro City. Being Plymothian, alarm bells rang at the Viridor because the ambitious Cornish club is nearer to where Matt lives than the one he has graced for the last two seasons. Matt was signed in 2016 after playing in Sweden, and secretary Andy Power has had his work cut out tying key players down on extended contracts. Travelling to Taunton is difficult for the captain as he plies his trade as a self-employed plumber based in Plymouth.

The club trusts it's players not only to look after themselves physically in between games but also stick to an appropriate diet. Matt concedes there can be bad weeks as far as that discipline is concerned but it's very few and far between. Empowerment and responsibility is a powerful motivator for grown men.

As he turns his head to watch his team-mates the Peacock's captain starts to look lost. Missing out tonight on such a big game for the club hurts. "It breaks me," he admits. He'll still be on duty in the changing room though. Like most football teams, the captain is the leader and is a major influence even in a non-playing capacity. They have an informal code of conduct and a fines system which Matt enforces for misdemeanours such as player's not cleaning their boots or even forgetting to bring shower gel. It's more light-hearted banter than a disciplinary measure, which improves team camaraderie and if you want to win football matches, this is vital.

And again, this makes me think there's a Sunday team spirit amongst the Taunton players and it's something which Matt Wright acknowledges. "We're bad losers, we'll fight to the end." confirming what I'd already seen at Bitton. He then adds that the team will have a go at each other, both on the pitch and in the changing room if it means getting the best out of each other. A case of we strive for perfection, excellence will be tolerated.

One thing I realise when listening to him is how far I've already climbed up the English football pyramid. Matt competes at level seven but sounds top level, 'football dictates my weekend.'

Apparently, he's single now after his girlfriend finished their relationship and is now temporarily living with his mum. There can be problems when a young girl latches onto a footballer. She wants to party but he can't. The modern footballer is an athlete and has to live his life that way to forge a career in the game. I'm guessing that players at this level get paid roughly £250 a week which supplements their main income but obviously is not enough to replace it.

There is also a huge downside to being a professional footballer especially at the top level. For all the obscene money they're paid, there's a price they have to pay as the press will have you believe they're fair game for anything they feel like printing. Apparently, there's an unwritten law in this country that states that the more money you earn, irrespective of the amount of talent you possess, the more your private life is allowed to be invaded. You are now owned by the general public. You want a nice meal in a quiet restaurant, then you're going to have to sign autographs and pose for selfies whether you want to or not. You want to protect your family and keep them secure? Tough! A long-range lens will still show them to the world and it's all your own doing. After all, it is you that dedicated yourself to your passion and grew to be brilliant at it.

A few years ago, Liverpool and England captain Steven Gerrard found himself splashed all over a Sunday tabloid, due to his lack of addictions, vices or infidelity. 'GERRARD IS BORING' screamed the headline. It seems that an ex-girlfriend of his had spilled the beans on their relationship and was paid a five-figure sum. She complained that Gerrard didn't drink, never stayed out late, didn't smoke and wasn't a violent person. The only thing he wanted to do as it transpires was to train hard, eat and drink the right things, lead his team at the top level and get a regular place for his country. What a monster!

Footballers can't win can they. If they're not being portrayed as drunken, violent bastards, fuelled by cocaine binges or running up gambling debts then they're slagged off for their dedication and professionalism.

I've just thought of a more appropriate headline ... 'GERRARD'S EX IS A TABLOID WHORE'.

Before Matt Wright heads off to the home changing room to wish his team-mates good luck, I noticed chairman Kev Sturmey applying the finishing touches to the lush green turf, as tonight he's doubling up as head groundsman. Leading by example he personifies the motto in Taunton's changing room, 'You're nothing without each other.' It's one in, all in here at the Viridor.

There is one burning question though that I decide not to ask captain Wright. Why does everyone call him 'Socky'? I'd only heard rumours as to why. The reason for the nickname according to some Peacock followers is something to do within his role when introducing himself to a new member of staff. The story goes that somehow he'll manage to obtain a sock from the latest acquisition and then wear it on a certain part of his anatomy. I must admit I never saw anything like that in a Sunday morning changing room!

Matt Wright is a credit to the club and to the game. Upfront and honest, he comes across as a decent guy and utterly professional. His passion is obvious. But there is one question being asked by all Taunton supporters in attendance tonight. How will we fare without our leader?

FA CUP THIRD QUALIFYING ROUND
WEDNESDAY 10TH OCTOBER
VIRIDOR STADIUM
ATTENDANCE – 595

TAUNTON TOWN 5 ST ALBANS CITY 2

"Intelligence is the ability to adapt to change.".
STEPHEN HAWKING

The answer is well. Very, very well. Manager Rob Dray may not be an expert in the field of theoretical physics, but he's bloody intelligent when it comes to tactical changes on the pitch and tonight throws the right dice. Resigned to the fact that he'll be missing his captain leading the attack, who would have played with his back to the opponents goal shielding the ball from big defenders, Rob deploys two quick strikers instead. The idea being that they'll split the visitor's four defenders and run them ragged in order to create goalscoring chances.

That's the theory anyway, but for it to work physically, Taunton will have to change their approach to this game. Tonight, there is no target man up front. They'll have to keep the ball on the deck, pass it to feet or push it in front of a quick team-mate to latch onto. Unfortunately, they're on auto pilot when the game starts, knocking long passes deep into St Alban's territory half-believing Matt Wright is out there with them. The visitor's two huge central defenders simply chew anything served up to them and spit it out with interest.

After twenty minutes, neither team has threatened to break the deadlock but all that is about to change spectacularly. Rocky Neal lives up to his nickname, battling through one challenge after another and eventually is awarded a free kick. Standing behind the goal Taunton are attacking, Mike and I are convinced the set piece is over hit as it seems to curl harmlessly through the air until it's headed back into the danger zone. Matt Buse's reactions are quicker than all Saints players who fear to tread and he stabs the ball into the net. As Mike would recall after the game, "he wanted it more"

Level seven 1 Level six 0.

St Albans respond but unbelievably concede a second goal just five minutes later. If the first goal was a product of determination then the second is absolutely exquisite. Rocky Neal yet again wins the ball with tenacity and puts Matt Buse in possession. The scorer of the first goal storms forward and suddenly remembering that his team has a different shape to their attack tonight, prods the ball between two defenders for Danny Sullivan to chase. Once again, the ball into the penalty area seems over hit but Ryan Brett audaciously flicks the ball into the net. It's a confident and skilful finish which sends the Peacock fans into dreamland and I can't stop applauding. "Beautiful!" I hear myself say, "absolutely beautiful!"

So far St Albans have offered virtually nothing in attack. Any half chance they try to grab is quickly snubbed out by a Taunton player who looks as fresh and sharp as the next one. The home team attack with even more energy and force a number of corner kicks which eventually results in a third goal. As the half time interval approaches, Ollie Chamberlain takes advantage of uncertain defending and takes the whole ground up into the stratosphere towards heaven. 3-0. Three bloody nil!

The Taunton fans stood behind the goal offer the goalkeeper some comfort, reminding him in their own lovely way that it's a helluva long way back to Hertfordshire on a Wednesday night, and even longer when you lose a Cup match. He's had to pick the ball out of his own net three times but can't be blamed for any of them. Mind you, there's always the second half. Ryan Brett almost scores another just before half time but the ball hits the crossbar. If this was a boxing match, after six rounds the referee would stop it. The visitors are dazed after being decked three times.

The whistle blows for the interval and the St Albans team can't get off the pitch quickly enough. They'll retreat to their den and lick their wounds. In contrast the Peacocks strut, proudly fanning their claret and blue plumage. Over a cider in the clubhouse, we manage to get a signal on our iPhones and YouTube St Alban's manager Ian Allinson scoring for Arsenal in a Cup semi-final against Tottenham. It's a moment to reflect. He scored the winning goal after north London's very own 'Rocky'; David Rocastle had set him up. A brilliant footballer, the game lost Rocky to cancer at a very young age. Appearing only a few times for England it was such a tragic waste of life and a natural talent. Down to earth, he always travelled by tube on his way to training. Twice a League champion, he left behind a wife and three children who are now supported by 'The David Rocastle Trust', along with the local community, all set up by Arsenal Football Club.

St Albans take the field for the second half, no doubt having being rollicked in the changing room. At 1-0 they shook, 2-0 and they look rattled, 3-0 and they were about to roll over. Taunton are playing rock 'n' roll football tonight. Elvis Presley, Chuck Berry and Jerry Lee Lewis may as well be on the scoresheet.

The visitors react to their manager's war cry and see a lot more of the ball but still can't carve out any chances. The next goal for them is crucial. Only one goal but it makes a big difference between trailing 4-0 or 3-1.

A chance at one end, a half chance at the other. That's the pattern of the game until disaster strikes for goalkeeper Dean Snedker who somehow lets a mishit shot from Ollie Chamberlain slip through his grasp and roll tamely into the net. 4-0! And in typical sporting fashion, the Taunton posse behind his goal show him sympathy …

> *'Four nil, and you're fucking shit,*
> *four nil, and you're fucking shit'*

Up to this point St Albans are the poorest side I've seen on my cup quest, but with half an hour of the game left, they score the best goal I've seen so far. New signing Ralston Gabriel receives the ball on the left-hand side of the pitch, drops his left shoulder, swerves to the right and beats two defenders before executing a brilliant curling shot into the far corner of Taunton's net. Kindon's curse on the away sides has lifted, and this is the cue for Ian Allinson to make two substitutions and go for it.

St Albans now dominate possession of the ball but Taunton's defence keep them at bay, for a while at least. It seems almost inevitable when the score becomes 4-2. Ten minutes after that stunning goal, defender Tom Bender takes his time when the ball finds him after a corner kick,and hammers the ball home. And this brings a situation into a game of football that only football fans, players and managers understand. It's now all psychological. If you would say to anyone outside of the game that with twenty minutes left the score is four goals to two, that person would be forgiven in thinking that the team winning is in a comfortable position. Not a bit of it! The reality is that if your four-goal lead is halved, especially when playing a higher-ranking team, semi-panic can set in. The crowd, no matter the size gets nervous. This in turn affects the players in the same way a dog can be affected by it's owner's mood. They sense a different feeling. The opposition having found a way to score have their tails up and can benefit from the other team's uncertainty and confusion by attacking the ever-growing fragile defence, which had previously stood firm.

This is where the Master of Psychology comes in; the manager. How will Rob Dray deal with this? He simply steps back and assesses the situation. A tactical change takes place and a double six is thrown. He substitutes a striker and replaces him with a defender which strengthens Taunton's rearguard. But the instruction from the Boss isn't just to defend. They attack just as they did before, and why not? We've scored four tonight so we can score a fifth. They nearly do so a couple of times before Matt Buse scores a great goal in the final minutes. A technically superb volley smashes it's way high up into the St Alban's net almost with an air of contempt. It means the visitors comeback doesn't change things. Taunton are in the next round. The last game was good, this one was brilliant.

At full-time the tired but happy home team walk off to their anthem 'I am a Cider Drinker' by the Wurzels, which no doubt the locals will carry out to the letter long into the night. The draw for the next round has already been made and the self-titled 'Pride Of Somerset' Club will be travelling to Essex to take on Billericay Town who are top of the same League that St Albans currently lie sixth in.

The drive home barely takes an hour. While Hurricane Michael batters Florida and other south eastern states in the USA, hurried

Michael Vallis storms through the wind and rain and I'm home by 11pm.

Early to rise on Thursday morning and walking to work, I bump into Ken 'Ted' Taylor. Ted was captain of a Saturday team I mainly made substitute appearances for in the Plymouth & District League before breaking my ankle in only my second start. Anyone who played in the same Sunday sides as me after 1990 will be shocked as to how I earned the nickname 'Merse' after Paul Merson, the Sky Sports pundit who at the time played for Arsenal and England. In my first and only full game for Ted's team I scored our only goal in a 4-1 defeat against Saltash United's first team during a Cup match. It happened seconds after going 2-0 down and I struck a left foot volley as sweetly as I've ever hit. Nobody was more surprised than me!

The 'Gooner' fraternity within the team have always referred to me as Merse since then, including Ted who I like to call 'Chippy' which was Arsenal playmaker Liam Brady's nickname. After that injury I concentrated on running a Sunday team and a year later when I played again, put myself in a defensive position where I cynically reasoned that if anyone was going to get hurt, it wasn't going to be me.

Ted is walking the opposite way to me and asks me about the Taunton game which he knew I was at due to that wonderful stalking invention, Facebook. Ted is walking his dog Otis, named after the legendary soul singer. No doubt Otis will soon be 'shitting on the block on the way'.

Chapter Six

FLYING WITH THE PEACOCKS

My day starts at 5am and it's going to be a long one; taxi to Plymouth Station for a ninety-minute journey to Taunton Station, followed by a short cab ride to the Viridor Stadium in Wordsworth Drive.

Instead of a cockerill crowing, the local residents are treated to an early morning peacock chorus of that all time sexist classic and football crowd chant 'Get your tits out for the lads' when one woman has the nerve to complain about being waken up at stupid o'clock by Callum the drummer boy.

I'm on one of two coaches which have cost 2.8K carrying supporters and players alike on the only way to Essex. Apparently Taunton Town would only get 3K for winning their League. It's heart-warming to see at this level how important the FA Cup is. On the same table as me are away travel manager Rob Wenham who doubles as head steward for home games, supporter Dan Carter who doubles as team mascot and a couple called Jo and Estelle who double as husband and wife. They've been married for eight years and live opposite the ground. They met while watching the Peacocks and you get the impression they would love to rise first thing every morning to the sound of music delivered by a drummer boy dressed in claret and blue.

There's a fair bit of banter between Dan and Estelle which starts when the latter says she's known the former since he was 'a bump in the belly'. Dan refutes this and claims that he discovered Estelle in a cardboard box and that the happily married lady is in fact a serial streaker.

Once again Taunton will be taking on a team one level higher up the pyramid. Billericay Town are top of the National League South and have been bankrolled by the second most powerful person in Essex, Glenn Tamplin to the tune of two million. The 'Blues' have recently managed to attract Ex-Premiership players such as Jermaine Pennant, Paul Konchesky and Jamie O'Hara and with that sort of clout, it's not hard to see why Taunton today are 7/1 against winning. All three players have appeared in FA Cup finals and in fact Konchesky scored in 2006 for West Ham against Liverpool and was just seconds away from a winner's medal when a bloke called Steven Gerrard smashed in an equaliser sending the game into football's version of Russian Roulette, the dreaded penalty shootout. But for that cruel ending, Paul Konchesky would have gone down in Cup history as the scorer of the winning goal whilst cementing himself as a West Ham legend.

Out of those three players, only Jamie O'Hara is expected to play which the more vociferous contingent on this coach is looking forward to. Nothing to do with the skill factor mind you, but having a tabloid friendly colourful personal life plays right into the hands of unforgiving, merciless opposition fans. Half the game is psychological and Dan reckons the Peacock followers will get inside O'Hara's head by reminding him of his marital indiscretions.

The general feeling on board is that Taunton will have to start the game like they did against St Albans if they've any chance of progressing onto the same stage they'd be sharing with professional footballers. Captain Matt Wright is available after suspension and according to Rob Wenham who's in constant communication with the team coach, the players are feeling positive.

Somewhere on the A303 in Southern England, our table including myself are preparing tickets for the traditional away day raffle. Rob reminisces about Taunton's cup exploits two years earlier when they reached the first round proper and received 30K in TV revenue, which the club is still living off. Success on a Cup journey can also have it's downside when you're a travelling supporter though. One notable absentee today called 'Natch' won't really be missed on a long journey. Apparently his non-stop jokes are torturous with everyone starting with his catchphrase of 'Have I told you ...' which sends his fellow peacocks into a semi-coma. He's a 'pringles' joketeller. Once he starts, he can't stop. When Taunton visited Shortwood United in Gloucestershire for the second season running recently, even a barmaid exclaimed, "Oh for fuck's sake! Not you again!" when he walked into the home team's clubhouse.

The raffle is drawn and yours truly wins first prize. As a genuine gesture I ask for it to be drawn again as I'd prefer it to go to a real Taunton supporter. The prize is a refund on the coach ticket which is then won by Trish who is sat near us. My gesture has sort of backfired as this is her first trip as an away fan.

A regular supporter called Kev comes down from the top deck to reward me for my 'nice touch' and plonks a can of cider in my hand. It's only 9.30am and like I said this is going to be a long day, but a memorable one! Other prestigious prizes in the draw are Taunton Town FC calendars and air horns for the game. Someone upstairs has won the annoyingly noisy things but returns it to be redrawn. Not in the name of generosity you understand, but because he's a grown up. This 'gesture' also backfires unfortunately because he wins it again. I've never seen such a disappointed or ungrateful winner of a raffle prize.

Most of these good people are from Somerset, mainly Taunton and Bridgwater, and have followed the Peacocks for anything from three to twenty years. Just like any football fan whose local team plays in the lower levels of the pyramid; they also follow the top glamorous teams. Chelsea, Manchester United and Liverpool are popular on this coach.

Today though is all about Taunton Town. Just get through this round and who knows? National TV coverage and extra revenue are waiting around the corner. They freely talk to me about their hopes and memories …

NAME	FAVOURITE PLAYER	BEST MEMORY	PREDICTION
Dan	Lloyd Irish	Reaching FA Cup first round two years ago	2-1 win
Estelle	Lloyd Irish	none	5-0 win
Jo	Lloyd Irish & Matt Wright	Winning league last season at level eight	3-1 win
Troy	Ollie Chamberlain	Winning league last season at level eight	3-2 win
Ian	Matt Buse	Play-off match versus Tiverton	2-0 win

The right-hand column shows just how optimistic (or fickle) a the football fan can be, and will always be. I'm introduced to Dave Webster, fourteen years a Taunton supporter and a living legend when it comes to away trips for the wrong reason. During a nine-hour journey to the north east two seasons ago, Dave committed the worst act anyone can inflict on any fellow supporter on such an arduous trip by blocking the toilet. This touching story puts me off the sausage roll I've just purchased at Fleet Services.

It was the FA Cup first round and not even a superb gesture from Barrow Town Football Club to fund the visitor's entrance fee could numb the pain of the numerous coach stops due to unbearable bladder pressure. Dave used to be a Manchester United supporter back in the day when you could turn up to Old Trafford five minutes before the kick off, pay cash at the turnstile and not be forced to pay through the nose online for a ticket to watch the team you grew up with. Or to put it another way, when they were crap.

He's level-headed, frank and honest. He makes three predictions which astonishingly will all come true. A 2-2 scoreline, a Taunton player to get sent off and Jamie O'Hara won't be a problem. He believes that manager Rob Dray's passion is mirrored on the pitch but there is a touch of indiscipline. Three red cards in the last five games is testament to that. Looking through the coach windscreen and into the future, he mutters, "cometh the hour, cometh the man". Dave is engaging company and has just returned with his son from South Africa where they took in Rorke's Drift, the site where the British Army bravely defended their station in 1879 against thousands of zulu warriors, as depicted in the film that made Michael Caine a household name. Maybe it's this humbling experience that keeps him realistic about a football match.

Turning back to Taunton Town matters he praises Rob Dray, who he tells me cleverly signs players who can play in two different positions so as to not to not weaken the strength of his numerically challenged squad. Sunday League football again! Later on this trip, Dave visits the on-board toilet which ignites a collective groan from those with fresh memories of the Barrow trip. On hearing the flush work perfectly, the other passengers' relief is almost tangible, but Dave looks confused when stepping out of the door. When he went in there was daylight, when he came out there is darkness. How long was he in there? "We're in the Dartford Tunnel," someone explains to him.

The Steward

The story goes that one of the regulars watching Taunton play at the Viridor was a veteran of the Met Police. That was the buzz around the clubhouse which led to chairman Kevin Sturmey approaching spectator Rob Wenham in the crowd and offering him the position of head steward. After serving twenty-five years in the met, Rob moved west to Taunton and quickly became a fan of the Peacocks, as well as his home team Millwall. If you were born in Lewisham, you either wanted to play football for the south east 'London Lions' or rip up seats watching them. After choosing the legal side of the law, he ended up playing for non-League sides Oxford City, Ebbsfleet United and the met police itself where he claims he never got to know his team-mates very well due to different shifts in the line of duty, which meant a different line up on the pitch every game. There were about sixty players in the squad, he reckons.

As for Taunton Town, who is his favourite player? "Every one of the buggers!" is the quick answer. Once you've met the imposing Rob Wenham you're unlikely to forget him; and one thing I'll never forget is the reply he gives when I ask him his favourite memory following the Peacocks. Invading the pitch at Hemel Hempstead isn't something you'd expect of an away travel manager/head steward, especially when he led it! You'd be forgiven in thinking that offering this match day responsibility to Rob is akin to handing an arsonist a box of matches, but in reality, he's a decent bloke with principles.

As well as loving the players equally, he takes care of the supporters and in his experience has never seen such a connection between those on and off the pitch. There's no top or bottom at this club. Ninety-five per cent of work at this club comes voluntarily by everyone whether they're named in the match programme or they're buying it. By this part of the journey I'm realising I couldn't be travelling with a better bunch.

Then I ask Rob a question that leaves not only him but everyone else in earshot something that no football fan in the country can answer without provoking a conflict of head and heart. I put it to them that if Taunton Town reached the further stages of the FA Cup and were drawn to play against the mega-rich Manchester City, would they prefer the glory of entertaining them at home, or reap the riches that playing up north at the Etihad Stadium would bring them? At first, the response is predictably romantic.

"Manchester City at home! We could pull off a shock result!" They wouldn't like it with two thousand cidermen breathing down their star-studded necks. But then the business side of the game takes over as heads rule hearts. Yes, it would be wonderful to see one of the best teams on the planet come to Taunton but that would be over in a day. The long-term future of this football club is vital, so a 50/50 share of a sixty thousand attendance in Manchester would be very welcome, thank you very much. I mean, what's the point in a lavish and glamorous wedding day feeling like royalty only to live like paupers during the marriage?

So, what would Taunton Town FC do with all that money? "We'd get better stewards!" chirps in Dan Carter.

As I've interviewed people from different aspects of running a football club so far on this Cup run, I've been asking the subject to sign my match programme. Later, I ask Rob to sign my copy of Billericay's 'Town Crier' to which he responds by signing it 'Big Rob Wenham' and for those who can't read, he then sketches a downscaled version I suspect of his meat and two veg. He's too big and mean looking I decide, to ask him if it's a self-portrait.

On the more serious side to his job, he has a word with another chap called Rob and his partner in crime Willie who I christen 'The Taunton Taunters' about their conduct today at an away ground. It seems that several goalkeepers have made complaints to the League through their respective clubs about the special brand of 'banter', which allegedly crosses the fine line between taking the piss and verbal abuse.

Rob tells me he's played "a bit of guitar" in his time. His claim to fame was backing Toyah Wilcox as a rhythm guitarist, a gig he earned after turning up for auditions in his area – an easy decision for the organisers as he was the only one who turned up. Whenever the eighties' punk icon would see Rob she would greet him with "Hello Baldy, seen you around!" His own personal highlight was playing at Birmingham Academy. The crowd could hear him play but couldn't see him as he was stuck in the wings off stage. Apparently, his guitar kept on unplugging. Rob's got personality and unlike one of Toyah's hits, it's not a mystery he's so sociable.

On board today there are sixty-five of us. At £15 a ticket that makes £975 but this coach costs another £325 to hire, so where does the shortfall come from? A little comes from the raffle and then the balance is subsidised by chairman Kev and vice-chairman Brian Pollard. They obviously don't have to and it's not their responsibility as the away club is independent of the football club, but these guys know the value of support on the road, so in return for the luxury coach ride, we're asked to perform a guard of honour when the team disembarks theirs.

It's a beautiful sunny day in Billericay whose football ground is set in a picturesque English landscape. A country lane is the only way to drive into the AGP Arena, surrounded by greenery, which today is amplified by gorgeous blue skies. The welcome for the Taunton players is as warm as the weather. Travelling Peacocks applaud Rob Dray and his team, followed by handshakes, fist pumps and high fives. Apart from the Taunton Taunters that is! Eastender Rob and Glaswegian Willie break ranks to greet the home players behind the wheels of dreamlike Mercedes and BMWs with their own warm welcome ...

'You're only here for the money. Here for the money, you're only here for the money ...'

Alcohol it seems can reduce grown men to excitable schoolboys. As the Taunton team coach pulls off to park at the rear of the ground I suddenly notice the all too familiar crest on the side of it. Coloured green with a white ship and four letters underneath, PAFC. Plymouth Argyle Football Club! The bond is complete. Now I feel like one of the gang and can't wait to get inside.

Last Saturday was 'non-League day'. With no games taking place in the top two levels of the pyramid due to international fixtures, football fans around the country were encouraged to attend their local team's game in the non-League to boost attendances and revenue. Prices were reduced which attracted hundreds more supporters. A sort of 'happy hour'. Thus Billericay Town, known as the Manchester City of the non-League, attracted a gate of over fourteen hundred spectators for their game against Gloucester City. How many will they get today, just one step away from a stage where their owner's investment demands they should be.

Inside the ground, Billericay Town FC is indeed impressive. The home team's colour of blue is everywhere to be seen. Not only the signage but every single seat, which fills both stands running the two lengths of the pitch. The ends behind the goals are standing areas and are covered. Owner Glenn Tamplin's money has been put to good use and the entire set up looks equipped for bigger things. The clubhouse is big. Numerous spacious bars easily accommodate supporters of both teams and even two hours before the kick-off, there's a fair few inside watching Chelsea play Manchester United on big screen HD televisions. The barmaids are Essex girls straight out of a reality programme; forced smiles for the supporters and fake eyelashes which no doubt will be fluttering at wannabee professional footballers after the game.

Callum commands the middle of the room as he starts to bang the beaten-up drum whipping up the excited cider fuelled claret shirts, singing in time. It's a football supporter's version of pissing in all four corners of the room. This is now Taunton territory. Outside, behind one of the goals, a flag stating 'Pride Of Somerset' is prominently decorated, laying claim to this part of England.

A few ciders later, the team news filters through. Dave Webster's first prediction is correct. His bold claim that Jamie O'Hara will be no threat is spot on as we hear that he's only on the substitute bench. And he's not the only star who's missing. Dan Carter has forgotten to collect his mascot's uniform from the coach, meaning there'll be no cat amongst the peacocks. What a pity! What I'd give to see an oversized pussycat on the pitch just before a game, provoking an ex-professional footballer about his alleged extra marital activities.

The word 'togetherness' is repeated time and time again by various supporters and staff from Taunton Town. One such fan is Kev who donated my breakfast drink. A supporter for forty years, he's never seen closeness such as this, and good days are ahead, he believes. This football club gives everyone something. It makes people's lives worth living, something to look forward to. The Viridor Stadium isn't just a football ground. It's a place of worship, the centre of a community.

Just before the kick off I'm introduced to Simon the kit man.

"All right mate," he greets me.

"Hello Simon, so how come Taunton play in claret and blue then?"

"Dunno mate," is the reply.

"Oh ok. Do you know why their away strip is yellow?"

"Dunno mate".

"Why are Taunton known as The Peacocks?"

"Dunno mate".

"Ok well, enjoy the game".

"Cheers mate".

You just can't get a word in with some people!

FA CUP FOURTH QUALIFYING ROUND
SATURDAY 20TH OCTOBER
AGP ARENA
ATTENDANCE – 976

BILLERICAY TOWN 2 TAUNTON TOWN 2

So, Dave Webster's second prediction came true. Two down, sadly one to go. I join the Peacock's support behind the goal Taunton are attacking in the first half. The Taunton Taunters, Rob and Willie, take up their usual strategic position a few yards away from the Billericay goalkeeper and offer him some useful tips as well as questioning his parenthood, sexuality and ethnicity.

As the service starts, the choir sing hymn numbers 237 and 345 from the bestselling songbook entitled 'Goading The Opposition Fans'...

'Where were you when you were shit,
where were you when you were shit'

Followed by their 'fair' comparison with Greater Manchester's ambitious non-League club...

'You're just a shit Salford City, shit Salford City,
you're just a shit Salford City'.

It's a decent enough start to the game. Corner kicks for both teams, but then Billericay start to turn the screw. After twenty minutes Moses Emmanuel scores for the hosts. It looks like a defensive mix up or was it offside? Doesn't matter. Taunton are already one down and so far everything is going the way of status. Gladly though, Billericay's lead lasts just two minutes. Taunton respond brilliantly as Shane White crosses to Rocky Neal whose subtle first touch enables him a chance to score, which he takes with no fuss.

Behind the goal, the Peacocks celebrate and pay tribute to one of their unsung heroes to the tune of Andy William's 'Can't Take My Eyes Off You', although I don't think the late crooner would approve of the revised lyrics.

'Oh Danny Sullivan you are the love of my life,
oh Danny Sullivan I'll let you shag my wife,
oh Danny Sullivan, I want ginger hair toooooo ...'

I suspect Danny Sullivan wants ginger hair too, as he's bald. I bet the dynamic attacker also wishes he was given the opportunity to score on the pitch as well as off it, as he's on the substitute's bench.

The sun is shining straight into the Billericay goalkeeper's eyes but I doubt if Rob Dray's team talk would include launching the ball into orbit in order to blind him. That would be a waste of his player's talents. The home team have lost their rhythm which heartens the travelling support. We will now sing our fourth hymn of the day, so please turn your songbooks to page 23 where you'll find 'Insults For The Opposing Owners'.

'He snorts to the left, he snorts to the right,
Glenn Tampon, he's snorting all night'.

So, the same rumour that is all over the westcountry is now audible in the east of England. Someone had told me back in Plymouth that the man who has funded this impressive set up was interested in white lines not only found on the pitch, but rumours aren't fact. I do know for a fact though that Mr Tamplin wouldn't appreciate the improvisation of his surname.

Meanwhile, the suited and booted Peacock's chairman accompanied by secretary Andy Power have joined the support behind the goal, having carrying out their obligatory duties in the host's boardroom. Togetherness.

A few minutes before half-time, Emmanuel scores his second goal after Billericay suddenly remember how to pass the ball and move into space. Incredibly, and yet again, the lead is short lived. Shane White puts Ben Adelsbury in possession who ice skates around the Billericay defence and sets up Matt Buse who scores from close range. Two goals each! And then it's half-time.

Back to the clubhouse. More forced smiles, more fake eyelashes fluttering, more drinking, more drumming, more singing.

Taunton start the second half strongly, their belief growing down to rattling the home team's cage, in quick reply to conceding those two goals. Ten minutes pass when Billericay pay their guests a compliment by making a serious substitution. Here comes Jamie O'Hara to not only take but claim the stage. The Blues' out of tune orchestra now has a conductor. Rob Dray's tactical response is a bold one when he introduces the bald one into the fray. Danny Sullivan changes the number of attackers from two to three, as his manager sacrifices personnel elsewhere on the pitch. It nearly pays off. Immediately Taunton take control of the game and are given a glorious chance to take the lead after Matt Wright's presence in the Billericay area unsettles a defender to concede a penalty kick.

Dave Webster's words are ringing in my ears. "Cometh the hour, cometh the man". The captain takes the penalty kick and smashes it so hard that the goalkeeper can only watch it … hit the crossbar! An inch lower and Taunton Town would have been in the big time. Typically, this doesn't douse the Peacock's fire and half chances are created but then, Dave Webster's third prediction comes true.

His favourite player Andrew 'Rocky' Neal is sent off for what the referee deems a late and dangerous tackle. For me, it's a yellow card at most for a reckless challenge, but the victim of this crime milks it by rolling around in mock agony resembling a scene from Platoon. The referee seems influenced by these amateur dramatics and pulls out the red card. That's Taunton's fourth in six games. Fair play however to Billericay goalkeeper Alan Julian who earns a round of applause from the visiting congregation, when he faces them shaking his head and mouths, "no way was that a sending off".

At the opposite end of the ground, Taunton goalkeeper and fan's favourite Lloyd Irish is the busiest player on the pitch as Billericay try to press home their numerical advantage. It's now an onslaught. More players in all yellow see the same-coloured cards. Challenges are misjudged as frustration and fatigue replace steel and skill. Crosses from both flanks bombard the Peacocks but Lloyd Irish handles them with an assurance some of his teammates are lacking.

As the full-time whistle nears, O'Hara instigates more chances for the home side, but he's playing against the clock as well as a gutsy football team. Where there is danger, Taunton's number one brings calmness. At last, the referee calls time and it seems like a moral victory for Taunton. Then I witness an interaction between players and supporters I've never seen before. The Taunton posse line up along the railings behind the goal as if to give the second guard of honour today. The players walk towards them in single file as if they are greeting opponents before a big game. Everyone in a football kit gives every proud fan from Somerset a high five, a handshake or a hug before disappearing towards the visitor's changing room. Togetherness.

Thirty minutes later the players enter the clubhouse. Matt Wright looks gutted and needlessly tweets an apology later on for missing that penalty. He's applauded as warmly as any of his team mates as the drumming falls silent. These Peacocks have strutted into an Essex coliseum and left with barely a feather ruffled.

1953 WINNERS – BLACKPOOL

What if Lloyd Irish had dropped the ball? What if that mistake had led to a winning goal for Billericay? As far as Taunton fans are concerned, well yes, obviously that would have been a huge disappointment, but no more than that. The Peacock's goalkeeper is a fan's favourite which means any mistake he makes is instantly forgiven and ultimately forgotten. They love him.

Now think of two England players who were both sent off in the World Cup and the nation's different reactions to them after going on to lose the two respective games on penalties.

David Beckham in 1998 and Wayne Rooney in 2006; both played for Manchester United and both received the red card after kicking out in retaliation. Why was Becks the most hated man in the country after we were eliminated, and why was Rooney given nationwide sympathy after England lost?

The answer lie in our own perception of the two footballers. Rooney, carrying an injury, went into the 2006 tournament as our great hope, the one player who could win a game single-handed, and the best we've produced since Paul Gascoigne. Beckham on the other hand, went into the 1998 tournament with a reputation of immature petulance. A few years before being made captain of England and furthermore a national icon, he represented a side to the game that most of us despise. Over exposed as a commodity and in a relationship with an equally over exposed pop star, his footballing skills were never in question. It was his attitude that most England fans felt never warranted him international appearances at that time.

Saying that, his sending off was a disgrace. A travesty of justice meted out by a weak referee who had let the Argentine team dictate their interpretation of the rules to pressurise him until he buckled. Constantly harassing and surrounding the referee, Argentina would do absolutely anything to beat a nation who they believe stole their islands in the south Atlantic.

Rooney's sending off was controversial because of Christiano Ronaldo's unsporting part in it, demanding a red card should be administered to his club team-mate and then slyly winking at his squad's bench when the Argentine referee agreed.

Both players had been stitched up. Both players had retaliated after being fouled. Both had been dismissed from the field of play for violent conduct; but one of them was the fan's favourite.

And that's why in coronation year the FA Cup final has forever been dubbed 'The Matthews Final' forever, even though Blackpool striker Stan Mortensen became the only player in the entire twentieth century to score three goals in it. Stanley Matthews was the nation's darling. The 'Wizard of Dribble' like all magical players, transcended the game and inspired poetry.

His skills were mesmerising. Opponents knew exactly what he was going to do but couldn't combat it. A symbol of a golden era in the game at a time when post war austerity seemed never ending. Not so much a light at the end of the tunnel, but a light inside the tunnel, shining through the gloom.

My generation were brought up on the legend of The Matthews Final and therefore never even heard of his team-mate Stan Mortensen. And that's the point. Both players had lost two previous finals for Blackpool in 1948 and 1951, so the nation wished for third time lucky in 1953. And lucky they were. For the record, they beat Bolton Wanderers 4–3 after trailing 3–1. The equalising goal which sealed Mortensen's hat trick was scored just seconds before the end of normal time ; then in added time, Matthews set up Bill Perry who dramatically scored the winner.

But the turning point of the whole game happened when Bolton's Eric Bell got injured. In an era before substitutes were even thought of, Bell was forced to limp on. Worse was to follow with just half hour of the game remaining, when Ralph Banks, direct opponent of Matthews, developed cramp. This gave Stanley Matthews the space, the time and more importantly, the speed to destroy the left side of the Bolton team. Time after time, he tormented the defence on that side with his dribbling skills but the final ball into the danger area was usually over hit.

But then the legend was born. With the score at three goals each, Matthews weaved towards the almost crippled Banks, then swerved by him before mishitting a pass that flatfooted the Bolton defenders. The ball found it's way to Perry who gleefully hit the net and thus ensure England's favourite footballer would receive the elusive FA Cup winners medal he craved.

In 1991 Stan Mortensen passed away. The only footballer in over one hundred FA Cup finals to score a hat trick but this was just a sub plot. As one national newspaper headlined it …'They'll probably call it The Matthews Funeral'.

Stanley Matthews joined his team–mate nine years later but in the world of football, he never died. Legends never do.

"His name is symbolic of the beauty of the game, his fame time-less and international, his sportsmanship and modesty univer-sally acclaimed. A magical player, of the people, for the people."
INSCRIPTION ON THE STATUE OF SIR STANLEY MATTHEWS

So who is your favourite player? Favourite goal? Favourite game? Before you can answer honestly, you have to separate your heart from your head. If someone ever asked you who you thought was the best player ever, would you answer with your favourite? Or who you really thought was the best.

These are my England favourites in my time as an England fan …

PLAYER – Glenn Hoddle.
GOAL – Michael Owen against Argentina, 1998 World Cup.
GAME – 4-1 versus Holland, 1996 European Championship.

And these in my opinion are England's best …

PLAYER – Paul Gascoigne.
GOAL – John Barnes against Brazil, 1984 friendly.
GAME – 5-1 versus Germany, 2001 World Cup Qualifier.

The bottom three are just my opinion and up for discussion or debate in a pub. But the top three are answered from the heart, a personal choice to which there is no argument. No one can tell your heart how it feels. You have your favourites. You have your magical memories. That's why you love the game.

My favourite Taunton player is Matt Wright. Today he missed a penalty. Unlucky mate, shit happens. Nobody on this coach is blaming him and rightly so. As well as the apology on Twitter, he also vows to make it up just a few days from now in the re-play at the Viridor. Strong character.

There's news of an accident somewhere on the A303 which slows our journey to Somerset. Somebody on board complains but is put in their place when Rob Wenham reminds them. "Someone may have died tonight; be thankful you're getting home in one piece." I'm dropped off near the M5 Motorway on the outskirts of Taunton with an hour to kill before my coach to Plymouth is due. I buy a coffee from a petrol station and as the supporter's coach heads off towards Wordsworth Drive, I wander lonely as a cloud.

Eventually, I get home at 3.30am on Sunday. It's twenty-two and a half hours to get to Essex and back; the same time it takes to fly to Australia. Overtired I just can't sleep. The day's events keeping my mind active. I desperately need to dull the enjoyment. Picking up my iPhone, I browse the FA's website and read up on their coaching courses. Within minutes I'm sleeping like a baby.

Chapter Seven

BILLERICAY BLUES

Awake at 10am the next day and feeling strangely refreshed even before my first coffee. I've already decided to attend the Taunton versus Billericay replay on Wednesday evening and book two tickets online for the ninety-minute train journey.

Whoever wins that night will play in the first round proper of the FA Cup. Basically 'proper' means there are no more qualifiers. This is where the competition goes national, and the nation starts to take notice. Teams from level three and four of the pyramid are now introduced into the fold and every one of them are full-time professionals. With bated breath I watch the BBC on Monday evening wondering where the next leg of my adventure takes me. How about Plymouth Argyle versus Taunton Town? That would be perfect!

Chesterfield! I'm going three hundred miles north to Chesterfield. But that's the deal! The numbered balls picked out of a machine by ex-professional footballer Dion Dublin dictates where I'm heading. Why does Dion Dublin dislike me? I only shouted at him in broad daylight from a moving car a few years ago for a bit of banter. One Saturday afternoon whilst driving down Western Approach in Plymouth city centre I spotted about twenty guys all dressed in black tracksuits walking out of the Copthorne Hotel. It was the yellow canary on the green background that gave it away. Norwich City were on their way to play Argyle.

Stuck at a red light I noticed Dion Dublin amongst them. As the traffic lights changed to the colours of Norwich's kit I shouted out, "Hey Dion!" He looked over at me as I pulled away shouting my prediction. "2-1!" The former Cambridge, Manchester United, Coventry, Aston Villa, Millwall, Leicester, Glasgow Celtic and England striker just smiled at me with a look that seemed to say 'Piss off you nobody!'

And 2-1 is the result! 2-1 to Norwich that is. And guess who scored the bloody winner? The same bloke who's now sending me on an arduous train journey to Derbyshire. As the ball nestled in the back of Argyle's net and the hotshot striker wheeled away in delight, I wonder if his mind wandered back to the mouthy tosser in the silver Audi.

Coincidentally, when venturing on their own Cup adventure five years previously, Mike Vallis and his son Paul also travelled to Chesterfield at precisely the same stage. The Spireites as they're known, will be favourites to win whoever wins the replay in Somerset as they compete at level five of the pyramid.

Wednesday evening comes and a colleague drops me off at Plymouth Train Station straight from work. The good news is that 'she who shall not be named' is accompanying me for the game and she's really looking forward to it. The bad news is that 'The Crimson Horror' (her words not mine) is paying it's monthly visit so joining the metre-high club tonight is out of the question.

The crowd at the Viridor Stadium exceeds fifteen hundred, a nice little earner for both football clubs. The funny thing is, I reckon there was that number attending the AGP Arena a few days ago but the official attendance was below a thousand spectators. As both clubs share the gate money right down the middle I'm pretty cynical about how Billericay came to this official number.

I introduce The Crimson Queen to Rob Wenham who's on stewarding duty just outside the ground and generously pays for one of us to get in. "Look after him, he's a good bloke!" he shouts after us. Inside the ground and into the clubhouse for the now traditional pint of cider. The Crimson Queen remarks on how friendly the place is and by the time we leave tonight, Taunton Town will be her third team as well. For the rest of the season we're both following the Peacock's results.

I take a couple of pics which I'll post on Facebook later of Dan the mascot (complete in cat uniform), The Crimson Queen and Big Rob Wenham (the Millwall Lion). I label them 'The Cat,

The Kitten and The Lion'. A year from tonight The Kitten will dump me by trading me in for an older model and ominously, the two images portray the future. In the first pic, she is facing me with her eyes closed and in the second, she is gazing up to her left at the taller older man.

On the pitch, Sully, Socky and Rocky put in a decent shift but Billericay's defence is watertight. They look serious tonight and there's no second bite of the cherry for the team I'm currently following. The only goal of the game is scored by the visitor's Sam Deering just before half-time, which signals the end of Taunton's brilliant Cup run. Jamie O'Hara is the stand out player and small world as it is, he's on Instagram pictured with my ex-team-mate, ex-colleague and fellow Plymothian James 'Coco' Cole, once a semi-professional himself.

My disappointment at Taunton's demise from this season's FA Cup is tempered by the fact that I've made a few friends here at this welcoming club, including Rob and Willie 'the Taunton Taunters'.

Chesterfield is known for it's famous crooked spire hence the nickname of the football team. It's a haunting site especially when dark, as it sits upon a gothic fourteenth century church. Local folklore has it that the Devil once visited the town and generally causing mischief, decided to hang onto the spire in order to desecrate the holy structure below, the townsfolk rang the church bells which frightened the hell out of our Lucifer who couldn't flee quick enough. However, the horned one forgot he had his tail wrapped around the spire which then twisted and bent over due to the force of his departure. Now I've heard some excuses for shoddy British workmanship but this one tops the lot!

I wonder where the little Devil fled. Did he hide for a few hundred years before summoning Isambard Kingdom Brunel and commissioned him to design a railway bridge into Cornwall?

Walking out of Chesterfield Train Station, the first thing you notice is the crooked spire on top of a hill directly in front of you. And as it turns out, that isn't the only crooked thing here. As it starts to rain, I jump into a waiting cab and tell the driver I'm going to the Proact Stadium. I've already checked the walking route on Google and it's quite straightforward. A twenty-five-minute hike along two main roads, so why is this driver literally 'going around the houses' when it's only a five-minute drive? Do I look like a mug? Just another tourist stepping off a train to take pictures of a crooked spire?

Pulling up at the ground of Chesterfield Football Club and he's charging me £7. I show him my iPhone and ask why he didn't take the direct route. It's like bartering with a market trader. Our voices are raised and the air turns blue. Time is on my side as it's over an hour to kick off and he's impatient for his next fare. We compromise on a fiver. It's now stopped raining. I should have walked!

The Proact Stadium is easily the biggest ground so far on this cup run. It holds a capacity of ten thousand supporters but less than a third of that will be watching today. Although playing in the National League which is the top tier of non-league football, Chesterfield Football Club are equipped to compete at a much higher level. Finished eight years ago, the Proact is one of the newest grounds in the country, modern enough to host concerts and international games at youth level.

The one feature which struck me not only as a football fan but a humanist also, is a remembrance garden at the back of the stadium commemorating all of the fallen in both world wars who wore the blue shirt of Chesterfield Football Club. It's very tasteful and the timing of my visit could hardly be better as tomorrow is Armistice Day. This weekend football supporters will stand in silence in respect for those who fought for King and Country never to return. In Chesterfield's garden names and pictures adorn the walls of those who were sacrificed. It's not just there on Remembrance Sunday but all year round. 'Lest We Forget' is a constant reminder at the Proact Stadium.

Chesterfield should have made FA Cup history in 1997 but were denied that glorious place simply because of the naked eye and human error. Only the seventh team to ever reach the semi-final from the third level of English football, they were on the verge of becoming the first to reach a Wembley final. The game was played at Old Trafford where their opponents were Premiership team Middlesbrough. Had VAR been around two decades ago the Spirerites would surely have won. With about twenty minutes remaining, they led by two goals to one when the ball crashed against the Middlesbrough crossbar and appeared to bounce past the goal line. As the players celebrated a third goal, the referee signalled for the game to play on judging that the ball hadn't crossed the line. Middlesbrough earlier had a player sent off and their ten men would have found a 3-1 reversal virtually impossible to claw back.

The final should have been giantkillers Chesterfield versus glamorous Chelsea, and that would have been as romantic and magical as anything that had gone before in FA Cup history. The very stuff everyone involved dreams about and the very spirit the world's oldest and most famous Cup was built upon.

But today I'm here for Billericay Town and a quick look at their history tells me we have a connection. When I watched them play Taunton, I found it strange seeing as the town is situated five miles from the sea, that the badge on their football shirt depicted a ship with words underneath saying 'Together we sail as one'. The ship in question just happens to be the Mayflower which set out for the new world four centuries before. The Mayflower had originally sailed from Boston in Lincolnshire carrying the Pilgrim Fathers before picking up several from the town of Billericay who had travelled to the waterside. One more stop in my home town of Plymouth before sailing west for the new world and a place in America which was named New England. Today there is a place in the state of Massachusetts called Billerica as well as another called Plymouth, and of course Boston, a famous city.

In English football both Plymouth Argyle and Boston United are known as 'The Pilgrims' with the Mayflower ship sailing proudly on the respective club crests. Billericay's nickname is simply 'The Blues' after their shirt colour. Today though as the away team they are obliged to wear their second-choice colours of all red due to a colour clash with the home side. Billericay

Blues for the next couple of hours will be 'Ricay Red', as their followers refer to them as.

As the teams enter the arena, the cry all around me is 'Essex! Essex!', but before the modern-day equivalent of a battle commences this Remembrance Weekend, silence descends on the red and blue corners as we pay respect to the lost ones.

> *"All we have of freedom, all we use or know.*
> *This our fathers bought for us, long and long ago."*
> RUDYARD KIPLING

After two minutes stood in absolute silence, a bugler poignantly plays 'The Last Post' stirring the senses to near sadness. If it hadn't been so sullen, it would have been beautiful. I hadn't heard a bugler since watching Argyle years ago, when he would perform the final call of the British Army whenever an opponent lay injured. It would have been impeccably observed too if it wasn't for one Essex wanker who shouted out at the very start of it. He was immediately hushed by his mates.

FA CUP FIRST ROUND
SATURDAY 10TH NOVEMBER
PROACT STADIUM
ATTENDANCE – 2952

CHESTERFIELD 1 BILLERICAY TOWN 1

It's a lively start to the bout. Two skilful boxers. In the red corner all the way from Essex, 'Billericay Dickie' and in the blue corner, local boy Chester 'the church spire' Field. Decent punches are thrown but taken well on the chin by both goalkeepers who look in fine form. Jamie O'Hara is on the substitute's bench so once again the Blues orchestra are playing without a conductor. Fear not, for all around me are the Essex Boys in good voice.

*'Singing aye aye Ricay Ricay aye, singing aye aye
Ricay Ricay aye. Singing aye aye Ricay,
we all love the Ricay, aye aye Ricay Ricay aye.'*

From a high vantage point in the east stand of the Proact, the one player that sticks out for me is the visitor's number eleven Jake Howell for all the wrong reasons. Even on the far side of the pitch it's clear to me he's out of sorts, lacking the pace that a wide position demands. He's struggling to get involved in the game as Chesterfield pass the ball around reducing him to appear as 'piggy in the middle'.

Howell's inability to get back quickly to support his defence on that side of the pitch is exposed a few times and Billericay manager Dean Brennan is just as slow before he would finally plug that gap. The defence are bombarded by the home team's crosses and slack marking in the danger area allows the home team to get in unchallenged headers which are wasted.

And then the inevitable happens. Defender Laurence Maguire, younger brother of England international Harry, heads home a goal from a free kick delivered from a wide position. Yet again the defence makes it easy. Chesterfield are now threatening to play 'Ricay' off the park until Jake Howells is moved to a more central position where he starts to justify his team selection as his skill, vision and delivery of the ball become more prominent. In fact, very quickly he shows himself to be the best player on the pitch.

'Correct tactical decision,' I record in my notebook, but underneath I then ask the question I've asked of most managers down the years. 'Why didn't you start him in that position?' Is it because I'm in a more advantageous seat than Dean Brennan? And if this is a better viewpoint, why don't managers position themselves higher up in the ground where they can clearly see the pattern of the game? A quick mobile call to the dugout at pitch level is sufficient enough to carry out his instructions via the coaching staff at pitch level.

Sat where I am, it's also obvious to see that Billericay's lone striker Jake Robinson is virtually isolated from his team-mates feeding on scraps from the odd aerial service. It's becoming a trend in modern football that managers and coaches prefer only to pick one player in attack.

The pitch here at the Proact Stadium resembles a bowling green compared to some of the playing surfaces I've witnessed so far on this journey. It's perfect for the ball to be rolled along the green turf but is being ignored; a wasteful tactic considering that the skilful Robinson himself and lively team-mate Moses Emmanuel playing miles away from him, would love to run at those big Chesterfield defenders and maybe pull off a surprise result.

So, when half-time arrives, 'Ricay are one goal down. Over a pint of lager in the concourse I overhear a supporter remind his mate that before the game, he said that Billericay just like Dracula, feared crosses. "That's why we're losing!" he reasons. Get that Essex boy on a coaching course to obtain his badges. Amazing how many football fans have something which the managers of their beloved teams lack; the ability to see the trees in the woods. Returning to my seat for the start of the second half, Billericay's fans compliment their hosts…

'Nice ground, shit fans. Nice ground, shit fans.'

Ironically echoing the Taunton choir at the AGP Arena in the previous round.

The Supporter

Maybe it's because he's a Londoner, that Keith Tuckwell loves London teams. Brought up in the west of the capital, he's a lifelong

Brentford fan but these days follows Billericay Town, as he now lives in their catchment area. He's travelled to Derbyshire this weekend to kill two birds with one stone. His daughter lives in this neck of the woods and so what better reason is there to visit her than by watching his adopted team in the FA Cup.

This reminds me of a story regarding my Wembley wife Mike Vallis. Five years ago, making the same trek as I'm doing now, he and his son Paul also travelled to the Proact. Not only did they come here for the first round, they also made the journey back to Chesterfield for the second round which took place shortly before Christmas. Deciding to kill the same number of birds using the same method as Keith Tuckwell, they diverted to Cambridge University to pick up daughter Jennifer and bring her back to Plymouth for the seasonal holiday. When she asked why they were heading north and not west, she despaired on being told they were all going to watch a football match, a game she didn't like. But like so many non-believers, Jen was surprised at the enjoyment she felt being part of the crowd, experiencing the atmosphere, hearing lewd songs and chants which she learned came under the banner of 'banter'.

Keith Tuckwell admits he's not fanatical about football but just appreciates a good game. "I like to see what TV doesn't show you," is one good reason to attend a match. I think I know what he means. These days, no TV station ever shows streakers invading the pitch. The game at the top of the pyramid he claims is from another galaxy. And it's even more bizarre on mainland Europe. Neymar, the Brazilian superstar has just signed for Paris St Germain and will be paid something like 700K a week! "Madness!" he says in exasperation. And it is madness when you consider that parents are funding children at grass roots level to play on the local park, and the teams they play for depend on volunteers, desperately trying to squeeze kit sponsorship from small businesses.

Meanwhile, the Essex contingent in the stadium taunt their opposite numbers by reminding them of where their proud club stood for many years in the past …

'Football League and you fucked it up,
Football League and you fucked it up!'

Moments later ecstasy hits Essex as the Billericay Blues celebrate a brilliant equaliser. Keith actually misses it because he's talking to me. Over his left shoulder, I see Moses part the blue sea of the Chesterfield defence and he strikes the ball so powerfully that the BBC will include it in every FA Cup programme for the rest of the season. The best goal for me so far!

I can see the potential headlines in tomorrow's sport pages if he does it again. 'MOSES TAKES BILLERICAY TO THE PROMISED LAND'.

When the cheers for their team fades back into jeers for the enemy, Keith tells me about Brentford Football Club's business model. "They don't take players on loan; they coach the youth," he explains. Even though the west London outfit don't necessarily run a youth academy as they can't compete with more glamorous neighbours such as Chelsea, they cleverly recruit young players who have been rejected by those teams, and develop them. It doesn't cost a lot either. Wannabe footballers offered a second chance to make it in the game will bite your hand off. They are coached, put in the reserve team and progress to such a standard they will either make it to the first team or be sold for a handsome profit if the player is seduced by bigger clubs. It's a simple but brilliant concept. Buy cheap, sell high, re-invest. No wonder a move to a bigger ground is just around the corner … literally!

At last Jamie O'Hara is off the bench and on the pitch but Chesterfield look the stronger outfit and dare I say it, professional. Although the Spirerites are a tough nut to crack this season they haven't won enough games so far to stay clear at the wrong end of the National League. Hovering dangerously above the relegation zone, the team have drawn exactly half their games and so the last thing they want is a long midweek trip to Essex to play a Cup replay interrupting preparations for next week's League game, where a win would give them a valuable three points.

With this in mind they attack Billericay with zest, sharpness and purpose. Shots rain in, forcing goalkeeper Alan Julian into making crucial saves and forcing the spectators behind the goal to take evasive action for the wilder efforts. With time running out, the Blues' defence grow in belief making well-timed tackles and well-hard challenges. Their defending is actually brilliant, placing any part of their anatomy in the way while behind them is a goalkeeper performing an impressive impersonation of Superman.

And a one-all draw is what they deserve at the end. Billericay supporters hail the men in red shirts and they strongly fancy their chances in the replay. And why not? After all, sitting ambitiously at the top of the National League South, the type of club they'll want to visit next season are Chesterfield themselves. If they get promoted that is, but 'if' is a big word in football.

The weather has cleared up, so I decide not to get in a debate over cab fares and walk back to the train station. Just enough time for a quick pint in a cocktail bar named 'Cocos' before a bloody long journey back to Plymouth. I'm the only one sat at the bar. Well actually there's two of us. Myself and a Christmas tree. A Christmas tree! It's not even mid-November and this place is already advertising the festive period!

And I thought it was just football on TV that was cynically commercial.

1956 WINNERS – MANCHESTER CITY

As an Englishman, I've always wondered how the nation of Germany mark the occasion of Armistice Day. No doubt they too remember the fallen, and maybe it's my ignorance but I believe it must be a time of major regret. Led by a dictator with hideous agendas, his rise to power was done very gradually and very deliberately.

Is it any wonder then that only a decade after the Second World War thankfully ended that nobody trusted a German? But who were we really at war with? The German people or the Nazis who controlled them? Fellow human beings or an idealist movement?

German Bert Trautmann was a paratrooper in the Luftwaffe who received no less than five medals that included the coveted Iron Cross. He became one of only nine per cent of his regiment that survived the war after being captured and spending four years as a prisoner of war in Lancashire. On his release after the war, he chose to live and work as a farm hand in the north west rather than go home. At over six feet and two inches tall, he was also a useful goalkeeper turning out for non-league St Helens Town but was quickly spotted and signed by Manchester City.

At a time of rationing, austerity and bitter feelings towards Germany there were surely going to be protests and demonstrations, but Trautmann not only won over the City fans, he also in time achieved a remarkable national acceptance when The Football Writers Association awarded him with the 'Footballer Of The Year' award.

It's one game in particular in which he's fondly remembered by English football fans. FA Cup finals down the years have presented us with memorable performances by individuals whose moments of magic have moved historians to wax lyrical, but no one else could match Bert Trautmann's bravery in May 1956.

Basically, during the game the German giant broke his neck and should have died. In the pre-substitute era of football, Trautmann received an almost fatal injury when throwing himself headlong into an opposing Birmingham City player's knee. A courageous act which would have ended tragically but for a miracle. Apparently, there are five vertebrae in a human being's neck and his second one had split in two. Unbelievably, the third vertebrae had smashed into it on impact and effectively held the second in position which cheated the Grim Reaper.

There were still twenty minutes of the game remaining and Manchester City were 3-1 up. Trautmann refused to come off for treatment and was there to climb the famous thirty-nine steps to the Royal Box to receive a winner's medal. Images capture a moment when Bert Trautmann can be seen leaving the Wembley pitch holding his medal in one hand whilst supporting his neck with the other. Amazingly he also made himself available for post-match interviews!

Back in the changing room, still holding his neck in an upright position, he could hardly raise a smile, let alone the famous trophy and it would be another four days before he or anyone at the club knew the true extent of the injury.

Maybe it should be allowed in the laws of the game that referees upon seeing a modern-day player feign injury after throwing himself to the deck should have the right to march over to the cheating bastard and utter just five words … 'Remember Bert Trautmann, get up!'

Ten days after the draw at the Proact Stadium, Chesterfield defeat Billericay in the replay by three goals to one. All three scored by striker Tom Denton. Spireites manager Martin Allen paid a tribute to The Blues by describing them as a League team in waiting, after seeing first-hand how the Essex club had transformed it's home ground under the second richest person in that county. Anyone who has ever visited the AGP Arena in recent years would certainly agree with that.

Chesterfield typically draw three more games in the League between the home game against Billericay Town and whoever they will face in round two. Monday evening arrives and once more I excitedly tune in to the BBC to see where I'm headed in December. My heart sinks a little when it shows that either Chesterfield or Billericay will entertain Grimsby Town, a level four team. So, this means that irrespective of whoever wins the replay, I'll be making a long trip back to somewhere I've already been, but that's the luck of the draw. When I find out it's a return to Derbyshire, I'm online buying a match ticket, booking a hotel room and hiring a car.

The price of love!

Chapter Eight

IT'S GRIMSBY UP NORTH

It's a long drive from Devon to Derbyshire but quite straight-forward. Apart from that is, numerous hold ups on the A38, M5, M42 and M1, due to roadworks and restrictions. As this is a Saturday afternoon (the game being played on a Sunday), there's not a maintenance worker in sight, so frustrations are driving motorists mad who never seem to feel the benefits of invisible improvements.

Keeping me company on this long trek are Talksport Radio, Absolute Radio and LBC which is holding heated debates on something called Brexit. It seems that two and a half years ago, 52% of those that chose to vote wanted a divorce from the European Union, but this failed marriage could get complicated and bitter.

I make a piss-stop a few hours in, because several signs are reminding me to. 'Tiredness Kills-Take A Break' they tell me, but what they'll never tell you is that motorway services will rip you off as soon as you set foot in there. Five miles outside Chesterfield on the A617, the famous crooked spire can be seen in the distance; lit up in all it's gothic, dramatic and haunting glory. The closer I get to it, the more mesmerising it becomes.

Checking into the hotel, I realise I've left my phone charger at home, so typically of people 'from around these parts', the girl on reception lends me hers and just tells me to leave it with her colleague the next morning. One thing I like about this part of the world are the people. The December night is dark and freezing but everyone I get to meet in Chesterfield are warm and welcoming.

Being the patriot that I am, my first pint of cold lager is in a pub called The Red Lion. A sign on the door states 'No Dogs Allowed' but there is a water filled dog bowl by the fireplace.

A hen party walks in, nine of them. All painted fingernails and false eyelashes, they claim two tables next to me. Handbags are placed in synchronisation on the table and mobile phones at the ready. For the duration of my stay the sides of their heads are attached to these devices, interrupted now and then by the speedy pushing of buttons as they are placed back on the table. Whatever happened to conversation?

The girl nearest to me smells like a powder room all by herself and asks if I will take a group photo of them with her iPhone. Of course ladies, happy to oblige. Standing in front of the two tables, I try not to laugh, as they all discard their mobiles in order to smile sweetly at just the one I'm holding. After the obligatory 'one for luck' pic, they immediately pick up said mobiles with more precision than any band who have ever performed at The Royal Edinburgh Military Tattoo. It's as if they've been temporarily parted from a new-born baby. LOL.

One girl speaks to me, probably because nobody wants to speak to anybody else, and soon comments on my accent 'not from around these parts'. I explain why I'm in Chesterfield and the trail that brought me here via the FA Cup. I also mention that I like to know something about the place I'm visiting, so the conversation inevitably turns to the crooked spire. Having read the story of the Devil's visit and the townsfolk chasing him off causing the spire to bend and twist, I ask her if it's known by everyone here. She says it is, and furthermore tells me part two of the legend. Apparently, one day, so the locals believe, the spire will straighten itself when a virgin bride walks up the aisle in the church it looms over. I look slowly around the tables and all I see are a bunch of young women dressed to the nines, advertising their sexiest look, hoping they'll be swept off their feet by a young bearded tattooed guy who with any luck, also has money and wears a man bun. I keep my thoughts to myself. Virgin bride? Fat chance!

On leaving The Red Lion, my attention is now on my own iPhone as a notification hits my email app. Result! Chesterfield Football Club have granted me an appointment to interview a long serving director before the game! Time for a few celebratory drinks. Two decent pubs, a genuine ale house and one McDonalds restaurant later, I'm back in my hotel room scribbling notes in preparation and iPhone on charge. I'm organised for a pre-match interview, followed by a match report, feeling just like a real football journalist.

Chesterfield Football Club is the heartbeat of the town. A genuinely friendly and community-based set up and so easy to reach. I park near the ground and make my way to 'Chester's Den' which is described on the club's website as a play café situated underneath one of the stands. Chester is actually the name of their official mascot which is a mouse. Why a mouse? What's the significance of that? Hang on a minute … it's a field mouse. Oh right! Got it now! CHESTER the FIELD mouse! I need to wake up. A cup of coffee is first on the agenda.

The Director

One of the fastest growing sports in the country is 'walking football'. As I write this, there are over thirty-five thousand participants in a game which was founded barely a decade ago. The man who pioneered this after raising it's profile on Sky Sports News and gave the game it's rules is John Croot, a director at Chesterfield Football Club for over thirty years. John mirrors the warmth of the people I've already met outside of the ground, from within these walls.

The idea of walking football entered John's head whilst driving back from a forum at The Cliff, former training ground of Manchester United back in 2008. As a representative of a community trust, he was challenged with the concept of including people over fifty-years old to participate in our national game. But how do you make the game both accessible and safe for those players in that age bracket? You do it by eliminating the two biggest health and injury threats which are running and slide tackling. As the latter is only effective after the former, this law goes hand in hand. And thus, the seeds were sown inside the mind of a Chesterfield director.

After inviting Sky Sports News to a few sessions, John's phone to use his words, went ballistic. He was so busy sending the rules to other football clubs and communities, that it never even crossed his mind to patent them. Had he done so he would be, to quote Del Boy 'a millionaire this time next year'. Helped by funding from the Football Foundation which is the Premier League's sports charity, John Croot had unwittingly invented a game which is now played all over Europe, Brexit or no Brexit. He only invented walking football recently. He'd obviously never seen me play!

England are known throughout the world as the fathers of football after inventing the rules of the game which we now know, evolving into something equally loved and mocked since the mid-nineteenth century. John is the unofficial father of walking football. Both sets of rules were made approximately ten miles apart between Sheffield and Chesterfield respectively. Must be something in the ale up here.

John Croot first became a director at Chesterfield amazingly at just twenty-three years old and in doing so, became the first football supporter to enter a boardroom which tells you everything about the bond between club and community. As chief executive of Chesterfield's community trust these days, he runs local successful programmes such as rehab centres, but it's inside the football club itself where the main impact is made. Impressionable young kids are made to feel part of it all. The Hub is the name of a state-of-the-art community facility situated at the back of the east stand, which is open to the general public apart from Christmas Day. You don't have to be a football fan to walk in off the street. It consists of Chester's Den café & play centre, a fitness gym, corporate meeting room, hydrotherapy pool, office space, classrooms and a multi-purpose sports hall; yet another of John's chestnut trees that grew from his idea the size of an acorn. It hosts roughly about twenty parties a week for small children which virtually guarantees future generations supporting

Chesterfield FC. Chester the fieldmouse visits schools with some of the playing squad; engaging with pupils and spreading the gospel of the Spirerites.

And he should know. In the late 1970's John attended St Mary's Catholic School right next to the original ground of Chesterfield Football Club, Saltergate. He would visit the ground every day asking for jobs and eventually became a programme seller. He's witnessed a lot. Expressed the whole range of emotions; promotion, relegation, a move away from Saltergate to the bigger, modern Proact Stadium. And he remembers everything.

Did I hear the name Saltergate? I smile at this, because as a Plymothian I feel a strange sense of rivalry start to kick in, and it's all to do with 1997. An event happened in the spring of that year that has gone down in Chesterfield and Plymouth Argyle's history as the most infamous game in both club's existence. The Battle Of Saltergate as it became known, broke league records for all the wrong reasons. Five players were sent off in the same game and all for violent conduct. The first red card was shown early on, but despite being one man down, Argyle went one goal up. With just a couple of minutes remaining, legendary ex-Liverpool goalkeeper Bruce Grobelaar, now playing for The Pilgrims was caught by a stray elbow which left him concussed.

The referee would later comment that what he witnessed on that day was frightening. Two boxing matches took place about twenty yards apart. No handbags; these were full on fist fights which then sparked a pitch invasion by the home fans. Mayhem ensued as blue and green shirts continued to trade blows. The referee managed to single out four culprits and off they went for an early bath. After an investigation, the police decided not to prosecute, possibly feeling justice had already been served in the shape of severe fines and suspensions handed out by the football authorities.

Recalling that incident, John tells me about future Premiership striker Kevin Davies running forty yards to get involved and then just walked off the pitch, not even waiting for the referee to show him his red card when everything calmed down. It would mean Chesterfield's main goalscoring threat missing an FA Cup game on their way to becoming only the seventh team in history to reach the semi-final of the competition from level three; and who were the team before that to reach the last four from the same level? – Plymouth Argyle thirteen years before.

Back to the director who's still wildly running down memory lane while I'm thinking about the uglier side of the game. His first game he ever attended was in the FA Cup away at Stoke City where World Cup winning goalkeeper Gordon Banks plied his trade. That's just one more reason why the Cup is loved the length and breadth of the country. It doesn't matter where you are in the football pyramid, everyone has an FA Cup memory.

And there's memorabilia all around this part of the ground regarding that semi-final run. The match programme is framed. A quick glance at it surprises me as I see the name of the captain, Sean Dyche. The future Burnley manager signed for Chesterfield in a deal organised by John Croot. A hard man in his playing days, I can picture the gravelly voiced ginger haired player giving as good as he got in the Saltergate shenanigans. The 1997 semi-final between Chesterfield and premiership Middlesbrough went to a replay so there are two sets of blue and red pennants adorning the wall. The best piece of memorabilia though is trustingly handed to me. The very shirt worn by striker Andy Morris who scored the first goal and frightened the hell out of their illustrious opponents. I hold it up, turn it around and see a white number nine, the same view which big Nigel Pearson of Middlesbrough would have had all too often that day at Old Trafford.

There's also a picture of a football team parading silverware. By the general look of the players who all resemble TV private investigator Magnum, I'm guessing it's taken in the late seventies/early eighties' era. The trophy in question was called The Anglo-Scottish Cup, a pre-season tournament which ran from 1975 to 1980, and coincidentally was first won by Middlesbrough. Twenty-four teams played in a round robin group stage which guaranteed four English and four Scottish clubs a place in the quarter-finals. The final itself was played over two legs and in the last ever one, Chesterfield defeated Notts County which now means the trophy has a permanent home at the Proact. On the way to the final, Chesterfield beat the mighty Glasgow Rangers by four goals to one.

John Croot has just given up an hour of his precious time on a big matchday and proves to be a gracious host. I dearly want Chesterfield to win today. Not only for these good people but most of all because John has promised me an interview with manager Martin 'Mad Dog' Allen, one of my favourite characters in the game, if the Spirerites make it to the third round. Mad Dog has an unusual approach to each game which includes his team practising Yoga on a huge inflatable mat an hour before kick-off. There's a room next to the boardroom reserved for this ancient Hindu discipline and when you think of the many physical and mental attributes required by players to win a football match, it sort of makes sense.

Now John leads me down the terracing to pitchside. On the way, he tells me about Chesterfield's strange claim to fame in this competition. From 1950 all the way to that semi-final appearance forty-seven years later, the Spirerites never got past the third round. They nearly did in 1979. Drawing at Peterborough United in the second round caused excitement in the town, as it meant that they would be in the hat for the third round (the draw being made before the replay), but premature celebrations were scuppered by losing at home to 'The Posh'.

There's a BBC camera on the side of the pitch which makes John chuckle. The game today will be hyped up to high heaven by the 'beeb'. They'll tell everyone about Chesterfield's wonderful Cup tradition due to 1997. They won't mention the fact that they rarely play an FA Cup match in January.

It's a lovely stadium, boasting some of the best supporter's facilities in the country, spawned in a portakabin years ago and managing to grow via the Supporter's Trust. To John's knowledge, it was Northampton Town Football Club that pioneered a bond between it's footballers and fans. Whilst holidaying in Tenerife, he bought a fanzine which had a cult readership called 'When

Saturday Comes' and included in detail what Northampton were trying to achieve. The supporters there created a pressure group which managed to convince the board of directors to involve them in the running of the club, and why not? Football clubs exist due to supporter's funding, which basically makes them unofficial shareholders.

Back in the portakabin years ago, there weren't even any partitions or working electrics but through business loans and League funding, Chesterfield were able to build The Hub for it's people, costing about £1.6 million pounds.

So, what is this director's view on the Premier League? He's not a big fan that's for sure. He admits that the game at the top level is now more professional but the problem is the top division itself. The Premiership is the FA's newest baby and therefore needs more care and attention than it's older brother, the FA Cup. Aided by TV revenue and elitist club owners, the vast majority of money pouring into the game stays there feeding the fat cats, while the rest of the pyramid struggles on scraps.

And this is the basic problem when you have two different organisations running our football. The rich look after themselves and couldn't really care less about the working class beneath them. There's a definite lack of empathy from the FA to any club outside of the promised land. But how did we get into this state of affairs? Why are England, the fathers of football, the only country in the world to have two footballing authorities? The answer to that lies in the late nineteenth century and the north/south divide, born out of the Industrial Revolution.

The very first footballing competition ever devised was the FA Cup. The very first final was played in 1872 and for the next decade football was dominated by amateur sides from the London area. The impoverished Northern players couldn't afford to play on an amateur basis and therefore their clubs wanted to adopt professionalism. The FA finally agreed to let them do that, and so clubs from both the midlands and the north formed their own competition called The Football League. Even though those teams were affiliated to the FA, they competed under the control of the League. This League grew and grew, eventually compassing ninety-two teams from the length and breadth of England. Due to their professionalism, they were also better than the original Cup winners; Aston Villa, Blackburn Rovers and Preston North End swept aside the likes of Wanderers, Royal Engineers and Old Etonians.

In time, the game also became professional in the south and until 1992 there remained an unofficial alliance between the Football League and the Football Association; and then something happened which shook the national game to it's very core and angered supporters whoever they followed. The FA, along with Sky TV, aided and abetted by the owners of the top clubs, hijacked Football League Division One and renamed it The FA Premiership. The idea they all claimed was to create a league of such quality that the England team would be successful for evermore; but within their walls a secret and selfish agenda was being formulated to create an elitist group taking all the money poured in by satellite TV. It was only after several meetings did they finally agreed to carry on the concept of promotion and relegation between the top two levels of the pyramid.

In my opinion the FA have done wonders for the promotion of football for all ages and for the women's game which has recently exploded, making it accessible to absolutely anyone, but the creation of the Premiership leaves the majority of the country to seek funding, cap in hand, from other sources. Even if a team is relegated from the Premiership, it's still 'rewarded' with something approaching a hundred million pounds meaning that teams competing in the levels below are being forced to compete financially but simply don't have the same money as those sliding down the pyramid. So, they borrow money beyond their means and virtually cripple themselves as they can't pay the loan back, due to low attendances and ridiculous wages.

Burnley Football Club are a good example of a 'yo-yo club', and also a good example of how to run a football club. Managed brilliantly by Sean Dyche, a Saltergate veteran, they were promoted to the Premiership through sheer footballing ability on the pitch, while sensibly spending within their means off it and therefore not risking their very existence. They were duly relegated by financial means (not having spent madly in the transfer market on better players) but received a windfall in the process doing so. The owners admirably and sensibly stood by Dyche who knew his squad inside out and simply then spent a lot of their relegation reward signing players and paying top wages, thus enabling an easy return to the Premiership. They then survived another season up there, received more money, invested it again, survived again, received even more and so on …

John Croot should have patented that walking football! He's been a brilliant host and we depart on an amusing anecdote which involves Chelsea fans. Whilst on an away trip, he and a few mates bumped into a crew from west London who took a liking for the Chesterfield contingent as their respective clubs shared the same initials, CFC.

After a while, the Chelsea lads came up with the idea of inviting John and his fellow Spirerites to a house party in the area. Okay then, nice one! Where is this party? "Don't know yet," replies one of them, "we'll find a place, bring a screwdriver."

Today John is expecting a feisty encounter against Grimsby, but what are the Grimsby fans expecting? I'm sharing a table with two of them drinking coffee in Chester's Den when I ask them their prediction. One of them looks out of the window and up at the overcast sky. "I think the rain will hold off," he says seriously. His mate just looks at me and shakes his head in despair.

FA CUP SECOND ROUND
SUNDAY 2ND DECEMBER
PROACT STADIUM
ATTENDANCE – 4537

CHESTERFIELD 0 GRIMSBY TOWN 2

The friendliness I've encountered from the locals on my second trip to Chesterfield doesn't extend to the travelling supporters …

is the welcoming chant.

Sitting in the ground on the opposite side to where I sat for the Billericay game, I look around and once again ask myself why this club isn't in the Football League. They've got the facilities and are financially stable enough to build a squad that could comfortably scale the pyramid, so why are they near the bottom of the fifth level?

A quick glance at their results so far in the match programme reminds me that Chesterfield are draw specialists. I should know, I've seen one! Only one point for a draw but everyone else are getting their fair share of wins and totting up three pointers. In a sequence of three games, a team could lose one but still pick up four or six points which would improve their League position. This team's problem is that although they remain largely unbeaten, in a sequence of three games they're only picking up three points. Teams below them in the League are leapfrogging them and into relative safety.

Striker Tom Denton is a giant on the pitch. His three goals at Billericay in the first round replay has ensured this cup-tie in front of a half-full stadium. He's the obvious target for the home team's aerial assault and looks threatening early on, but this proves to be a false dawn. A goalmouth scramble in the Grimsby penalty area near the start of the game is as good as it's going to get for Chesterfield today.

The Grimsby contingent fill the away end to my left and there must be over a thousand of them who have made the trip and are making all the noise. They're not very happy with the referee however. They claim he's wearing a Chesterfield shirt and masturbates for a hobby. My attention falls on the two managers from a brilliant vantage point just above the player's tunnel. It's fascinating to watch their body language in the respective dug outs and sometimes it is more entertaining than the game. It's easy to see why Martin Allen is known as Mad Dog. To say he's animated is an understatement as he constantly moves around barking orders. Cupping his hands around his mouth, shouting at the top of his voice. I can hear him but can't make out his instructions. "They can't hear you!" shouts a supporter next to me, somehow imagining that Mad Dog can hear him!

Playing chalk to Martin Allen's cheese, Grimsby manager Michael Jolley simply stands there with his hands in his pockets. He carries the same demeanour as Gareth Southgate. Tall, slim and dressed very smartly, he transmits calmness to his players while his opposite number seems to instil panic into his. At one point, Allen nearly loses his footing as he goes to pat one of his team on the back only to completely miss. This triggers sniggers all around me. It's fair to say that after only a few minutes of this game, there doesn't seem to be a lot of love here for Mad Dog.

On the pitch, Tom Denton wins everything played towards him but he's all alone. There's no support around him and he lacks pace, making Grimsby's defenders look comfortable against a one dimensional and very predictable attack. And after thirty-five minutes the visitors score. Charles Vernam hits the net to my right, and to my left Grimsby folk go wild. Imagine poking a stick into a black and white striped wasps nest and you'll get the picture. All the home fans can do is sit and watch them, waiting for it all to calm down. Grimsby Town, known as 'The Mariners' leave the pitch at half time with a 1-0 lead to the sound of their happy supporters singing.

'We only sing when we're fishing, sing when we're fishing ...'

The second half starts the same way as most of the first played out, but then Chesterfield get a free kick in a promising position. Three men stand around the ball. The referee blows the whistle. Two players make a dart into the Grimsby area in an attempt to confuse the defence, but the third player just stands there, confused. Nothing. Derbyshire accents all around me sound like neighbouring Yorkshire ones. Roars of disapproval descend upon the pitch, quickly followed by a resignated laughter. Did they work on that set piece in training? Martin Allen covers his eyes with his hands.

This is his cue to change the shape of his attack. He simultaneously makes two substitutions that changes his side's formation. Off comes the lonely Tom Denton and a team-mate, to be replaced by two very quick strikers. They both attack with zest and force corner kick after corner kick. But guess what? It's these very corner kicks where Denton would have had chances to score and his big presence is now missed. And then guess what happens! From one of those corner kicks Grimsby break away and make it 2-0. Harry Clifton races away with Chesterfield defenders in hot pursuit. He shoots but is brilliantly denied by goalkeeper Callum Burton, only for the rebound to fall at Clifton's feet. And this time he finds the net.

Grimsby's black and white wasps sting when they're winning. Chesterfield fans are hurting as the goalscorer milks it in front of his.

'He's one of our own, he's one of our owwwnnnn,
Harry Clifton, he's one of our own.'

A few minutes after the killer goal, I'm asked by two home fans sitting next to me whether I'm a scout on a mission here looking for talent, given that I'm scribbling like mad in my notebook. "Well if I was a scout, I wouldn't be here watching any of your shit!" They just laugh. Then I ask them about their manager, Martin Allen, who according to them, only signs mediocre players; players with no pace, who are always found out against decent opponents.

Right on cue, Grimsby fans taunt Allen with …

*'Sacked in the morning, you're gonna
get sacked in the morning ...'*

Astonishingly, the Chesterfield fans join in! Meanwhile, back on the pitch, the sharks from the fishing town sense blood in the water, relentlessly attacking in a near frenzy. The game ends. The fans represented by Mad Dog are going mad,the fans represented by Michael Jolley are ... well, jolly.

*"Some cause happiness wherever they go,
others whenever they go."*
OSCAR WILDE

Immediately after the game Martin Allen promises a clear out at the Proact Stadium, but obviously that wouldn't include himself. The writing is on the wall though as it's announced that a serving director of the club who is pro-Allen resigns. The board of directors act on both sets of the supporter's cruel prediction, and sack him.

It's no surprise when it happens. As one ex-manager put it: "There's only two certainties in life. People die and football managers get the sack."

At the back of my mind however, I can't help thinking that one day, Martin 'Mad Dog' Allen will end up managing Plymouth Argyle.

1988 WINNERS – WIMBLEDON

So how much control can a manager have on a football team? The answer ranges from none at all to absolutely everything.

Martin Allen's touchline antics seemed to inhibit his players rather than inspire them. So maybe the question that should be asked is 'how much influence can a manager have?'

To me football management is straightforward. You pick the best players (i.e. the players who are in good form), then choose a formation and style that suits them. This ensures that all eleven players play in a position where they can all play to their strengths, and therefore their weaknesses won't be exposed. And unless your name is Pele, every footballer ever born has at least one weakness.

In a team full of brilliant players, this method of team selection and formation can be devastating to their opponents. But what if you haven't got brilliant players? Ladies and gentlemen I give you Dave Bassett. 'Harry' as he was known at Wimbledon, was appointed manager in 1981 and just a few months later, saw his team promoted from level four to level three of the League pyramid. Unfortunately, 'The Wombles' were relegated back to level four the very next season, but crazily promoted again the following year, this time as League champions. And under Bassett they never looked back.

Yet another promotion quickly followed to see them at level two, where understandably Bassett was starting to get attention from other clubs. He decided to stay however as he felt there was unfinished business at Wimbledon, and then in 1986, incredibly, this tiny football club in south west London reached the top level, brushing shoulders with many established big teams. And those bigger teams found out the physical way that Wimbledon weren't just there to make up the numbers.

After finishing brilliantly in sixth position of what then was called Football League Division One and reaching the FA Cup quarter-finals, the manager then decided it was time to move on, as he believed he couldn't take them any higher, and so left to take over at his native Watford. The year was 1987. In just six seasons under the stewardship of Dave 'Harry' Bassett, Wimbledon had propelled themselves from the backwaters of the Football League to the heady heights of the best division in the world. How did he achieve this?

To find out the answer you have to go back to just his second season in charge when they were relegated. Bassett learnt a harsh lesson that he couldn't deploy a pretty style of football with limited resources and playing ability if you wanted to survive at the more physical stage of the pyramid. The whole team's style had to change. Wimbledon then adopted a more robust direct style of football which eradicated taking risks in defence that had punished his one-dimensional playing staff. The ball was played quickly forward to put the opposing defence under pressure. It had been done before but not with such regularity and ruthlessness. Opponents couldn't handle this aggressive onslaught. They knew all about it, but very rarely came up with anything effective to combat it.

Harry's philosophy was simple. Playing the game this way suited his numerically small squad. The sum of the parts became greater than the whole team. There was one miscalculation on his part though. He left Wimbledon one year too soon, because as BBC commentator John Motson would brilliantly put it in May 1988 … "The Crazy Gang have beaten The Culture Club!"

Under new manager Bobby Gould, Wimbledon had caused an upset by beating Liverpool in the FA Cup final, but was it the massive shock that most football reporters and fans alike have believed it to be?

For me it isn't. A surprise, yes, but a shock? No. Liverpool were the best team in the country at the time but Wimbledon had, for the second year running, finished in the top third of the top League. By the reaction from football folk after the final you would have thought the Wombles had never been in the top flight to start with. They weren't given a prayer before the game but the bookies hadn't reckoned on the spirit of Bassett which still prevailed in every corner of the club. The players knew each other's game inside out and played a basic style reinforced by big physical players such as Vinnie Jones and John 'Fash The Bash' Fashanu. It wasn't pretty to watch, but they were real characters.

History records show that the only goal of the game was scored by Lawrie Sanchez. It also gave us the first ever penalty to be saved in a Wembley FA Cup final making a hero of goalkeeper Dave Beasant. But it shouldn't have been that way, because early in the game, Liverpool had a perfectly good goal ruled out due to hastiness on the part of the referee.

Peter Beardsley was fouled but recovered on his feet, jinking into the Wimbledon penalty area before skilfully chipping the ball over the oncoming Beasant's body. As he turned to celebrate, his toothless grin turned to jaw dropping disbelief as he realised that the man in black had already stopped the game for the initial foul and had failed to play the advantage rule. It was a poor decision which even early on, turned out to be the biggest turning point.

Had Liverpool gone 1-0 up, you could never have seen Wimbledon's crude style of football threaten the classiest team in the land. Liverpool were too cute to let a lead slip against anything their opposition threw at them. They would have been too good in possession and on such a hot day inside the cauldron of Wembley Stadium, Wimbledon players I believe would have exhausted themselves chasing the ball around. As it turned out, Sanchez put his team one up and thus gave The Wombles a shot in the arm and something tangible to fight for. On the day a clever tactical decision by Bobby Gould and his experienced assistant Don Howe (also assistant with the England team) ensured that Footballer Of The Year John Barnes was effectively starved of the ball by deploying one of their players as a human shield. Whenever Liverpool were in possession, the player simply stood between the ball and Barnes, cutting off the danger man's supply.

Through the years, I've often wondered what Dave Bassett was doing on that day and how he felt when realising that the team he had built lifted the most famous trophy in the most famous football stadium. While Wimbledon were reaping the rewards that Bassett's football savvy had sown, the man himself was in the middle of a relegation battle with Sheffield United after having been sacked at Watford a few months before.

Could things get any worse for him that season? It's bad enough that the two teams you managed that year both get relegated, but then you have to witness another manager bathing in the glory and achieving something that even their most optimistic fans would never even dare to daydream of. It's like running a marathon only to fall about a mile from the end and watching helplessly as someone else takes your medal.

Things got worse for Wimbledon. A lot worse. Their players left one by one, enticed by bigger clubs as profiles within the club were raised spectacularly. They lost their home ground Plough Lane and were forced to play their 'home' games at Crystal Palace FC in Croydon. And as they say these things happen in threes; they actually lost their identity when hijacked by a takeover bid based in Milton Keynes, eventually becoming known as MK Dons.

The spirit of the original club lives on however, and after a new club was founded by supporters in 2002 at the bottom of the pyramid, AFC Wimbledon rose like a phoenix from the ashes to once again play in the Football League. This astonishing comeback built on sheer resilience may not have resulted in silverware but is as dramatic of that famous Cup victory back in '88, and I always smile whenever I see them above MK Dons in the League table.

I can't really raise a smile though when I think back to that final. An underdog's win at Wembley is supposed to be remembered by the neutral as part of the competition's enduring fairytale finals. The 'in your face' brand of battling football bending the rules of the game (and sometimes breaking bones) makes the average fan wince rather than wax lyrical.

But that would never bother Fash, Vinnie and co. it's the way things were at Wimbledon.

And so it begins...

Callum Martindale, the reason I started my journey at Saltash United.

*Pictured with ex team mates John Nickson and Steve Cooksley
at Westbury in Wiltshire. Sadly we were two decades early to audition
for a remake of Last Of The Summer Wine.*

*I was impressed with the set up at Bitton.
Even if they didn't have enough match programmes on the day.*

This team ethic at Taunton Town FC is spot on, and it showed on the pitch.

Selfie with the brilliant Paul Gascoigne.
What a privilege bumping into a legend… he told me.

147

Rob & Willie, The Taunton Taunters. Scourge of many a non-league goalkeeper.

At the home of Billericay Town FC, a club designed for bigger things.

John Croot, director at Chesterfield FC. The inventor of Walking Football.

*Lest We Forget is an all year round message
in Chesterfield's Garden Of Remembrance.*

*Cod Army ensemble. Grimsby fans enjoying themselves
before taking on Crystal Palace.*

*Great effort by the Grimsby team narrowly losing at a Premiership club
and appreciated by their travelling support.*

Paying through the nose to get a ticket for Crystal Palace v Tottenham.
The only way I could obtain one was to get a seat in their Legends Suite.
Overall this adventure cost me more than two grand!

Crystal Palace legend Neil Shipperley in the shirt and tie.
As no nonsense off the pitch as he was on it.

The Keepmoat Stadium, home of Doncaster Rovers. Surrounded by greenery and a lake, it must be the most picturesque football ground in England.

The sun breaks through the Yorkshire clouds and lights up the Keepmoat.

Doncaster mascot Donny the Dog. I was disappointed to find out he wasn't real.

Trevor Higgins at Elburton Villa FC. Surveying all he helped to build.

Watford Honorary Life President Sir Elton John pictured with a David Kindon lookalike.

Match tickets are rare for a Cup Quarter Final, forcing me yet again to pay over the odds for one via Watford's VIP suite. But at least I managed to get a press pass just to the left of my glass of wine. Attending the post-match press conference was a real eye opener.

*Crystal Palace manager Roy Hodgson being helped to his chair
by his carer at the press conference.*

*Last minute of the semi final at Wembley Stadium and Watford Captain Troy
Deeney scores a dramatic penalty kick to send the tie into extra time against Wolves.*

Cup Final Day. Magic Mike and myself pictured on Wembley Way.

*Mission accomplished! Every match programme from my journey,
and each one signed by someone featured in each chapter.*

Chapter Nine

SHINE THROUGH THE GLOOM

After the long drive back from Chesterfield, I took the next day off work. In the evening The Crimson Queen met me in Plymouth city centre after she finished work, so we went for a few drinks. I was so excited and couldn't stop checking my watch as it took an eternity to reach 7pm, the time for the third round draw.

This is the stage of the competition when the FA Cup by tradition, takes on the magic of football. There are now sixty-four teams left, comprising of survivors from the previous rounds and the big teams from the top two levels of the game. Anything goes now. Anyone can be drawn to play anyone, irrespective of geography, size, history or status.

I'm now following Grimsby Town. Will I be travelling all the way to Cleethorpes in Lincolnshire where strangely they play their home games (why aren't they called Cleethorpes Town?), or will I be traveling somewhere closer to home, maybe a Premiership venue? And Premiership team it is! Eventually Grimsby's number is drawn and they'll be playing away to … Crystal Palace! South London here I come! I went there to watch Plymouth Argyle play with my then colleagues Barry Hawkings, Pete Ridgeon and Mike Reed. It was 1987 as I drove us up in my gold metallic Capri. Okay then, in for a penny, in for a pound. I also wore a gold earring and sported a mullet of blond highlighted hair. Hey, it was the eighties!

Another tradition of the FA Cup is that the third round is always played in the first weekend of the New Year, so that gives me a month to obtain a ticket online. Before then, The Crimson Queen and myself fulfil a promise we made to each other for Christmas. Engagement? Holiday abroad? No, we promised each other we'd return to the Viridor Stadium to watch Taunton

Town; and it was a cracking game! A top of the table clash ended with a 3-3 draw against Weymouth in front of a bumper crowd. It was good to see some of the lads from the Billericay trip. Rob Wenham greeted us in the clubhouse and presented me with a Peacock's calendar which The Crimson Queen had secretly paid for as a belated Christmas gift. A quick flick through the months and I realised that Rob had personalised it for me. There was a picture that I posted on Facebook mentioned in the previous chapter of The Cat, The Kitten and The Lion, on the February page. She wasn't expecting that! We finished our drinks before I escorted Miss February to a standing position behind the goal which Taunton were attacking.

The Mascot

I've already described Dan Carter as a cat amongst the peacocks. As mascot for Taunton Town Football Club, he is understandably emotionally connected to the team that represents the place where he was born. "My true heart lies here," he told me. Not surprisingly, he volunteers to help out in other areas at the Viridor, including attending to the changing rooms, ensuring that they are clean on matchdays and even giving them the odd lick of paint.

He can't speak highly enough of chairman Kev Sturmey and vice-chairman Brian Pollard who both, in his words, gave him a chance in life and taught him that an active mind is a healthy mind. You see, Dan, like so many men aged between twenty and fifty years old has suffered from mental health issues including Post Trauma Stress Disorder (PTSD) and borderline personality disorder after a traumatic episode he experienced in his childhood. When diagnosed, he thought that no one would ever have the time of day for him and confined himself to his house; but there were three things that he loved in his life which kept him going and ultimately drove him to seek help; namely his two daughters and Taunton Town F.C.

There's no doubt in Dan's mind that football saved his life and through the club he met some amazing people in both staff and players; but why does a football team nicknamed 'The Peacocks' have a cat for a mascot? Apparently, a few years ago, the local operatic society for reasons only known to themselves, dumped a cat suit over the gates of Taunton's football ground. Picked up by the ground staff the following morning, the new addition to the family was christened Wordsworth after the street where the club is situated.

I first met Dan when we shared the same coach table on the way to Billericay. He spoke with honesty and an open heart going into detail of his history of depression which resonated with me, as I have experienced the same thing.

> "We enter the world alone, we leave alone,
> so it's better to be alone."
> UNKNOWN

I can trace my depression back to the age of eleven. A small kid attending a huge comprehensive school (about 1600 pupils), I was quite bright, but years of paranoia had turned me into the class clown. By the age of fifteen I had managed to fail all of my 'mock' exams and had just six months left to salvage decent grades.

But I didn't care. I couldn't put my finger on it at the time but I knew something wasn't right at home, something to do with me. I had a lot of friends but felt like a loner and too often, preferred my own company. Luckily, someone did care; Mr Brimacombe at Southway School. He pulled me to one side at the end of one lesson for a heart-to-heart discussion. I could feel myself smirking but saw in his eyes genuine concern. It didn't sink in at first but when I thought long and hard about it I realised that I should pour all of my efforts into the three subjects in which I had the same three teachers throughout those five years. I didn't want to let them down, especially Mr Brimacombe, and I passed all three exams.

Apart from justifying their very existence as teachers, getting those grades didn't mean anything to me personally, as I didn't know what to do with my life and I didn't have a clue what the hell life was about. I loved music and football and never looked past the next weekend. Mind you, I was still decent enough to write a letter to Mr Goddard, the headmaster of the school, and asked him to pass on my thanks to those three teachers who had motivated me to make that last effort there. Mr Brimacombe, Mr Coules and Mr Wilkins.

Sunday 9th May 1982. It may seem like strange timing when my mum sat me down in the kitchen to tell me my father's true identity. I was about to take those exams when she told me that my dad in fact, wasn't my dad and that I was a result of an affair she'd had with another married man. That's why the old man hated me! Now it all made sense. She felt she had to tell me now because he'd reached breaking point. Basically, he wanted to break me in half and had invited me outside for a fistfight. I can't put into words how upset I was. I ran over to see my best mate Phil Marshall who couldn't believe it. His advice to me was to leave home. For the next twenty-four hours I was in a state of shock until my mum made the confession. I felt relief and even a little elation. What irony though. I always thought he was a bastard, but all along it was me!

The emotional impact of that deceit however was huge. The chip on my shoulder grew ever bigger as time went on. I became ever more distant to the other three members of the household and bore a grudge against the man who had threatened me.

Sometime later I was within a whisker of wreaking revenge. Older, bigger but not too wiser, I confronted him in the passageway. It's hard to explain and goes against my true nature but; as we walked towards each other I instinctively and deliberately barged into him in order to provoke a reaction. "What's wrong with you?" he shouted. I didn't respond but just stood side on to him, slightly crouched with my right fist clenched. I'm looking into his right eye and dying for him to take a step forward; patiently waiting to put three years of anger and bitter frustration behind me with just one punch. The silence was deafening!. And then he walked away. I felt great satisfaction if a little cheated. Looking back, I'm glad I never hit him. The emotional damage would have been greater than anything physical and we wouldn't have made it up two decades later.

I always recall two telephone conversations. One in January 2002 and the other in January 2011.

The first was made to Jim Kindon, my dad. Not my biological father, but the dad who had brought me up; the same bloke I had once hated and wanted to punch. I'd just gone through my second traumatic experience when I got wind that he wanted to meet me. He was now a grandfather to two girls and apparently looked differently at life. I was told he had major regrets about the way he'd treated me. He was no longer the cruellest person I'd met, so I made the call and told him it would be nice to come up for a coffee. I also told him before I hung up that he was my dad. He'd brought me up and I had his name.

We had some sort of relationship for a couple of years but then I stopped visiting him. I just didn't want a lot to do with family. I didn't feel any bond and never understood those who have. I've always respected other people's family life but never felt that connection myself.

The second phone call nine years later was made to me by a neighbour of his who informed me that Jim Kindon had died. I went silent, feeling nothing. I think I may have thought of my sister at this point who was his daughter by blood. The voice at the other end said, "Dave? Are you there? Are you okay?" I heard myself say, "Jim Kindon died in 1982." And hung up. I've never had any regrets about not attending his funeral.

So then, who or what was the cruellest thing in my life? An ex-girlfriend who now lives in New Zealand not only finished our relationship in the New Year of 2002 but also made the decision to have an abortion. It all happened in the space of a few days and I had no say in either of those two things. The first instance is anyone's privilege and the other is dictated by law. She was twenty weeks pregnant and was rushed to Bournemouth for the termination. I've never seen her since the night we split and never want to. The poor little boy was delivered stillborn so they told me, as per procedure, but never got a funeral as per law. He was going to be named Travis, a name she liked. When she told me that was what she wanted our baby to be called, I showed her a framed black and white film still hanging on my passage wall of Robert De Niro in Taxi Driver. The character's name he played was Travis and the reason I bought it was because when I rented the video years before, I felt an affinity with him.

In my early twenties, I was still living in the house I'd been brought up in. I virtually lived upstairs, Jim Kindon would usually be downstairs and our paths never crossed. I'd just leave my rent in the kitchen every Friday evening. Talk about the odd couple! I had a good social life at the weekends but during the week I'd get to work early, drive a lorry for a plumber's merchants, come home usually with a rented video and crash out. When I first saw Taxi Driver, I felt as if I could have played that role. Travis was a loner who drove for a living, lived alone, talked to himself and felt that society was on a downward slope. A few years later I bought the picture to remind me of how important it is to stay in touch with the human race. Loneliness is an illness.

And now I was going to be a dad. I couldn't believe it! I didn't even want children before that because I didn't want them to hate me the way I hated my dad. But the day my girlfriend told me we were expecting it changed the whole way I looked at life. It wasn't going to stop there. She was qualified to live in New Zealand due to a former relationship and we spoke about making a new life there. Strangely, it was another Robert De Niro film 'Heat' where his character wanted to do the same but never quite got there. I was thrilled to be an expectant dad and she prepared me to be one by including me in every meeting she had with her doctor, pre-natal classes and a scan. At the scan she claimed the unborn boy was boxing in the womb. I said Travis Kindon would either be a boxer or a footballer. I talked to him through the wall of the womb and felt him kick now and then and couldn't wait for a definitive due date. This lad was going to change my life for the better and for the first time ever I had felt true love. It was all coming together. The bitterness about family betrayal was going to go away as now, I looked forward to a brighter future. Everything I was going to do from then on would be for my family and I would do anything to make them happy.

And then it was taken away. The shock hit me for six. I sank into depression and attended private counselling arranged through my work, but to be honest, neither that nor anti-depressants helped. The only thing that my counsellor Peggy (a retired midwife) showed me was that I was in fact a loner. She explained that by placing four ornaments around a circular rug on the floor and told me to sit in the middle. The four different ornaments represented my family, my friends, my colleagues and football team-mates. She told me that I was in the middle, keeping them all at arms' length. Now and then, I might join them on the circumference but always returned to the middle where I'd be on my own. There was no constant in my life she said. I replied that the baby and my own family would have been that constant had I been a better boyfriend. I failed in that respect. All she said in answer to that was that I would know how to deal with it if it happened again.

Apart from visiting my dad during this time (now he was forgiven), I don't recall a lot about those first few months of 2002. All I can tell you is that suffering from a mental illness is like being in a long, dark and very cold tunnel, with no light at the end of it. If you break a bone in your body, the comfort comes from knowing that it's healing every day and will become strong again. When your mind is broken however, nothing is healing. This leads to adopting dark thoughts and very dangerous ones.

As I approached my thirty-sixth birthday in May, I started to come out of depression, or so I thought. Alcohol was masking the misery. When sober, I had a terrible demeanour and a negative aura, cynical about life and sarcastic in the workplace. When drinking I could make anyone laugh and felt good about myself. I didn't realise it then but I didn't even like myself.

Through it all though was that guardian angel called football, both watching and playing it. Just like Dan Carter at Taunton Town FC, it kept me alive and gave me something to look forward to. Off the pitch I was nobody, on it I was somebody, part of a team. A bond between brothers fighting for the same cause, followed by the obligatory piss up. My team-mates were my family, people I could trust and grew to love. Football it seemed was the glue that held my family together, but I was kidding myself. In truth, football was always there to fall back on but it was women who were both the problem and the solution. They were capable of breaking me or making me. Throughout my life, they've been both my downfall and my salvation.

Anyone who has a mental health disorder and/or addicted to substances such as drugs or alcohol are in self-denial until they recognise that the person in the mirror needs professional help. Everyone else can already see it, and it wasn't until January 2017 when the inevitable emotional crash happened when I broke down at work. For the previous two months I had been kept awake by having horrific nightmares after a woman I was briefly involved with told me that her ex-husband had forced her to have an abortion. Images of stillborn babies invaded my psyche and when I awoke, I would blame myself for the lost son I desperately wanted. It was clearly my fault wasn't it. I was a lousy boyfriend and he had met his end horribly and never saw the light of day. Worst images were to follow as my subconscious took over my tired mind. Being a Beatles fan, I know a thing or two about them. I know for example that in America, one of their albums had an infamous cover which showed the Fab Four laughing and holding dismembered and bloodied baby dolls wearing white aprons. Known as 'The Butcher Album'; at one fell swoop, they had blown away their loveable moptop image on the other side of the Atlantic, and all I could see at night was the blood on my hands, not theirs.

In work they made me make an emergency appointment with my GP which I'll be eternally grateful for. Sorry to break this to all you lovely colleagues of mine, but you're my family now. Even those who aren't lovely! I was immediately prescribed sleeping pills and an anti-depressant called Sertraline, a drug which releases chemicals into your brain in order to balance it. Basically, it makes you think normally.

During the appointment I could feel tears running down my face. It's easier to talk to a stranger about things you'd be ashamed of than saying it to anyone you know. In a strange way you're protecting them. I could hear what I was saying, but I couldn't believe what I was saying. It was like an out of body experience. Surely these weren't my words! But it was and at the same time came the realisation that I'd been getting away with it for years. I should have sought help sooner. Alcohol had fooled me that everything was all right. Feeling down the next day I thought was just coming off the booze. Alcohol itself wasn't a problem with me and never was. I could take it or leave it in that respect. It was my mental state that was the problem. Getting drunk was just papering over the cracks.

These days I still get struck by anxiety attacks which last about five minutes. I tremble, feel sick and can feel tears run down my face but strangely, there's no sadness and usually no one around to witness it. It's happened a few times in the workplace when I've suffered a new 'low' in my life and I've always tried to tell people in the middle of these attacks that I'll be okay, but it's difficult to get the words out as I stammer when it happens. Only a handful of colleagues, a few doctors and a couple of psychiatric teams have been there when this occurs. No close friend or family member has seen me in this state. Even though I look a desperate sight on the outside, inside I'm okay as I know through experience that it soon passes. It's like an alcoholic walking up a high street. They pass several bars and can smell the alcohol beckoning them in, but they know that all they need to do is to keep walking and the enticing odour disappears. Their target is then reached, the end of the street; no more anxiety for a while.

On the 9th January 2017, I had my first assessment at Plympton Health Clinic after being referred there by my GP. In the report it's mentioned that I was tearful and full of remorse for the lost baby. It also mentions a fixation with Jack Daniels and cocodamol as a way of keeping the nightmares away. However my dark sense of humour would prevail now and then. When asked if I'd ever practised self-harm, my answer was "I bought a Plymouth Argyle season ticket once!"

Christmas 2016 was the worst one of my life. An ongoing struggle to face the day, even before it got light. Regular as clockwork it started with those nightmares. Waking up trembling, I would swig from a bottle of Jack Daniels which would calm me down for a bit. Never getting hungry, I'd spend most of the days in pubs; only broken up by the walks between them. When I reached home the anxiety would start. The paranoia I had as a child was creatively thinking ways of ending it all. More trembling followed by more Jack Daniels. Wouldn't it be so easy just to down a full bottle with a load of cocodamol and slip away painlessly. I could do it on Christmas Day, the one day of the year that I was completely (by choice) on my own and nobody there to stop me. Not like those who walk to a bridge to jump off, hoping that someone will talk them out of it. I wasn't due back in work until January 2nd, over a week away. Even then the door would have to be bust open; and probably by the police. Let them discover me, not anyone I know. They are trained to deal with it after all. That's your problem Kindon, even when you're thinking about taking your own life, you're so considerate!

Eventually and obviously I got better and became normal thanks to the medication and support from those heroes in the NHS. On the 27th April, I was assessed for the final time in an Exeter clinic by a psychiatrist. It was now reported that I was well-kempt, made good eye contact and engaging warmly in the conversation. My speech was good, as was my self-esteem and my thought processes normal. Most importantly though was that I had a good amount of insight into the two forms of PTSD I had experienced in 1982 & 2002. It was then agreed I could go on a programme where my medication could be reduced and eventually stopped.

The following month I ran the Plymouth half-marathon, raising money for the PDSA, my preferred charity.

I'll end the first half of this chapter with three brilliant bits of advice given to me by three friends in January 2002; words I have never forgotten and that, even through my darkest hours, could shine through the gloom that had possessed my mind. The three stages if you like of coming through depression ...

ADRIAN CHARLES – "Dave, stay low. Keep a low profile."
DAVE HARPER – "Dave, don't change. You're a good bloke."
CAROLINE McVICKER – "Dave ... fuck 'em!"

1979 WINNERS – ARSENAL

'Shine through the gloom and point me to the skies ...' so sang both sets of supporters on Cup Final Day 1979, but any Arsenal or Manchester United fan belting out football's most famous hymn 'Abide With Me' would never dare guess what they were going to witness in this game.

And neither would anyone at home. For eighty-five minutes the game was ordinary, and we were about to go through the motions as Arsenal comfortably led 2-0 and were expected to descend the steps from the Royal Box clutching their winner's medals. In the event the players representing the red side of north London would win the FA Cup but only after the game suddenly had everyone out of their seats both at home and inside Wembley for a finale so amazing that it became known as the 'Five-minute Final'.

But it shouldn't have been. If Stan Mortensen was denied immortality in 1953 for scoring a hat trick, then 1979 dealt the same blow to a brilliant midfielder called Liam Brady. It's said that the talented Irishman was so disgusted with his performance twelve months previously when Arsenal lost the 1978 final to Ipswich

Town, that he vowed if ever given the chance again, he would make Wembley Stadium his own. And that's exactly what he did.

At half-time, The Gunners led by two goals, both engineered by Brady's superb dribbling skills and executing perfect deliveries to unlock Manchester United's defence. Early in the match, he collected the ball and beat a couple of opponents with ease before slotting a pass inside the United area for team-mate David Price. Price then flat footed the defence by pulling the ball back for the oncoming Brian Talbot to score the first goal. The bookies lost a lot of money because of this. A lot of fans had bet on Talbot to score the first goal simply because he'd won the Cup playing for Ipswich against Arsenal the year before. It was a fun bet, but many punters saw it as fate and cashed in; to their delight.

The second goal came about half an hour later and it was all Brady's creation. Again, beating defenders with ease before chipping the ball invitingly across the goalmouth for his compatriot Frank Stapleton to head the second. For most of the second half the game was okay with both teams getting half chances to score but the clock ticked on for an anti-climatic formality. Or so we thought.

With five minutes remaining, United had a free kick which was crossed into the area and suddenly the ball was in the back of the Arsenal net after defender Gordon McQueen instinctively swept his left foot across it. The United players just jogged back to the halfway line feeling that this was just a consolation goal, but incredibly, just sixty seconds later, they had equalised. It seemed just a token gesture when the ball was floated to the edge of the Arsenal penalty area, more in hope than expectation. Arsenal players seemed to freeze however, as United players desperately tried to knock the ball towards goal. It found it's way to Sammy McIlroy who took an eternity to hit a tame shot past goalkeeper Pat Jennings. Time slowed down as the ball softly rolled into the net and send the red half of Manchester into ecstasy.

Arsenal players were beaten. They sat on the lush green turf in absolute shock at the same time as the sun sapped their strength. They had nothing left as United players sensed this was their day after all. It was inevitable now that the final would go to extra time and Manchester United would win one of the most dramatic and exciting FA Cup finals in years. In homes all around the country viewers were convinced now that the famous silver trophy was going back to Old Trafford for the second time in three seasons.

But nobody told Liam Brady the script and he would not be denied glory for the second year running. Within seconds of Arsenal kicking off again he received the ball and caught half of the United side (and the commentators) off guard as he ran deep into enemy territory before laying the ball off to winger Graham Rix who in turn crossed to the far post. Goalkeeper Gary Bailey misjudged the flight of the ball and Arsenal striker Alan Sunderland met the cross a few yards from United's goal before scoring the winner and running deliriously towards his disbelieving team-mates.

At the final whistle, everybody was stunned. Players from both sides collapsed and both managers could hardly get their words out to waiting microphones for the two major terrestrial channels. Collecting their respective medals from royalty it was hard to see which player had played for which club as a lot of them had respectfully swapped shirts with emotionally shattered opponents. The Football Association would ensure that this would never happen again, by issuing a directive that all players must wear their team colours at all times on Cup Final Day. Ominously, Frank Stapleton who scored Arsenal's second goal was wearing a Manchester United top and would later join and go on to win the Cup with four years later.

So, Liam Brady got his winner's medal. Incredibly twelve months later Arsenal would reach the final for the third consecutive year but lost to West Ham, and Brady was off to play for Juventus in Italy where his superb technique would be more appreciated. Because of that five-minute rollercoaster of a finish, he never got the universal recognition he deserved in 1979, but for Arsenal fans who remember this brilliant Irish footballer, this was indeed 'The Liam Brady Final'.

The day before Crystal Palace played Grimsby, I rocked up at Avis Car Rental in Plymouth to pick up a smooth ride with digital radio. The girl at reception called Emma asked me out of interest why I was going to London, so I told her about the whole adventure. She was impressed as she likes football and told me about a racehorse she partly owns called 'Iwilldoit' which was running in the 2.50 at Bangor on Tuesday afternoon. The jockey wears Argyle colours as they are all part of the Green Army and they were going to make a day of it in north Wales. I went on to the Skybet website and stuck a fiver each way at odds of 14/1. It had no chance of winning she told me, but it would be a fun day out.

Early the next morning, I set off for the capital avoiding horrible grey motorways and choosing instead to take in the beautiful scenery of southern England. As the sun comes up on a clear cold day, there's a bright blue sky overlooking white frozen countryside – Manchester City colours. An omen? Taking my time, I drive past Stonehenge before merging with the M3 motorway which will virtually take me into south London. This is where it gets ugly. Heavy traffic everywhere and some parts resemble third world countries, rather than the capital of the third biggest contributor to the European Union. Why aren't we getting our own house in order?

There are also parts of London which are very religious and spiritual. There are mosques and methodist churches in the same borough of which one has a notice board which I read when stopped at traffic lights. It's advertising a psychic meeting at 7.30pm. on Tuesday evening. But if it's being attended by psychics, then why display it? Surely they should already know?

Online I found a very reasonably priced hotel for my overnight stay in Croydon and just a twenty-five-minute walk to the ground. It's a Best Western hotel and although it looks old on the outside, it resembles a Premier Inn on the inside with a cosy bar and restaurant. For just under £30 I've got a bargain. Okay, they've run out of draught beer but the carpets are nice. Rather than pay an extra tenner to park and register the car on the hotel grounds, I find a very quiet and convenient cul de sac fifty yards away. I'm told at reception that I need photo I.D. if I want to stay such as a driving licence which I've left at home.

"I've come by train," I lie.

"Have you got a passport?" she asks.

"I didn't know I needed one to get into Croydon!"

She insists I must have some sort of visual proof, so I pull my iPhone out and show her my Facebook profile pic. However I'm having difficulty trying to replicate the image as it was a drunken selfie taken on Christmas Eve. By now, her boss is laughing his head off and tells me that it's okay and I just have to sign a form. Surely that's proof enough if you sign a form, as long as you have a pre-signed credit or debit card to hand.

It's freezing cold and drizzly as I walk down a hill towards Crystal Palace Football Club. The houses are quite old but tidy and well-kept in Whitehorse Lane as the floodlights can be glimpsed now and then, tantalisingly through gaps between the driveways. Only the cars have changed in these streets for decades I reckon. I walk past the ground as I remember a pub about two hundred yards down this road where I've been twice before; and there it is, these days reserved for away supporters. It's absolutely wall to wall with Grimsby fans inside the Prince George. Is this where William and Kate conceived their firstborn? I've been here amongst Crystal Palace and Manchester United fans, both raucous sets of supporters, but this lot today are making the best atmosphere and I can't wait to get into the ground to sample more.

The kick-off is 5.30pm on a Saturday, so inside the pub all TV screens are showing Jeff Stelling on Sky Sports and his cult show 'Soccer Saturday' where live goal flashes hit the screen the moment the ball hits the back of the net. The sound is off because there's a party going on with Grimsby fans in good voice. The DJ is playing all the classics and everybody joins in to Neil Diamond.

'Sweeeet Caroline, dah dah dah,
good times never seemed so goooood ...'.

I'm leaning with my back against the bar in a corner keeping myself to myself and loving the atmosphere. Then all of a sudden there's booing and insults shouted at the big screen. Scunthorpe, Grimsby's hated rivals, have only gone and scored! And I'm the only one laughing. Then a goal for Argyle flashes up, and I'm the only one cheering. A few of them look at me but I tell them I'm on their side today, and after all they're known as The Mariners. And who played for us before making it big? Paul Mariner! But most of them are too young to remember him.

Opposite the pub, a number of Grimsby supporters are congregated outside Costcutters, apt name for a level four club where fans are taking group photos. It's thirty minutes before kick-off so I make my way back to the ground. The entrance for away supporters is called The Arthur Wait Stand, presumably after a bloke called Arthur who took a helluva long time to get through the turnstiles. This may be a Premiership club but the facilities are piss poor including the gent's toilets, obviously. Outside the entrances I'm wondering why one of the turnstiles has twice as many fans queuing up than all the others. Then as I get nearer I realise that it's the only one with a female steward who's frisking every one of them and giggling at their lewd comments. Welcome to Planet Retro, the sexist side of the game.

Ironically my mate Barry Hawkings with whom I came here with in 1987 and is a Crystal Palace fan would have loved to be part of the Grimsby crowd today. When we worked together, he instilled in me a passion for away support. "Geez!" he'd address me, "Look at the away end! They're all pissed up and loving it!" Inside, the stewards are friendly and they let all Grimsby fans stand up rather than force them to sit down in cheap cold plastic seats. It's a good view I've got, about twenty rows back and overlooking the halfway line. There's a display on the pitch involving a ceremonial eagle and it's owner. The magnificent bird of prey takes flight from one end of the pitch before swooping and landing gracefully onto the crossbar at the other end, much to the Palace fan's delight. Crystal Palace have been known as The Eagles since the 1970's, replacing their former and not so intimidating 'The Glaziers' nicknamed after the all glass structure in Hyde Park which symbolised the British Empire's industrial dominance in the mid nineteenth century before sadly burning down.

Future England manager Terry Venables cut his managerial teeth here in the late seventies, a time of cautious tactics replacing flair on the pitch and ugliness off it. Playing an all-London Cup match against Chelsea one day, there was a punch up when one Palace fan threw himself at a few dozen opposing supporters from the other side of the River Thames and was quickly arrested. As he was frogmarched around one side of the pitch towards the exit, there was a hold up in the game, due to an injury and Venables noticed the thug being escorted out by two police officers. He had a shaven head, wore braces that held his bleached jeans up, helping to reveal a mean pair of eighteen holed Doc Marten boots. Chewing gum and putting up no resistance whatsoever, he looked down at the dugout where the Palace coaching staff were sat and addressed Venables with "Blimey! The fings I do for you Tel!"

Today's Palace manager is ex-England boss Roy Hodgson whose secretary hasn't replied to my emails asking whether I could grab a few minutes sometime for an interview. No doubt he's busy not only with preparation but with all of the media responsibilities that come with having a top job in football nowadays. I then tried to contact Grimsby manager Michael Jolley but to no avail. I wouldn't think he would be as busy as a Premiership manager in that respect, but then I read up on him and I suspect he doesn't trust anyone after an unsavoury incident ten years ago.

For twelve months he was registered as a sex offender and banned from coaching in football after pleading guilty to having sexual intercourse with an underage girl. He and a friend had met three young women in a nightclub one Saturday night who told them they were nineteen. After consensual sex with one of them, all of the girls asked to borrow money to get a cab home but Jolley was skint after the night out. The girls then demanded money and started to cause a scene which included him being struck in the face with a broken bottle prompting a neighbour to call the police. After everyone was questioned Jolley was informed that he had in fact had sex with a girl who was a few months short of her sixteenth birthday. He resigned from Falkirk Football Club in Scotland and his name placed on the sex offender's register. A year later it was decided he wasn't a sexual predator and that he had been lied to by the girls in question so taken off the register and able to get another job in football. The law is the law and if you break it then take the punishment.

People will moralise on whether or not it's all right to have consentual intercourse with a younger woman even if she's above the age of consent and that all depends on your point of view. But one question bugs me about the whole business. How the hell did these girls get into a nightclub? If Michael Jolley had broken the letter of the law, why wasn't the proprietor of that drinking establishment prosecuted?.

FA CUP THIRD ROUND
SATURDAY 5TH JANUARY
SELHURST PARK
ATTENDANCE – 19967

CRYSTAL PALACE 1 GRIMSBY TOWN 0

Crystal Palace fans in the Holmesdale End to my left are making it a carnival atmosphere. Smack bang in the middle of this red and blue tribe is a drummer who calls the tune. When he starts to drum, thousands of them start to sing, starting with his mates who stand around him and spreading infectiously. Visually it's just as good as the place starts to jump in ripples spreading around the complete end behind that goal. That was the end where I stood watching Argyle in '87 a few feet away from Michael Foot MP who was suitably dressed in a donkey jacket, jeans and steel toe-cap boots. Apparently, he used to do impressions of a politician.

Although this game would be decided by a late goal, the turning point comes in the first few seconds. Brilliant winger Andros

Townsend appears to be tripped by an over eager Grimsby player whose adrenaline has got the better of him. Townsend gets the free kick but is remonstrating with the referee and pointed to a ripped sock. After a VAR interruption the perpetrator is sent off. Not even the second minute and the underdogs are down to ten men! At the time it didn't seem that bad of a challenge but at half time modern technology shows the tackle to be a very bad one as Grimsby folk replay the incident on iPhones.

Referee Martin Atkinson had initially just given the free kick and nothing else; but someone in a room somewhere has had a word in his ear and the correct decision was made. The problem is nearly twenty thousand spectators didn't have a clue why. No communication. I feel for the travelling support at this stage. Paying through the nose to get here, watching a game at a Premiership club, staying in a hotel due to the late kick off and traveling back the next day. And now they're right up against it on the pitch. Their usual chant of 'We only sing when we're fishing' is now replaced by …

'One-nil to the referee, one-nil to the referee.'

Memo to the Football Association … if you want the officials to be shown more respect then why not let everyone in the ground know why they are making game changing decisions?

The Grimsby players battle magnificently and their followers sing wholeheartedly.

'Mar-in-ers!'

… is the cry from a thousand people in black and white striped shirts. The Palace fans respond loudly and it's an enjoyable affair. On such a cold day everyone is allowed to stand and the place is rocking. Around me the 'Cod Army' mock and cheer every Crystal Palace attack that comes to nothing and make up their own special song for Andros Townsend; he of the ripped sock.

'Wanker! Wanker! Wanker!'

... rings out every time he touches the ball.

The home team are getting frustrated by the valiant efforts of the numerically challenged side from three levels below. This however isn't affecting their core support who give a great rendition of The Dave Clark Five's 'Glad All Over', their Cup Final song from 1990. Grimsby respond with ...

'We've only got ten men, we've only got ten men, we've only got ten men ...'

Holmesdale End sing ...

'We're Palace, we're Palace, we're Palace, and that's the way we like it, we like it, we like it, whooooaaaaahhh ...'

They in turn are taunted with ...

'Premiership, you're having a laugh! Premiership, you're having a laugh!'

This is so entertaining I almost forget there's a football match being played. The game is a bit of a damp squib compared to the heat on the terraces and the Cod Army sense headlines in tomorrow's papers but cruelly with just four minutes remaining Palace substitute Jordan Ayew scores a header right in front of the Holmesdale End. The devastation around me is almost tangible and for the second time today I feel for these people. How they would have loved to get a Premiership team back at their place! And judging by today's performance by Crystal Palace, Grimsby would have a good chance of turning them over.

The full-time whistle is blown and Grimsby players applaud Grimsby supporters and vice versa. Everyone on and off the pitch are wearing black and white GTFC shirts and it's the best show of unity I've seen since Taunton. Back at the hotel bar/restaurant I'm talking with a nineteen-year-old Grimsby fan called Bailey over a pint and a pizza. Like most 'Mariners' he was born in Cleethorpes where strangely Grimsby play. Then again, Crystal Palace play in an area called Thornton Heath and not Crystal Palace. He was just a toddler when his dad took him to his first game so obviously he can't tell me anything about it. He believes the referee was right to send off defender Andrew Fox for that challenge on Andros Townsend but is so proud of his team and their efforts today. He loves the atmosphere at football matches and speaks with great affection about the tussles Grimsby have with nearby rivals Lincoln City.

However, he would rather England win a major tournament than watch Grimsby play at Wembley in a Cup final and he goes on to say that it's such a shame his home team didn't go on a cup run, as it would mean so much money pouring into the club; in regards to prize money and TV revenue.

What a difference from myself and my mates roughly the same age watching Plymouth Argyle reach the semi-final in 1984 at Villa Park. Money never came into it. It was all about the magic and the glory. Bailey and I were born a thousand years apart. I'm still a Cup final kid, he's a Premiership baby.

Chapter Ten

MONEY MAKES THE BALL GO ROUND

Talking to the young Grimsby supporter just confirmed the way football fans of my generation feel about modern Cup finals. Money has replaced the magic. Money makes the world go round and indeed the wheels of our national game. I know football clubs have always been run like businesses because that's how they survive, but in the present era there is just too much emphasis on the value of everything which basically cheats those who love the game. Finishing in fourth place in the Premiership is more sought after than reaching the Cup final for the foreign owners of the top teams. They are light years away from the very people who matter, the supporters who are funding broken dreams.

Premiership football is like a new sports car. It's slicker, more glamorous, sexy to look at, quicker and a lovely drive, but we're still nostalgic for the classic sports car. Whoever designs the new shape has forgotten one very important thing. No matter what year the car is manufactured, it's the sheer passion that drives it.

On a more financially positive note, the racehorse I stuck a cheeky tenner on called 'Iwilldoit' only went and bloody did it! A fiver each way at 14/1 makes me a happy bunny in work as I followed the race online. I wasn't the only one in work who benefited either. Mark Tutten in our warehouse also stuck a bet on; both of us not knowing that the other had done so. I told him about Emma who works for the car rental company, telling me about her part ownership. Turns out it's his ex-girlfriend who's also let him know about it. This world just gets smaller and smaller.

Next up on the agenda is an all-London clash between two Premiership teams. I'm returning to Selhurst Park to watch Crystal Palace take on one of the best teams in Europe, Tottenham Hotspur, a club whose name is synonymous with the FA Cup. I check both club's websites on a daily basis only to find brick walls in the way of getting a ticket. No, I'm not a member or a season ticket holder; but I am a football fan on a mission and nothing's going to stop me going. There's only twenty-five thousand tickets available and as matchday gets nearer I'm getting desperate. A seat for a south versus north London clash is as rare as you know what from a rocking horse.

My last chance so it seems of obtaining a ticket is to pay over £200 for a seat in the Eagle's Legend Suite. Mind you, it does come complete with a match programme so at least I don't have to pay for one! Apparently, former Crystal Palace player Clint Morrison will be our host speaking before and after the game, so I'm preparing notes to interview him. The Legends Suite is actually built on top of a Sainsbury's supermarket which is amusing to look at on a Saturday afternoon watching tribesmen dressed in red and blue shirts sharing entrances with the blue rinse brigade. I can see my chapter heading already … 'Morrison's at Sainsburys'.

In order to cover the costs of hiring a car, petrol money, staying in London overnight and entrance to a football match which blows my monthly budget, I access the Skybet website on a Tuesday evening hoping to recoup my expenditure and even make a small profit. Quiet night in, make spaghetti Bolognese, drink a bottle of white plonk and put an Indie mix on the YouTube channel as my iPhone notifies me with goal flashes regarding my bets.

With ten minutes remaining in all of the games I've bet on I still need six goals spread across five games to win £390 but experience has taught me this never happens, so I go against my principles and tap the 'cash out' button for a fraction of the sum I would win, or as I call it, 'the pussy button'. I then call up Miss February but keep on hearing pings in my right ear signifying goals being scored. They're being banged in left, right and centre and she confirms my fears that I've made a mistake of cashing out for £34. When we finish talking I walk back into my living room only to hear and see the video 'Lucky Man' by The Verve. You couldn't make it up! And unfortunately I haven't.

A few days later I'm walking to the bus stop to get into town and collect another rented car when I bump into my neighbour Sally. She's a very nice lady in her late sixties struggling to make ends meet. She's just coming back from the churchyard where her late husband is buried and has been laying flowers on the grave. He was a reckless gambler she tells me, who almost broke her financially. Managing to salvage her savings and a few insurance pay-outs before he got his hands on it, she then hid it. When he passed on Sally then paid for a deposit on her house she now lives in. Beats getting a free pen from Michael Parkinson!

Trying to cheer her up a little whilst subtlely changing the subject, I comment about her new fella, the one I've seen her with a few times. "Oh no," she says, "I had to dump him as he was an alcoholic." I tell her she needs to complete the full set by getting involved with a drug addict, but apparently he was the one before the alcoholic! "Sally! Where do you meet these guys?" I ask her in exasperation. "Church," is her straight faced reply.

Oh God!

Driving to London the next morning but this time I'm taking the non-scenic route via the M5 & M4 motorways. Same old signs are telling me regularly to take a break as tiredness kills. I pull into one after three hours of driving for a cup of coffee. I answer a call of nature in the gents and as I wash my hands I look up to see a poster advertising an online football game which I reckon my girlfriend's son Jacob might like, so I take out my phone and take a picture. I'm dressed smart casual as I'll be in the Legends Suite and this lad mopping the floor notices me taking pictures. Wearing a long black coat, I reckon he mistakes me for some sort of services inspector, and he disappears swiftly through the door. I walk into the coffee bar where he's tipping off two young girls who are behind the counter about me, so I carry the illusion on by walking around the place snapping more pics.

Ordering a cappuccino one of them says; "This one's on the house" and they'll bring it over to me. "Mister ...?"

"My name's Dave."

The unusual thing about this place though isn't blagging a free coffee but this is a Starbucks lounge and not one run by that conglomerate hell bent on world domination, Costa Coffee.

The M25 motorway must be Britain's most expensive practical joke. With three lanes turning into four and then back to three, this monstrosity that orbits London resembles more of an American freeway. Basically, the highway code doesn't exist here and anything goes. Stretches of the surface are in terrible condition and you feel as if you're driving on four flat tyres.

Leaving on any junction from the M25 into south London it's very easy to get lost so that's what I did. Somewhere near Sutton I spot a geezer (he's called a bloke in any other part of the country) wearing a jacket over his head, shielding himself from the pouring rain which reveals a Crystal Palace shirt. Result! I pull over and offer him a lift to the game if he'll navigate me to the ground. Once there I know where I am as I'm staying in the same hotel as three weeks before. We shake hands and he introduces himself as Wayne. "My name's Dave."

On the way to Thornton Heath my new 'bezzie' tells me the story of how the Holmesdale drummer came to be and the supporter's relationship with Palace chairman Steve Parish. There's an agreement between the two parties that the drummer can command the centre of one stand behind the goal so long as he whips the crowd into a frenzy and therefore creates an atmosphere, which in turn lifts the team. Mr Parish is streetwise enough to know that marginal gains like this can give the team a psychological edge, win games and generate more money within the club. The balance is right. For the fan and owner it's an intoxicating mixture of football and finance working together.

I saw it, heard it and felt it at the Grimsby game. This is a tribal club and they're proud of being the only club in south central London. Millwall and Charlton play in the south east, Wimbledon in the south west. Wherever Palace play in the country, the chairman makes sure the drummer is positioned in a prominent place. And then I remember the 2016 Cup final, where high up in Wembley Stadium, I watched this spectacular red and blue wave synchronised with the drumbeat from behind one of the goals. A constant soundtrack to the flight of the Eagles.

Wayne was also at that final and the one in 1990, both against Manchester United, and echoes my generation's fondness of the competition's past and shares his concerns for it's future. I drop him off at the home fan's watering hole where we shake hands and I wish him good luck. In the event, Palace wouldn't need any.

I was really looking forward to watching Tottenham play as it's not often a neutral football fan gets to see a top-quality side but the Law of Sod decrees that both England captain Harry Kane and precocious talent Dele Alli are injured, while the underrated South Korean Son Heung-Min is also absent due to international duty in the Asian Cup. Nevermind, there's always Danish international Christian Eriksen to watch; a class footballer.

To his credit, Tottenham manager Mauricio Pochettino never complains about his depleted squad. Compare that to other Premiership managers such as Sam Allardyce who when at Bolton would moan about losing some of his players to foreign tournaments like the African Nations Cup. But did Big Sam have a point? I mean, how selfish of these footballers who choose to play for their country of birth over the club in which they, (like the managers), are just custodians of. Why the hell aren't they snubbing the highest honour their nation can bestow on them?

Ah but, I hear some of you say, the clubs are the ones paying their wages aren't they. Well, here's an idea, stop paying them obscene wages or even stop signing international players. No, here's a better idea, simply keep quiet and stop embarrassing yourself.

Against an understrength Spurs side, Crystal Palace must fancy their chances. They also have in their ranks ex-Spurs player Andros Townsend, the darling of Grimsby Town, and he may just have a score to settle; but then at the pre match press conference, Palace boss Roy Hodgson states that Premiership survival is his priority so he's going to pick a weakened team for this Cup match. Pity he didn't say it BEFORE the supporters bought their tickets but he wouldn't, would he. That would just reduce the attendance and probably affect his bonus money. And anyway, only fifty-seven countries around the globe will be tuning in to watch this football match. That's only a quarter of the planet.

I've never understood why managers or head coaches pick weakened teams in any competition. Any team who wins football matches never suffers from fatigue. As I've mentioned before, half the game is psychological and that in turn affects the body. A winning team is a confident one just as a losing team dents confidence and will affect your psyche and support, one way or the other. And without the proverbial twelfth man on the terraces, you're making your position a helluva lot harder. Managers call this type of team selection 'squad rotation'. Supporters call it 'taking the piss'.

I'm treated like royalty at Palace. Mini-quiches on entry to the Legends Suite and escorted to my table by a glamorous Posh Spice lookalike. Mackerel fillets and charred cucumber are served for starters. Main meal is chicken breast, green beans and aubergine. Chocolate and spiced plum mousse for dessert and all washed down with a glass of 'Eagle' white wine. I Just hope it's stronger than Roy Hodgson's team selection.

About an hour before kick-off, ex-Crystal Palace player Darren Ambrose takes the mic and tells us that both managers are taking the mick. Pochettino has left Eriksson out of the Tottenham line up, in fact he's not even named as substitute. It seems that 'Poch' is putting all of his eggs (some broken) into the European Champions League basket, so no wonder he never complained about his absentees earlier in the week. Basically, he doesn't give a damn about the FA Cup.

Ambrose tells it from the player's point of view. "The FA Cup is magical," he says, "No one wants to be rested. Spurs have no strikers on show today, mind you," he adds, "Palace haven't all season!"

Maybe us football fans are being too hard on managers in regards to team selection. Can you really blame them for concentrating on League status and sacrificing Cup competitions? They receive a much bigger bonus from their employers for the former and they're only human after all. One day they'll get the sack anyway, so they may as well look after themselves and their loved ones financially.

There really is nothing to lose. In a twenty-team Premier League a manager will become an instant millionaire just by avoiding the bottom three relegation positions. If you fail to survive and take your team down to level two, the inevitable sack is heading your way but so is a big pay off. What a crazy industry! Getting rewarded handsomely for failing at your job. Who cares then if you do alienate the supporters. They are there for life but you are not, and it's only a matter of time on the so-called managerial merry-go-round before another Premiership club comes knocking on your door anyway. Jose Mourinho is a case in point. At Manchester United he virtually ticked every box to get himself sacked, and when he did he became even more wealthy. At the top-heavy end of the pyramid, money really does make the ball go round.

1981 WINNERS – TOTTENHAM HOTSPUR

Not only did Mauricio Pochettino insult his club's history, he also disappointed two of his compatriots in Spurs legends Osvaldo Ardiles and Ricardo Villa.

Eyebrows were raised in the summer of 1978 when fresh from winning the World Cup with Argentina, the duo signed for the north London club. It wasn't common knowledge in White Hart Lane at the time but 'Ossie' Ardiles had always dreamed of playing at Wembley and that dream came true three years later when Tottenham reached the FA Cup final to play Manchester City.

Even before a ball was kicked, you sensed something different about this one. Something special. It was classic north versus south. Two teams attractive to watch, neither one of them were favourites. It was on the day. Chaz 'n Dave, Spurs fans, were flying high in the charts with 'Ossie's Dream', a song dedicated to the maestro's desire to perform in the most famous football stadium in the world for Tottenham. Or as he pronounced it in the song – "Tottingham".

The atmosphere was electric and came straight at you through the TV set. The pitch was greasy after downpours of rain which was something we weren't used to as Cup finals at Wembley always signalled the end of spring and the start of summer. There was also something else we weren't used to. This final went to extra time, the first in eleven years.

The game wasn't brilliant but was absorbing and very dramatic. It mainly featured a strange quirk of fate involving the oldest player on the pitch, ex-Scottish international Tommy Hutchison. In the first half he had scored a great diving header to put Man City one goal up and that's the way it stayed until late in the game. Then a cruel twist occurred which made Hutchison hit the next day's mixed headlines.

Spurs were awarded a free kick about twenty yards from goal. Hutchison took his position in the defensive wall. Those of us who wanted Tottenham to win the cup looked on with bated breath as Glenn Hoddle, worshipped by half of north London, sized it up for measure. As he caressed the ball in an attempt to curl it around the wall, Hutchison broke ranks in order to block it, only for the shot to strike his shoulder and divert the ball into the opposite side of the net from where City's excellent goalkeeper Joe Corrigan was diving. Corrigan could only help him to his feet as the hapless veteran crouched on his haunches holding his head in his hands. History had been made, and Tommy Hutchison became the first player to score for both teams in an FA Cup final.

Extra time was astonishing as one by one, players of both teams went down with cramp. They had given everything on the strength sapping surface. Poor on quality but rich in endeavour the 1981 final went to a replay which for most of my generation, would be the best we'd see.

If the first game was about Tommy Hutchison, then the second was all about three players in Tottenham shirts. Ricky Villa of Argentina who would score a memorable winning goal to add to the one he broke the deadlock with earlier in the game. Ossie Ardiles of Argentina whose dream came true, and England international Glenn Hoddle who was blessed ironically with South American skill.

Villa may not have even started the game given his performance the previous Saturday. Substituted at 1-0 down he walked with his head bowed in disconsolation towards the player's tunnel giving a brilliant impression of 'The Incredible Sulk'. But his manager Keith Burkinshaw selected him again and saw his faith rewarded as a determined Villa scored from close range to give Spurs the lead. Hoddle who was already making an impact nearly scored when his curling free kick hit Manchester City's post. That was just after the equalizer, the greatest goal scored in a final that no one would remember.

Steve Mackenzie scored a beautiful volley which rocketed into the Tottenham net but is never talked about. Why? Because City lost, that's why. And football folklore is as fickle as the fans who follow it.

In the second half, Manchester City were awarded a penalty kick which was successfully converted by Kevin Reeves. Two goals to one. Enter Glenn Hoddle. Just as a magician takes centre stage, so the most gifted English player of his generation (and other generations come to that) took hold of the game, first forcing Joe Corrigan into a good save then delightfully chipping the ball into the City's penalty area, the same way a professional golfer chips one onto the green.

Tottenham's two strikers, Steve Archibald and Garth Crooks, pursued the ball which broke via backspin to the latter who gleefully smashed it into the net. Two goals each and the best was yet to come.

Ricky Villa received the ball about ten yards inside the City's half and ran at the defence. Inside the penalty area he dropped a shoulder and swerved to his right beating opponents. He then seemed to stumble a little, but the big man stayed on his feet to calmly sidefoot the winning goal. Wembley erupted and all around the country backsides left the sofas. A fantastic goal to end a fantastic final and one year before the Falklands War broke out, two Argentinians had captured our imaginations and hearts.

FA CUP FOURTH ROUND
SUNDAY 27TH JANUARY
SELHURST PARK
ATTENDANCE – 19491

CRYSTAL PALACE 2 TOTTENHAM HOTSPUR 0

Did Argentinian Pochettino throw this away? Later he would comment that his ambitions weren't in domestic Cups but suspected the club's were different.

He names a side that contains only three players of note. World Cup semi-finalists Eric Dier and Kieran Trippier of England, Jan Vertonghen of Belgium. In fact the seven players on the substitute's bench today look stronger than the eleven he's put out on the pitch. That's not what amuses me though. Ever since their Cup final appearance in 1990 Crystal Palace have run out to the tune of 'Glad All Over' by The Dave Clark Five, a song the squad back then covered in an era when an appearance on Top Of The Pops was traditional two days before the final.

Knowing my musical history as I do, especially The Beatles, I know that this song both sides have entered the arena to, knocked the Fab Four from the top of the charts in the early sixties. At the time everybody joked it was the end of The Beatles and that the Mersey Beat so the music critics claimed, had been replaced by, wait for it … The Tottenham Sound!

The game kicks off and I'm in a superb position that can see every inch of the pitch, comfortably sat outside the Legend's Suite behind one of the goals with an unhindered view. Vertonghen looks composed, Townsend sharp. Dier prowls like a panther but can't seem to keep pace with the young red and blue young antelope he hunts. A Spurs fan next to me shouts out in frustration. "No one wants the fackin' ball do they!"

Palace's Jeffrey Schlupp senses Spurs lack of drive and dances into the Tottenham penalty area. No one can get near him and with just nine minutes of the game played, he crosses the ball for Connor Wickham to complete the formalities. Tottenham so far are just not competing, much to the despair of those around me. And then two penalty kicks are given in quick succession that settle this tie even before the half-time whistle. Townsend scores the first one to put his present side 2-0 up against his former side before Tottenham get one at the other end.

This doesn't spell hope however for Mr 'half empty glass' next to me who turns to me and says, "There's no one to fackin' take it. They're all at the fackin' doctors!" I'm guessing Dier will take it after brilliantly scoring the winner in that very rare penalty shoot success for England in the World Cup, but it's Trippier, another successful England penalty taker who steps forward. "Watch this!" Mr 'I don't think my glass has even that much in it' goes on, "he's gonna put it fackin' wide!" And you know what? That's exactly what Trippier does. Now I'm impressed with this bloke. He can see into the future! I might ask him to predict my fackin' lottery numbers.

The Spurs fans are laughing at it all at half time back in the suite. A few of them are even saying they wouldn't mind if Poch left. Back out for the second half and the Tottenham fans below us are enjoying laughing at themselves. They're taking the piss out of themselves and the club's tradititional Jewish history by chanting ...

'Yid Army!'

Followed by ...

'We sang it in France, and we sang it in Spain, we sang it in the sun, and we sang it in the rain. They tried to stop us but look what it did, the thing I love most is being a Yid.'.

Eric Dier sets up a chance to reduce the arrears. What is he doing, hey Poch? For attempting to get his side back into a Cup match, he's immediately substituted. Goalkeeping and defending well, Julian Speroni and Joel Ward (my Man of the Match) of Palace, respectively catch the eye. Ward is flawless while Speroni is in the right mood to celebrate setting a new Crystal Palace record of appearances for a goalkeeper.

After the game and back in the Legend's Suite, I ask another ex-Palace player for an interview. He can't right now as he's doing his corporate thing but he gives me his mobile number and says to ring him the next morning. We shake hands and he asks me my name. "My name's Dave," I say for the third time today.

The player in question is Neil Shipperley and he is an absolute legend here at Selhurst Park. He's old school and pulls no punches on the microphone when addressing the room. He's disappointed with Roy Hodgson's team selection because he loves the FA Cup and today Palace were lucky simply because Pochettino fielded an even weaker team. He tells the Tottenham contingent with typical forthrightness. "You lot got what you deserved," and they nod their heads back in agreement. He also noticed that Poch (who it's rumoured is being pursued by Manchester United) didn't get out of his seat once. "Read into that what you will." I'm not sure though. I genuinely believe he didn't get out of his seat because quite simply, he wasn't that interested.

Then Darren Ambrose takes over. He speaks of the enigma that is naturally talented Wilfred Zaha. He wishes that Zaha had the same work-rate as Andros Townsend because if he did, he would be unstoppable.

Darren Ambrose is a lovely bloke, very friendly and engaging. We have a drink together when he invites me to join the table with him and his wife. He tells me that Pochettino will be manager at Manchester United next season and that his replacement at Tottenham will be ex-Chelsea boss Antonio Conte who was at the game today. It's a done deal he claims.

I'm surprised when I hear that the official attendance is five hundred less than the Grimsby game. Maybe both sets of supporters know the score when it comes to team selection. Why bother going out in the cold to watch weakened teams when you can sit in the warm and watch it on the box for less money. Miss February is watching the game on TV and messages me saying there were a lot of empty seats. There were in fact about six thousand of them, so how come a football fan like myself struggled to get one and had to pay over £200 just to get a ticket; but that's the way it goes when you're not a native, and didn't I sign up to this contract last August when I attended the preliminaries?

An icy wind blasts down the A212 and into my face. I'm spending Sunday night in Croydon so a few pints are the order of the day. Head bowed against the elements I walk into the pub nearest my hotel, ironically called The White Hart, which shares the same name as Tottenham's home ground. In this weather Guinness is a more substantial draught to drink, so I sit in a warm corner and people watch. Not one football fan in here. I'm in the wrong part of Croydon as far as the round ball game is concerned. This Sunday evening is about as lively as Tottenham's performance.

Driving back to Plymouth the next morning, I think of Paul Smith, husband of my colleague Kim. He's a lifelong Tottenham fan, so much so that their two sons are named after Jimmy Greaves and Glenn Hoddle. He put a fiver on Palace to win the Cup a couple of months ago and now they're in the last sixteen. The price was 33/1 and now a lot shorter as there aren't many Premiership teams left. When I see him next I ask him what he thinks about his team's exit from the competition. To him it's not that big a deal. In this day and age he half expects a club with a great FA Cup tradition to crash out as a lot of them don't want to be part of it. Twenty of them join in at the New Year but just a few rounds later hardly any of them are still in it. Silverware is sacrificed for status survival. Welcome to the half-empty cup.

I pull into Taunton Services and dial the number an ex-Palace legend has given me. He answers within seconds …

The Hero

"I passionately believe in heroes, but I think the world has changed it's criteria in determining who it describes as a hero."
RICHARD ATTENBOROUGH

What is your definition of a hero? A firefighter? An ambulance person? A war veteran?

Walk around Croydon and it's a good bet that football folk from there will tell you it's Neil Shipperley, former Crystal Palace player whose legendary status was sealed when scoring the winning goal in the 2004 play-off final, which sent the Eagles flying into the Premiership. As a professional footballer, Shipperley had two spells with Crystal Palace and also played for Chelsea, Watford, Southampton, Nottingham Forest, Barnsley, Wimbledon, Sheffield United and Brentford. Between 1993 and 1995 he represented England at under-21 level alongside Liverpool's Robbie Fowler and scored three goals in seven games; the average return for a recognised goalscorer.

After this journeyman career he then completed his coaching badges whilst managing non-league teams, currently holding a UEFA 'B' coaching badge which is the second highest level in European football and mandatory if you want to manage at a certain level. It also covers youth football up to the age of sixteen and allows the individual to work as an assistant in the professional game; but what about the question I've always asked people in the game? The same question I've emailed several sports journalists, football managers and even the Football Association.

'Why, I mean WHY does a manager need coaching badges?' They're two different jobs aren't they? A coach trains the players and a manager picks the team. That's how Alex Ferguson, the most successful in the business worked. He was nowhere near the training pitch. Neither was Brian Clough, for my money the greatest manager since the War. You'll find the problem with coaches picking football teams is that they work to a system which players have to adhere to. Square pegs in round holes comes to mind. A manager on the other hand, will pick his players and then select a system that suits them. It's because of this mindset I've always carried in my head that I have a deep mistrust of the coaching system. The only answer to my question that came back to me via email is simply because it's part of the criteria to manage at a certain level. In other words, nobody really knows why Sir Alex was facilitated by somebody half his age, with no experience in picking a football team and had never won anything in the game.

Although 'old school', Neil Shipperley loved obtaining his coaching badges however and that was because he was taught by a chap called Jim Hicks who made it enjoyable. Neil isn't sure whether Hicks ever played the game but as a teacher, he was spot on; explaining to his class how to get the message across to players rather than how to play the game. He empowered them, therefore they had freedom of opinion. So how would Mr Shipperley pick a team? "There are two tactical approaches," he explains, "If their team is better than yours, then you pay them respect and nullify the midfield by outnumbering them. If their team is weaker or the same strength, then you face them toe to toe, counting on the belief you hold in your players."

And there speaks the voice of experience; someone who has played with and under some of the biggest names in British football.

What about the managers he played under? Surely signing on with that many clubs he'll come up with a famous name or two. He doesn't disappoint. As well as experienced and successful men such as Neil Warnock and Dave Bassett he comes up with a trio of very talented players who if they played in a fantasy team would make a formidable midfield. Alan Ball, Glenn Hoddle and Graeme Souness.

So, if he was THEIR manager, how would boss Neil Shipperley deploy them on the pitch? "You can talk about systems all you want," he tells me, "but ultimately it's man management that motivates players. And in that respect Bassett and Warnock were the best. Alan Ball was a lovely man, Hoddle was tactically brilliant but very aloof."

There's no doubt that Dave 'Harry' Bassett was Neil Shipperley's favourite. "He would pat you on the back if you'd played well or tell you straight if you hadn't." In fact he liked Bassett so much, he played under him at three different clubs.

But was he stereotyped under him in that 'big target man/ small speedy trickster' twin striker partnership? Batman and Robin so to speak. "No because I played in an era where every team played that way with the exception of Matt Le Tissier at Southampton. He was the best striking partner but like me was also a big man. We were the exception to the rule." As he went on about the man they call 'Le God' on the south coast it's becoming clearer that maverick Le Tissier was the exception to most rules. A man with a gift and not allowed to share it with England fans due to a deep mistrust of flair that sadly prevailed in manager's minds for decades. Is it any wonder that our national team has only won just one tournament in it's history, and that was on home soil. According to Shipperley, Matt Le Tissier became a luxury player and nobody knew what he was going to do on the pitch, such was his genius.

Dougie Freedman at Palace was a good striking partner and the most productive partnership was with Irish international David Connelly at Wimbledon, but his favourite was Andy Johnson who got into the England squad. How close was Neil Shipperley to playing for his country? He says he isn't aware if he was in any England manager's thoughts. He suspects not a lot; as at the time the pecking order was Alan Shearer, Teddy Sheringham, Robbie Fowler, Andy Cole,Ian Wright, Stan Collymore and later Michael Owen.

What are his views on the present England team? "I'm like any other England fan. Before the 2018 World Cup I'd fallen out of love with them due to lack of desire and sheer mediocrity; but now it's enjoyable to watch, with all of these youngsters breaking through."

And his most memorable moment in football? "Obviously, it was scoring the winner against West Ham in the 2004 play-off final, while my biggest disappointment was four years previously playing for Barnsley in the same final and losing to Ipswich." He likes play-off finals because they give genuine fans a big day out.

Will there be a big day out for Crystal Palace on May 18th at Wembley? "Roy Hodgson has to play his strongest side for that to happen. If he doesn't there will be so much unrest amongst the supporters."

Finally, I ask him if he could put me in touch with an agent who I could interview. He doesn't know any. That is, he doesn't want to know any. In fact, his reply and choice of words is something I've decided not to include in this book. Yep! Neil Shipperley is old school all right! I wonder what Richard Attenborough would have made of him. Neil comes across as the sort of bloke he would want in his crew secretly digging three tunnels called Tom, Dick and Harry, in order to make a great escape from a German prisoner of war camp.

Listening to Talksport Radio on the remainder of my journey I hear back-to-back tributes being paid to probably Britain's finest sportswriter Hugh McIlvaney who has passed away at the age of eighty-five. A son of a Scottish miner, the common theme by commentators, journalists and athletes was that he was of the people and wrote for the people.

I once saw a brilliant documentary written by him entitled: 'The Football Men', which detailed the lives of three Scottish managers who became immortal. Jock Stein, Matt Busby and Bill Shankly were also sons of miners, born and raised in the same county. Respectively, they turned Glasgow Celtic, Manchester United and Liverpool into the world-famous clubs they are now with their footballing knowledge, work ethic, passion and sharp razor wit; four attributes McIlvaney possessed. It not only shone through in print but also at press conferences.

One such occasion was before a heavyweight boxing match featuring Joe Bugner who was renowned as a skilled fighter but unable to deliver a knockout punch, a reputation he was fed up with and constantly reminded about. Quite indignantly he announced to the gathering Press: "Give me Jesus Christ and I'll fight him!"

Hugh Mcilvaney's put down came quicker than a counter-punch. "Joe, you're only saying that because you've seen the state of his hands!"

Chapter Eleven

ROY AT THE ROVERS

John Allen is laughing at me. The bar manager of the Navy Inn on Plymouth's Barbican isn't too happy with his team's demise in the FA Cup and therefore isn't interested in the fifth round draw the BBC are currently showing live. As a Tottenham fan, John has his own special memories watching Paul Gascoigne virtually single-handedly drag the north London team through the rounds and all the way to the final in 1991 before beating Nottingham Forest in a crazy game. Gazza got injured, Brian Clough failed to rouse his players with a team talk just before extra time, England's captain and top goalscorer Gary Lineker missed a penalty, and on top of all that, the country's best defender, Des Walker, scored an own goal which handed the silverware to Tottenham.

The reason for John's laughter is my face, or rather the disappointed look on it as my smile has just left because Crystal Palace, Tottenham's conquerors have been drawn to play away at Doncaster in Yorkshire. The longest trek of my adventure so far and one which cheers him up a little. I've driven back from south London that morning, dropped the car off at the rental depot, walked across the small swingbridge that spans Sutton Harbour and past the Mayflower Steps where the Pilgrim Fathers departed for the new world four centuries ago. Happy with my interview with Neil Shipperley, I'm going to reward myself with a mini pub crawl. My excitement is diminished when I realise my eleventh game is going to hit my wallet hard yet again. But like I've always said, that's the deal.

Six months ago over seven hundred teams entered the FA Cup and now we're left with just sixteen. Win three more games and you're in the final. I console myself with the thought that

if Doncaster Rovers from level three beat Premiership opposition then I would be there to witness a romantic event, and
given Roy Hodgson's weakened team selections in the last two
rounds, a surprise result is possible. The BBC feel the same way
as it's quickly announced they'll be showing the game live. But
then the bad news. As TV dictates kick off times after choosing
games, it's then announced Doncaster versus Crystal Palace will
start late afternoon on a Sunday. No thought whatsoever for the
visiting fans who will have to travel back from Yorkshire to the
capital on a Sunday night when most of them will have to get up
early the following day for work. Just like Sheffield Wednesday
supporters who have just had to travel the same mileage in the
opposite direction the same time of day this past weekend after
a defeat at Chelsea.

When I get home later that evening, there's yet another offer in the post from Sky TV to re-subscribe to all sorts of pack-
ages and deals they only tempt you with after you've left them.
Why not offer me this when I was a paying customer? In an age
where TV runs the national game it's not only supporters inside
the grounds who spend a chunk of their wages watching the very
thing they love whilst subsidising multi-millionaire footballers,
it's the armchair fans too. At least football is democratic though.
No one makes you pay to watch. You're not going to court for
ignoring anything that comes through the letterbox. It's a free
country and half the country doesn't give a toss about football.
None of their wages are going towards the player's inflated salaries or their partner's extravagant lifestyles but you'll find that
they are the first people to moan about 'overpaid ponces kicking
a bag of wind around a field.' The democratic process in football
is simple. You vote with your remote.

Cup competitions are more exciting than League campaigns
as the sheer nature of sudden death football is the shortest route
to success. Experiencing it in 1984 I watched Plymouth Argyle
battle through two rounds against Southend United and non-
league Barking Town before the big boys joined the party. We
quietly slipped through the next two games against Newport

County and Darlington when all of a sudden we were in the last sixteen. And that's why the Cup is magic. Manchester United and Liverpool had already been knocked out but we were still in it! Wembley is three games away and it's the luck of the draw. In the fifth round Argyle caused an upset at level one West Bromwich Albion winning 1-0 and all of a sudden became a national sensation. Plymouth Argyle are in the quarter-finals of the FA Cup! Now everyone wants to be our friend! The small kid at school who doesn't get to play with anyone in the playground is now the most popular. The BBC's Saturday afternoon sports programme Grandstand starts at the Tamar Bridge which the presenter says will be carrying a huge Cornish support to join us 'janners' at Home Park which today will hold thirty-five thousand fans. Another surprise result happened as Argyle got past Derby County and in doing so came from underneath the radar and smashed the air traffic controller in the face.

The fairy-tale ended at the semi-final stage when losing to Watford at Aston Villa's ground, the most memorable game I've attended. But the 'Little Green Giants' as we were dubbed had made their mark and charmed everyone we had met on our travels. Villa Park stewards stating we were the best supporters they'd ever seen at a ground that had hosted World Cup games in 1966. I'd never known anything like that Cup run before and haven't ever since. For years afterwards when attending a course or just visiting another part of the country, if asked where I was from I'd reply 'Plymouth' and other guys would say, 'Oh yeah! I remember when you were in the semi-finals of the Cup.'

And that was at a time when the clubs at the top of the pyramid took the FA Cup seriously which made the run even more remarkable. However these days the feeling of romance, pride and excitement isn't extinct. Take a bow then Pep Guardiola, genial manager of Manchester City who continues to pick strong sides and therefore shows total respect for the country's finest competition. The man is a class act.

The drive to Yorkshire is straightforward with no hold ups. Flying past more signs telling me to take a break and another sign which states 'This Sign Not In Use'. What? I'm accompanied by Talksport Radio, Absolute Radio (my favourite station) and LBC which stands for Leading Britain's Conversation where they're still banging on about Brexit. Today they've asked two ex-England players to add their thoughts on a subject most of the country is absolutely fed up with. Gary Lineker and Peter Shilton who both made their names with Leicester City and are veterans of the thrilling 1990 World Cup held in Italy.

Shilton voted leave and Lineker is a remainer and debate amongst themselves about Brexit, which for me is a waste of air time. Nothing's going to be sorted out today on a radio station is it? But the real reason they're speaking to the nation today is the passing of another ex-Leicester and England player Gordon Banks, a World Cup winner from '66. Has there ever been a better goalkeeper for England than Banks? He played nine games in two tournaments and only conceded four goals. He should have played a tenth game, but on the morning of the World Cup quarter-final in 1970, he went down with a mysterious 24 hour illness and we lost our crown. Banks always claimed that somebody had spiked his drink the night before, which disabled the world's best goalkeeper. As well as tributes pouring in and anecdotes, television is constantly repeating that fantastic save he made against Pele during the classic England versus Brazil game. Kids who have never seen it are showing it on social media. An astonishing piece of athleticism which led Pele, the greatest player who's ever lived to say that it was the greatest save he'd ever seen.

Doncaster Rover's Keepmoat Stadium is ideal for away supporters. In all, it's only taken me four and a half hours to drive here, such is it's easiness to arrive at. On the outskirts of Doncaster and only a ten-minute walk from the impressive Lakeside shopping village, it's set in stunning scenery. Even on a grey day like today it's a pretty sight, surrounded by greenery and a huge lake. Resembling a spaceship that somebody has just landed in a piece of England's green and pleasant land, almost the way HG Wells described at the start of his novel War Of The Worlds.

Just as impressive is the organisation. Obviously the local authorities and the football club have worked together into segregating fans, whilst treating them with respect. Pubs near the shopping village are designated for the visiting Crystal Palace supporters today while the 'Donny' faithful will be enjoying the anticipation of a big fixture in the town centre. The Beefeater pub however seems unprepared for the influx of Palace fans who have travelled up from London and apparently the invasion isn't complete. We hear that a load more supporters have had trouble getting out of the capital due to a bomb scare, or is it a strike on the underground, or just heavy traffic on the M1. No one's sure.

I walk to the ground by the picturesque lake and into the 'Belle Vue' bar which is named after Doncaster's former ground. You can feel the excitement just stood at the bar surrounded by Yorkshire people, donning red and white hooped football shirts. I order a pint of 'Rovers 1879', the year they were formed as a football club but they've run out of their specialist ale. An older guy who has been served just before me has managed to have the last one poured and turns to speak to me. Apparently he prayed to God last night asking the almighty to get behind Rovers today and help them win. "You believe in that then?" I ask him. His reply is that I myself have just seen proof of his existence as God has ensured he got the last pint of Rovers 1879 and I have to settle for a pint of lager. I can see a line in marketing now. 'Fosters, the pint for atheists!' He's still talking to me as he automatically picks up the pint next to him which just happens to be my lager and disappears amongst the hordes, leaving me no choice but to swipe the Rovers 1879. The Lord really does work in mysterious ways.

Right outside the Belle Vue bar, Doncaster have set up a fan's park and why not? It's a big day for the home club and their biggest game for sixty years; but unfortunately, the choice of music entertainment doesn't live up to the occasion. On a day like this before a game of this magnitude, surely the music should be upbeat, something raucous to get the crowd in good spirits. Maybe a few rock classics or party anthems to raise the feelgood factor and warm up northern folk on a cold day. Instead we're treated to a couple of students from nearby Hull University who are bringing down the mood with their own compositions. It's sort of folk music mixed with depressing blues and sounds as bleak as the weather. The atmosphere around their makeshift stage is absolutely flat and after about twenty minutes, east Yorkshire's answer to Bob Dylan give it up and start to pack their gear. As they do so, the sun suddenly breaks through the clouds which brings out an almighty cheer around me. Shine through the gloom lads!

The sun stays out and lights up the Keepmoat. Inside the ground there's a decent atmosphere with the home fans performing their own gig.

'We've got McCann, super Grant McCann'

… is the opening number sang in homage to the manager of Doncaster Rovers. I'm seen on BBC1 by Mike Vallis during the minute's appreciation for the life of Gordon Banks as all four sides of the ground sing …

'England! England England's number one, England!'

… as I'm literally the nearest spectator to the only big screen in the ground which shows the image of our nation's greatest goalkeeper. Mike picks me out easily. Hands above my head clapping and singing like everyone else. I wonder if Gordon Banks knew how much we all loved him when he was alive?

DONCASTER ROVERS 0 CRYSTAL PALACE 2

True to form, Roy Hodgson has made six changes to his team. His opposite number Grant McCann has made just two from Donny's last game and one of them is enforced due to suspension. I dearly want to interview a manager for this book, but have had nothing back from either club regarding my emailed requests. Similar to the Tottenham game, Palace win 2-0 with both goals scored before half-time; and again, the opener is scored within the first ten minutes. A quick counter-attack sees Jeffrey Schlupp race down the left-hand side of the pitch before shooting at goal from an acute angle. The shot is deflected which leaves Rover's goalkeeper Marosi flat footed. Already 1-0 down against a Premiership team who never look back.

The Eagles dominate the game and it's no surprise to anyone inside the ground or watching on TV when it becomes 2-0. This time, the goalscorer is Max Meyer with a close-range header after a simple cross by Andros Townsend evades Doncaster's defenders. Half-time comes and I enjoy a resurrected pint of Rovers 1879 in the concourse. As I'm about to take my seat for the start of the second half, I spot 'Donny The Dog'. It's not that hard to spot in truth. Six foot two brown fluffy mascots wearing a bright white football kit with red hoops aren't these days. He slowly walks my way then stops. Now he's looking at me and pointing to the TV screen in the bar showing the scoreline before wiping imaginary tears from his droopy eyes. Underneath that costume I suspect is a grown man shedding real tears.

Doncaster come out fighting at the restart but only create one chance to score. A header is wasted and that is as good as it's going to get for the level three outfit. The stats after the game though are surprising. They show that total possession of the ball is only split 53% percent to 47% percent in favour of Crystal Palace. Doncaster actually have had more attempts on goal but those figures obviously include wild efforts which only threaten wildlife in the air which aren't eagles. The game is largely uneventful and towards the end I get the idea to write a note to Roy Hodgson and somehow get it to him outside the player's entrance. In it I ask him for a little of his time before the quarter-final, as I'm now following his team into a fourth game, the most rounds I've followed any club on this run; and just like a Canadian mountie, I WILL get my man!

The Crystal Palace team coach is parked directly outside the player's entrance and is cordoned off in the same way that convicted criminals escape the glare of the general public after being found guilty. There's a big bloke in a smart suit who's head of security standing yards from me so I hand him the note and ask him to give it to Mr Hodgson. He promises to do so. In the note I've written my mobile number and invite the call anytime day or night. Also waiting outside in the cold is an older guy called Dave who wants to meet Gary Lineker and get his autograph. The ex-England goalscorer is today presenting the game for the BBC who have chosen this fixture hoping millions of viewers will witness a giant-killing act. Sadly, not today. Dave tells me he's been waiting for two hours and is freezing. Two hours? Didn't he watch the game? No he didn't, because he doesn't enjoy it anymore. It's not as good as it used to be. He remembers going to Anfield in 1969 when Doncaster lost to the mighty Liverpool 2-0 in front of nearly fifty thousand spectators. The two goalscorers were World Cup winner Roger Hunt and England squad member Ian Callaghan and yes, Liverpool did play a full-strength team.

Watching the news back in my hotel room and Roy Hodgson praises Doncaster Rovers. He says Donny gave them a tough game and Grant McCann can be proud of all his players. My personal analysis is although losing only by two goals to a Premiership side is no disgrace, I felt that Donny had played within themselves. The players didn't perform as they could have, given the amount of changes in the Palace side. They played the occasion and not the game, as the saying goes. The former England manager then comments on the pitch saying that it was a factor in the game, as both sides tried to get the ball down to play good football but found it difficult. From my position in the ground, the pitch looked fine to me and never cut up during the match, and Jeffrey Schlupp didn't seem to have a problem dribbling at pace to score the first goal.

Roy Hodgson dresses very smartly. He wears a suit and looks like a football manager but in reality he is a coach. In fact there's a belief in the game is that his strength is coaching coaches and not picking football teams. His team talks so they say, can be confusing and contain too much detail for a footballer to take in which can compromise a desire to win.

There are things about Roy Hodgson that I like. Now in his seventies, his enthusiasm for the game has never waned and despite all those years performing in a high-pressured job, he looks a lot younger. Football has kept him young, so have his forthright views I suspect. And he's got bottle. His courage is born of his convictions and he tells it as it is. If he lived next door to me, I can imagine plenty of conversations and debate regarding the beautiful game; although I don't think we would agree on most things.

Driving home the next morning and now Roy is being interviewed about the game on Talksport Radio. Never mind the professional broadcasters Roy, I want MY interview! He's making it clear that Premiership survival is more important than reaching the FA Cup final, and I might even agree with him if his team were in a relegation battle, but they're not. Crystal Palace are comfortably placed in the League table. What Roy really means (or really wants according to my cynical mind) is that his bonus is much bigger with every position climbed in the Premiership and is more important than supporters having a day out at Wembley.

Nearly two hundred miles later my mobile rings from a small compartment near the gearstick. Glancing down, I don't recognise the number. Is it Roy?!!! Did he read my note on the coach and decide to ring me? Excited beyond belief I pull over at the nearest services and check my voicemail. I can imagine the conversation between us with his unfortunate speech impediment … 'Well Dave I can meet you bwiefly for a chat before the next wound. It would be weally intewesting, so get back to me. Wegards, Woy …'

But alas, it's not the ex-England manager. Instead it's Tom Symons, one half of a lovely and generous couple who sat at the head of the table on my wedding day. He's left a message saying that it's his eighty-first birthday today and would like me to visit him. I call him back and offer a better day. I'll pick him up, drop the rental car back and we'll walk around the corner to meet our mate Charlie in one of Plymouth's smallest pubs, The Fareham. Charlie (Adrian Charles) is one month older than me and was brought up in the same street, although we had nothing to do with each other due to the fact that I lived in a council house and he was raised at the posh end of the street. We did have something in common though. We supported a team called Plymouth Argyle and anyone who has been through the same hardship will understand the bond. Years later as player/manager of a Sunday football team, Charlie was my goalkeeper and along with a couple of pedigree players and mostly mongrels, we won a Cup final together at a local football club named Elburton Villa.

The Manager

Trevor Higgins dresses as a coach but in reality is a manager at Elburton Villa F.C, a semi-professional set up which incorporates youth football teams. That's at the weekends for his pure enjoyment, as he earns a crust working for the car rental company I've been using on this journey. He's invited me over to the club on a Saturday morning to look at the set up over a cup of coffee and bacon sarnie. On one of the smaller pitches there's an under-ten's game taking place and as we walk over to watch, he simply tells me…"This is where the fun is."

"Football has to be fun for kids or it doesn't make sense."
JOHAN CRUYFF

Trev, (we're mates now) introduces me to his partner in crime Jake who has experience as a coach but is now taking over as manager, because of the former's work commitments. Even though Trev has handed the reins over he's still a figurehead here at the club as he played an important part in it's growth. The kids' teams play in the DJM League (Devon Junior & Minor) which has exploded with new clubs over the last two decades as youth football becomes ever more popular, with family funding.

Born in 1973 we both sing from the same hymn sheet although I don't think 'Talkin Bout My Generation' by The Who was ever covered by any choir, so maybe he can answer my long burning question. Why does a manager need coaching badges?

"It's all about safeguarding at this level," he explains and then tells me about the FA Level One coaching badge he's obtained by attending two weeks of practical coaching and three classroom sessions per week, spread over a couple of months. Basic development is key for youngsters from the age of seven upwards as well as First Aid training and diversity in the game. "It's all about encouragement at this age, you won't find any world beaters." But what if you suddenly did have a world beater on your hands? A Lionel Messi? Someone who could dribble past opponents just for fun?

Trev then admits there was one lad who could always do something special so he kept him on the pitch for as long as he was allowed, even though there were lesser talented kids who needed encouragement by playing. "This lad was treated differently than the rest," he admits. Now this may seem a contradiction in a team game, but Trevor Higgins has just shown himself to be a football manager. He doesn't think the same way as a coach. He doesn't bring the training pitch to the ground on matchday. He uses something called game management.

The young player he referred to could score goals with his eyes shut but Elburton lost him to the Plymouth Argyle academy.

These days he plays in defence and isn't even allowed to cross the halfway line. However, this means that he can learn the game from another angle and so in Trev's words "will become complete". And that reminds me of an article I once read about brilliant Dutch international and Arsenal star Dennis Bergkamp who when at Ajax of Amsterdam was taught to play in every position so he could anticipate his opponent's next move. When he finally became an imaginative attacking player he knew what defenders were thinking and didn't have to rely on pace to beat them. The first few yards are in your head. Bergkamp was raised in the Netherlands where they preached 'Total Football'; a system so designed that any outfield player could cover any team mate if he was ever out of position. Johan Cruyff personified this way of intelligent football in the seventies when the Dutch seduced worldwide audiences and reached two World Cup finals back-to-back, only to lose to the host nation on both occasions.

As we walk and talk, I'm watching two youth teams warm up for their match by jogging and then practising 'two touch' football, the first touch controls the ball and the second passes it to a team-mate. These days the game at this infant level is a helluva lot more technical than it was when my friends and I dreamed of playing in the FA Cup final. In fact, we played on pitches as big as Wembley! This generation plays on smaller ones and also have smaller goals which are scaled down to their average height and build. There's more emphasis on control and technique. Kids are becoming tactically aware and the ethos which has come all the way down from England manager Gareth Southgate is that every player, all over the country, starting at a young age must be comfortable on the ball. It's to be applauded as it's a big step forward and has already made an impact at youth international level, but there's one thing that bugs me. Where is the next Gazza? I'm seeing plenty of pass & move, pass & move, pass & move but I don't see any individual taking on or attempting to dribble past an opponent. If these lads have any natural talent as Paul Gascoigne had at a young age, my fear is that it may be coached out of them; and for me, the best physical quality any footballer could have is to beat an opponent one on one, and therefore open up the tightest game.

As a manager, Trev then makes another admission. Even here with lads at an impressionable age, he'll sacrifice the technical side of the game and get his team to play in a more primitive style in order to win a match. There's a fine line between craving silverware and doing what's best for the young footballer. I've come to the conclusion that coaching is a very important part of the game, especially at grass roots level, but there should be less emphasis on the badges higher up the football pyramid where I believe more natural skill and imagination should be encouraged.

Elburton Villa is a great little set up. Their senior men's team may only be at level eleven in the pyramid and therefore ineligible to enter this season's FA Cup, but the facilities here outshine those at Saltash United. The FA constantly change the criteria regarding standards of improving amateur football grounds but offer little or no funding to help these clubs make the grade. Every spring, clubs up and down the country are assessed and if there's so much as a floodlight not working on that particular day, then your spot in next season's FA Cup may be taken away. Imagine doing that to a top club! Mind you, the managers at Tottenham and Crystal Palace may welcome refusal in regards to entering the Cup.

Trevor Higgins has also been commercial manager here at Haye Road, Elburton. When he took over, the club was in debt but he and several donators helped build the whole set up not only with cash on the gate but enterprising ideas also, such as; car boot sales, food sales, building relationships with local businesses and residents alike drumming up support. Tradesmen know the public and soon word got around. Talking to Trev, I can just picture him pursuing sponsorship with vigour, his eyes burning with passion. He told me this is where the fun is. I can see this is also where his heart is. Appropriately, the current sponsors are local firm LTC Scaffolding who know a thing or two about building.

So, what got him into the commercial side of the game? Well, he was a bored newsagent and saw an ad in the local paper requiring a commercial manager here. His gran's house was nearby so he could always see the ground from her window and when he applied for the job, he saw up close the true potential this club had as he walked around the site. Years before he arrived, Elburton Villa Football Club were founded in 1982 and marked this with a friendly against Watford who had just gained promotion to the top level. Watford! I don't dislike Watford but their bloody name comes up time and time again. Beating Argyle in the '84 semi-final and breaking Pilgrim's hearts and guess where I'm going following Crystal Palace in the next round? Bloody Watford!

Before I leave Elburton, Trev asks me if I've ever heard of Hashtag United. I haven't. He advises me to google it as they are a fairy-tale club. Originally called Spencer FC after it's founder Spencer Owen, the club started as recently as 2016. They played exhibition matches against ex-professionals and then showed it on YouTube. After a few games, they gained thousands of followers not only on that channel but also on Instagram and Twitter. Based in Essex, they joined the football pyramid in 2018, by entering the Eastern Counties League at level nine as they passed certain criteria regarding their ground. This is a real life fairy-tale! Mr Owen (I'll refer to him out of respect), is living the digital dream. He started a team with his mates and now plays in the FA Cup. So that's where I went wrong! My mistake was to start a Sunday team and not a Saturday one!

The highest I could achieve on the day of rest would have been to reach the Devon Sunday Senior Cup final, but even if I'd won that, there would be no European competition to compete in the following season, whereas Hashtag United are only eight steps away from the biggest and most glamorous trophy in domestic football.

Hashtag United versus Real Madrid in the European Champions League! Don't laugh too loud. In this game, dreams can come true …

1973 WINNERS – SUNDERLAND

This has got to be the most magical final of all time and the biggest shock. You can't make magic happen, not even magicians can, they just create an illusion. And if anyone said before the 1973 FA Cup final that Sunderland would beat Leeds United, they would be accused of being disillusioned; but at Wembley Stadium that day there was no illusion, a giant-killing act occurred and the bookies lost millions. Sunderland became the first side from the second level to win the Cup for over forty years and in doing so, beat the mighty Leeds, a team both hated and feared.

David 1 Goliath 0.

This was current holders Leeds' third appearance in the final in just four years, whereas their opponents hadn't been to Wembley since 1937. A decent team who had finished sixth in their league under the stewardship of likeable manager Bob Stokoe who had sailed this ship into calmer waters away from a relegation storm. Both Manchester City and Arsenal in the earlier rounds had found to their cost that underestimating the north east outfit was fatal and all of a sudden, the wearsiders were in the final. But surely that's where the fun would stop. No way could they beat a team full of talented internationals whose superiority would wipe the floor with them, just absolutely no way.

Sunderland had some good players though. Billy Hughes was the poor man's George Best. Dennis Tueart and Dave Watson would both later play for England while Ian Porterfield had a superb left foot. But it was his other foot that scored the only goal of the game after half an hour, cushioning the ball on his left thigh before smashing it with his right boot high into the Leeds net. It was Clint Eastwood shooting a scumbag holding his Magnum 44 with the weaker hand, and to the same devastating impact.

The incredible thing about this final that ultimately makes it memorable though wasn't the winning goal, it was a save (or rather a double save) so astonishing it seemed to defy the laws of physics. Goalkeeper Jim Montgomery had played thirteen years for Sunderland and was in the twilight of a generally unremarkable career until one moment late in the game made him a national hero.

To say that Leeds were turning the screw against their plucky opponents is an understatement. They grew stronger as the game went on and their big game experience was taking its toll on the weary wearsiders who could hardly get out of their own half. The pressure was at breaking point.

And then came that moment of magic. A deep cross from the right-hand side of Leeds attack arrowed into the Sunderland penalty area which was met by a diving header from defender Trevor Cherry. Montgomery was equal to it and pulled off a good save which left him laid out on the pitch as the ball fell very invitingly at the feet of one of the hardest shots in British football, Peter Lorimer. The Scottish international pulled the trigger from point blank range and virtually turned to celebrate. Brian Moore, ITV commentator shouted, 'GOAL!' David Coleman, BBC commentator shouted, 'ONE-ONE!' What the …! The ball isn't in the net!

From a horizontal position, 'Monty' had somehow lifted himself from the turf and instinctively made contact with the ball with his left hand and onto the crossbar astonishing everyone on the pitch, everyone in the ground and everyone watching at home.

From that moment it was Leeds who seemed to tire. Maybe they had sensed it wasn't going to be their day and in fact Sunderland broke away on a counter-attack almost scoring a second goal. When the final whistle blew, Wembley erupted with red and white stripes as players from both sides collapsed displaying two extremes of emotions. Bob Stokoe raced onto the pitch to embrace Jim Montgomery. The manager was now a messiah in a part of England where unemployment and gloom were a way of life. But he shone through it, the knight on his steed in a Disney fairy-tale. People were now saying that he had brought the magic to Sunderland, but typically the man himself played it down. "The magic's always been here," he said, "I was just lucky enough to find it."

Years later, Montgomery was invited onto Sky Sports to sit through and relive the entire final as he spoke warmly about his team-mates. He came across as a quiet man and very humble, a reluctant hero. He remembered everything about the game itself but amazingly couldn't remember something that happened after it, something that made him emotional as he realised he hadn't taken it all in on the day. Because In 1973 and for the last time, after both sets of players received their medals from the Royal Box, they lined up to stand for the national anthem AFTER the final. 'God Save The Queen' rang around Wembley Stadium as the TV pictures showed twenty-two heads bowed, half of them clutching winner's medals in almost sheer disbelief, and I admit, I felt emotional watching him get emotional. Even though Jim Montgomery will always be remembered for that save, he himself has a regret which most Cup finalists live with. The fact that he didn't fully take in the occasion, but I reckon if he had, then he wouldn't have concentrated fully on the game and give football fans a moment to treasure forever.

Was 'Monty's Magic Save' the greatest of all time? In my opinion it is, even better than Gordon Banks against Pele simply because it turned a big game which won a Cup final. It's obviously open to debate but here's my top three …

JIM MONTGOMERY V LEEDS UNITED
1973 FA CUP FINAL.
GORDON BANKS V BRAZIL
1970 WORLD CUP GROUP GAME.
ADRIAN CHARLES V PLYMPTON RANGERS
1994 KAY TRANSPORT CUP SEMI- FINAL.

What? Who's that at number three? None other than me ol' mate Charlie! Just like Montgomery, he pulled off a brilliant save late in the game which effectively won the game, and just like Montgomery, he was loyal to one club.

The Sunday team I started in 1991 ran for seven years in total and Adrian Charles was there for every single game even if he can't remember half of them. In 1994 we reached our divisional semi-final. The day before Manchester United had won the FA Cup and completed their first ever Cup/League title double which meant that the 'reds' in our team celebrated into the night, not the best preparation for a big game. Half the team was hungover and started to wilt on a very warm Sunday morning. Luckily, we had teenager James Cole who scored two goals in a Man of the Match winning performance. In the last minute we led 2-1 but the referee had inexplicably found six added minutes from somewhere. Maybe his watch had stopped, and all the older players on the pitch were on my team with the high noon sunshine beating down on us as our younger opponents did a 'Leeds' by turning the screw as the minutes turned into hours.

Our backs were firmly against the wall as we held on by our chewed fingernails when Dean Newport, their captain and best player, collected the ball and ran straight at me. They say in such situations that the defending player shouldn't dive in with a committed challenge and I didn't. Nothing to do with tactical awareness but simply because I didn't have the energy to! Staying on my feet and refusing to be hypnotised by quick opponent's footwork I managed to manoeuvre him into a position where I knew he wouldn't shoot … or so I thought. He unleashed a shot with his left foot so powerful that I can still hear it whistle as it flew by me, and as I turned to watch it's flight my heart jumped out of my chest. It was flying towards the goal net just inside the post but in a split second through a crowd of players appeared Charlie's right hand which fingertipped the certain goal away from a demoralising extra thirty minutes of extra time. It was an utterly brilliant save which stunned all of us and we were too exhausted even to comment, "well done mate!"

That save was virtually the last act of the game as a few seconds later the referee blew the whistle for full-time. Some of us collapsed to our knees in the heat but were so happy to have reached a Cup final together, one we would win.

A week later I was driving around the player's houses or ringing their landline (no mobiles back then), to inform them that the final had been postponed and would take place the following weekend. It was a Saturday and that night I enjoyed a few beers with Charlie in his local social club. I thought it was the booze talking when he promised me that he wouldn't concede a goal in the final itself but being the mate he is, he did just that in a 2-0 victory, something he's quick to remind me of.

After our session I caught a cab back to my local 'The Old Road Inn' which sadly like a lot of estate pubs is no longer around having been converted into a block of flats. I was stood at the bar having a drink with a guy called Pete Hodgess who worked for the Royal Mail telling him about Charlie's wonder save and how I felt that maybe it was a sign of something meant to be. Postman Pete then turned to me and said, "So what you're saying Dave is that your mate Charlie didn't make that save, but actually fate made it."

"Nah Pete," I replied, "Fate would never had have reached it!"

Chapter Twelve

THE EAGLES ARE LANDED

We're at the quarter-final stage and now there's only eight teams left in the Cup. For the fourth game in succession I'll be watching Crystal Palace, but where? This is the last round where home advantage can be crucial to a team's fortunes, but strangely, The Eagles are the exception to the rule as their away form is better than the should-be fortress of Selhurst Park.

Looking at the eight survivors in this season's competition, I'm thinking about who I'd like to see in the final. No doubt in my mind; an all-Manchester clash between City and United will do very nicely and the atmosphere at Wembley on the day would be brilliant. The draw is made and thankfully both sides are kept apart. The reds of United will be playing at Wolverhampton while sky blue neighbours City will be travelling to Swansea. In the other two ties, Millwall will be at home to Brighton, a fixture Big Rob Wenham at Taunton will be delighted with, and yours truly will be driving to Watford who take on Palace.

Watford. Easy to get to but bringing back painful FA Cup memories. As a teenager I went to their home ground Vicarage Road in 1983 to watch Argyle lose 2-0 when The Hornets, as they're known, finished as the second-best team in the country behind Liverpool. It was their turn that year. What I mean by that is, every team seemed to take it in turns finishing behind Liverpool in the title race, in fact it was seen as a huge shock if the red half of Merseyside weren't celebrating winning the League in May. The two-goal loss happened in the New Year and plenty of us travelled up to generate an amazing atmosphere behind one of the goals with an antiquated roof helping the acoustics.

The following year was the semi-final defeat. A 1-0 loss this time at Aston Villa's ground and the most memorable game I've ever been to. Glorious sunshine, spectacular colour, great game but oh so heartbreaking. The then Watford manager Graham Taylor paid tribute to Plymouth both on and off the pitch, as he described players and fans alike as "magnificent".

1984 WINNERS – EVERTON

Everton versus Plymouth Argyle in the FA Cup final! It nearly happened. Most of us present at Villa Park in the previous round believed it should have been but instead Watford chairman Elton John got his day out at Wembley and wept through the traditional Cup final hymn 'Abide With Me' in the Royal Box. Fair play to Rocketman. He invested a lot of money into the club he's loved since he was a small boy and through his funding Watford FC went through a remarkable transition as they became known as the country's first family club. There was never any trouble by visiting supporters at Vicarage Road thanks to Elton's profound idea of treating football fans like human beings and arranging a shuttle service from Watford Station at his own cost, whilst on the pitch Taylor's teams were always disciplined. The Hertfordshire outfit were a throwback to decades long gone.

The football Watford played was also a throwback to a golden age of the English game. Back in the day virtually every side played a 'long ball game' which basically meant defences kicking the bag of leather yards up the touchline where quick and dazzling wingers would eagerly give chase. Blackpool had Stanley Matthews and thirty years later Watford had John Barnes. This style of football was seen as the norm in post war England, but in the Eighties the purists and romantics in the game saw it as a crude way to play the game. You can judge all you want but Watford supporters never complained when this direct approach put Barnes in possession, who would turn in exciting performances week after week whilst also supplying ammunition for striker Luther Blissett and later Maurice Johnston to hit the target. To compliment his way of playing, Taylor deployed four attackers which took a helluva lot of guts in an era when negative and defensive football was the fashion. They put opposing teams under pressure and scored good goals.

Their rise to the top level was a Hertfordshire hurricane and reaching the Cup final, finishing runners up in the League, entering European competition and their manager taking over as England boss in 1990 is a testament to the radical theories successfully put into practise by Watford.

As for Everton, most football fans were bewildered as to how they got there. In fact, most Evertonians were too. A few months before, 'Toffees' legend Howard Kendall was as a manager lambasted by the blue half of Merseyside demanding his head on a silver platter, which at the time would be the only thing silver in their club! But here at Wembley in May 1984, Everton were about to win their first silverware in fourteen years, which would ignite a run of success which most fans attending Goodison Park would never dare dream about. Two League titles and a European trophy were achieved in the next few years as the fighters in the blue corner went toe to toe with their more accomplished neighbours in the red corner.

It was tough on us Argyle fans to watch the traditional build up to the final on TV. It should have been us and all the celebrities were there. Freddie Starr representing Everton against Michael Barrymore representing Watford was a comical start to proceedings on a split screen which was followed by actress Susan George sending the Blue's squad a sexy good luck message that caused even smooth presenter Des Lynam to get a little hot under the collar on the BBC.

But it was when the two teams took the long walk from the tunnel behind the right-hand goal to the halfway line that really saddened us. That's what the new Wembley lacks so badly, that fantastic walk across the cinder track and onto the lush green turf which took a couple of minutes and was lapped up by every single supporter in the stadium. I can still see Graham Taylor, proud as punch, leading his players out with a smile that even a defeated semi-finalist like myself couldn't begrudge. It was an explosion of noise and colour. The blue and white of Everton opposite the red and yellow of Watford. The best walk in sport. No stadium music required, no light show or firework displays; just a genuine self-generated atmosphere of joy and hope, and it hurt. Like watching your ex-girlfriend walk down the street with a richer and luckier man.

After the explosive entry, the game itself was a bit of a damp squib. Early Watford chances weren't taken. In the event Everton scored twice, both goals converted by Scots Graeme Sharp and Andy Gray. Another Scottish international, Maurice Johnston, had a goal disallowed later on but I don't think it would have made a difference in regards to a Watford comeback. Their opponents on the day seemed more determined to win. Watford just seemed happy just to have reached Wembley. 2-0 was the final score and that was that. Everton won the most famous trophy in the world, Watford were runners up while Plymouth Argyle became just another semi-finalist; but for those of us that were there on that sunny spring day at Villa Park, it would never be forgotten.

Meanwhile, back to the future, it's March 2019 and football has gone crazy. They say things happen in threes and our national game showed us the blood, the mad and the ugly. Firstly, in the League Cup final at Wembley, Manchester City defeated Chelsea after a penalty shoot out; but only after a bizarre incident involving the latter's goalkeeper which overshadowed the previous two hours of football.

Chelsea manager Maurizio Sarri had to be restrained by one of his players as he went to confront goalkeeper Kepa Arrizabalaga who blatantly ignored Sarri's decision to substitute him and stayed on the field of play. The idea was to replace him with Willy Caballero who had a reputation of a specialist penalty saver. The goalkeeper's petulance possibly cost Chelsea the first domestic silverware of the season and it's to the west London club's shame that not only did he escape punishment, but the owners refused to condemn him and back their manager. In any other industry there would be disciplinary measures. But this is football and the players it seems, can have too much power.

Around the same time West Bromwich Albion sacked their manager Darren Moore even though he had done a sterling job in guiding the west midlands club to a possible promotion. In a league of twenty-four teams, they were lying in fourth place and ready to pounce for promotion, with just a couple of months of the season remaining. The dismissal was baffling and in the event, West Brom didn't get promoted anyway. What I found even stranger about it was that the footballing authorities have always preached about diversity and a wide representation of minorities in the game, yet the silence was deafening from the hierarchy when a black manager was sacked for doing a great job.

The most unsavoury incident happened in the 'Second City Derby' between Aston Villa and Birmingham City. A Blues supporter managed to get onto the pitch and assaulted Villa captain Jack Grealish, who never saw it coming. Thankfully Grealish although shaken, wasn't seriously hurt and what's more, karma came knocking when he scored the winning goal later on. Birmingham were fined 42K and the assailant was jailed for fourteen weeks; a satisfactory end to a bizarre month.

In the middle of all this madness, once again I have to pay well over the odds to watch a game as tickets are now getting almost impossible to obtain this far into the competition. On top of that, more of my emails are getting standard replies from Crystal Palace in regardings to interviewing Roy Hodgson. Just a few minutes of his time either electronically or over the phone and I'd be happy. But the emails coming back are predictable … 'I'm sorry but Mr Hodgson is busy preparing …' 'We wish you good look luck with the book …' 'The manager is not available at this time …'

Then I get an idea. Where and when is the best place and time to ask a football manager a question? In a press conference of course! Now I've just got to think of a way of getting into one, so I look up Watford's media email address in an initial attempt to make contact with anyone in the club that can help me in my quest. I am utterly determined to ask the ex-England manager at least one question. To my surprise, I get a swift response from a chap called Richard Walker, head of media, just a few hours later. 'Dear Dave, we have organised for you to access the media centre after the game. Your press pass will be ready to collect, with your match ticket.' What a result! Watford really are a friendly club, and as I find out on the day of the game, so is a local resident.

The ground itself is as easy to find as the journey itself to Hertfordshire, but the parking is virtually impossible. All roads near to Vicarage Road are for permit holders only and my frustration comes to the fore as I'm driving away from the stadium I've just passed. Impatiently I double back and soon find a cul de sac just a ten-minute walk from Watford FC. The only space I can park in without blocking any other motorist is in someone's private driveway. Memories of that Saltash resident come flooding back as I knock on the door of the property. A man answers the door as I tell him I need to get to the game quickly to collect a press pass and match ticket and can't find anywhere to park.

"Not a problem mate," he cheerfully tells me. "The missus has got the car and won't be back for hours."

Feeling grateful I give him a fiver and say, "you're a star, have a drink on me mate."

English football is a non-summer game ergo the majority of games are played in inclement weather and today is no exception. The short walk to the ground is freezing as a savage wind blows but I stay out in it anyway as I now have a little time to kill. The police are out in force and Vicarage Road is cut off to all vehicles, the only traffic being those in yellow and black football shirts outside of the main entrance. This end of the stadium looks nothing like it did to me in 1983, so I wander around the side to see if anything's familiar. Walking past a couple of stewards and into a car park I realise it's a dead end, so I turn back to go around the other side. Approaching the stewards, I ask them where I can pick up my press pass. I'm wearing glasses and a black coat with windswept spiky hair looking like a Chuckle Brother;

but before they tell me to get lost a Ferrari pulls up. Out of the passenger side, Crystal Palace and Sheffield Wednesday legend Mark Bright steps out. The former striking partner of Ian Wright and veteran of two FA Cup finals beams from ear to ear as I ask for a selfie and kindly obliges. The pic says it all about 'Brighty'. He seems happy go lucky, very friendly and talks a bit about the game coming up; but who's driving the Ferrari? It's Palace chairman Steve Parish. He's tall, very slightly built and obviously dyes his hair. We shake hands and he too is smiling. I tell him I've travelled from Plymouth to hopefully watch his team reach the semi-final and he thanks me. He doesn't however thank me when I ask how his girlfriend Susanna Reid of Good Morning Britain is as they've just split up. Whoops! Time for a sharp exit. They disappear through the director's entrance and I turn back towards the bleak grey elements holding my collars up.

On the opposite side is an impressive built for Premiership structure called The Sir Elton John Stand but a small lane literally divides something which cost about eight million quid and rundown properties. Broken glass, boarded up windows and ankle-deep grass are just a backdrop to abandoned sofas. You couldn't have a more black and white image of rags and riches.

I finally walk around the corner to the entrance where I supported Plymouth Argyle when I was sixteen and it's nothing like I remember. This side of the ground is bigger and modern. You can see where Premiership money goes. Opposite the entrance used to be a walkway where an away fan would step onto after the shuttle ride from the train station; but now there's just a concrete wall and peering over it I see allotments and crumbling masonry surrounding a disused railway track. Is this still a family club? Elton looked after football fans. Instead of being herded from pen to pen, he paid for a means of transport which showed the travelling supporter respect and inside the ground, they would reciprocate.

I've never met Richard Walker head of Watford FC media, but if he ever reads this, I want to thank him for delivering his promise because my press pass and ID badge is indeed waiting when I collect my match ticket. Through the entrance and into the concourse I make my way up some stairs towards the Horizon Suite. Security escorts me to a huge table which is mine alone. It overlooks half of the pitch and there's a free bar. Typical, I'm driving! I'm served lovely food and take in the rest of the lounge just people watching. Nothing like your working-class football fan in here, they look and dress middle class and definitely there's no one I can find common ground with, so I just browse the match programme.

Pictured on the front is thirty-eight-year-old Brazilian Heurelho Gomes, second choice goalkeeper. He's popular here at Watford and very much a cult figure. His smile reflects the gratitude he feels inside for still playing the game. He's been picked today and this is probably going to be his last ever appearance at Vicarage Road as he's retiring at the end of the season, hence front-page coverage. For him, this would be an emotional occasion.

Watford Football Club certainly has changed. In 1983 the only atmosphere would come from the away end but here in 2019 the previously muted home support has been replaced by an amazing and colourful reception as yellow and black tickertape welcome the gladiators. It's Saturday lunchtime and this is the first of the four quarter-finals being televised live.

FA CUP QUARTER FINAL
SATURDAY 16TH MARCH
VICARAGE ROAD
ATTENDANCE – 18104

WATFORD 2 CRYSTAL PALACE 1

The star of the show is Watford mascot Harry the Hornet. He is both cheerleader and comedian, one minute conducting the Watford choir to my right, and next making every home supporter laugh by stamping on the red and blue opponent's balloons which the wind brings from the away end to my left. Unfortunately, he gets carried away and attempts to chase a Crystal Palace balloon which has strayed onto the pitch and almost collides with the referee's assistant on this side which forces the man in the middle to bring proceedings to a halt. Now the Eagles are laughing as it was Watford on the attack when the whistle sounded. Everyone around me is giving the mascot what for, while I'm laughing my head off watching a football official reprimand a six-and-a-half-foot hornet who has his head bowed in shame like a naughty schoolboy. Harry walks away with his head down looking really sorry for himself with antennae blowing wildly in the wind. He finds a corner of the ground to sit in and hasn't got the zest for livening up the atmosphere, not yet anyway. For now, the balloons are safe.

Crystal Palace enjoy a lot of possession early on and Andros Townsend in particular is a threat. Spaniard Gerard Deulofeu of Watford then ominously comes into the game more; showing delightful touches and forcing early saves. After half an hour the place erupts as Watford take the lead. It's a scrappy goal but the home fans don't care. Frenchman Etienne Capoue is the goalscorer. Two minutes later, Deulofeu almost makes it 2-0 and Palace are all over the place. Despite their brilliant noisy support the players look shell shocked and nobody in white shirts is taking responsibility. Another ten minutes pass before Deulofeu yet again torments the Eagle's defence before being denied by goalkeeper and compatriot Vincente Guaita. The half-time whistle is a great relief to the visitors who can now regroup in the sanctuary of their dressing room. Deulofeu has quite simply played brilliantly while team-mate Will Hughes has also caught the eye.

So are Watford still a family club? I ask myself as I reach the warmth and hospitality of the Horizons suite. The answer is no. Friendly yes, but modern-day Premiership set-ups cater for those of financial gain and not for those who are family orientated. To offset that though there is plenty of passion inside the ground, something that wasn't there in the eighties. Some of the comments around me in the second half confirm what I'm thinking, "Linesman! Stick your flag up you cunt! He's fucking miles offside!" is one of the nicest things shouted at the officials as the game was reaching it's nail-biting conclusion. Another Watford fan then shouts at one of his own players as nervousness gets the better of him, "How much have Palace paid you, you fucking Chelsea reject!" I take it this guy doesn't think the player in question is having a good game.

Watford claim to have a family stand but today it is filled with Eagle fans who never stop singing to the beat of the drum.

*'Cause we support The Palace, The Palace, The Palace,
and that's the way we like it, we like it, we like it,
whooaaaahhh … Whooaaaahhh …'*

But what really baffles me is that as the players run out for the second half is how can Watford honestly portray themselves as a family club when 'Gimme Shelter' by The Rolling Stones blasts it's way around the stadium's sound system. Mick Jagger's vocals screaming

'Rape, murder, is just a shot away, just a shot away …'

Isn't the sort of thing you play to kids.

Crystal Palace restart the game, firing on all cylinders with Andros Townsend typically leading the charge nearly scoring on two occasions; but it's Watford captain Troy Deeney who really impresses me with not only his physical attributes in attack but also his organisational qualities. As Palace attack through a succession of free kicks and corners, Deeney, standing on the halfway line, points out to his team-mates the positions they should be taking up to snuff out any potential danger. Off the pitch he apparently has turned his life around and away from the wrong side of the law. They love him here at Watford, and it's clear that yellow and black stripes sear through his veins.

He can do nothing whatsoever though about the equaliser which has been threatening this half as it comes from a defensive mistake. Belgian Michy Batshuayi takes advantage of an error by defender Adrian Mariappa and closes in on goalkeeper Gomez, he is the calmest person in the ground as he coolly sidefoots the ball into the bottom corner of the net to send the Eagles flying out of their seats. He'd almost scored a couple of minutes before with a half-chance and Watford are now really up against it in their own back garden. Harry the Hornet continues to sit with his head in his hands.

Watford then respond brilliantly and attack as much as Palace. This is now a gripping game and hard to call. Both sets of fans are getting noisier but it's the visiting fans on my left who sing with more optimism. Both goalkeepers are kept busy and then comes the moment which decides the outcome. To Will Hughes' disappointment (and mine) he is substituted and replaced by Andre Gray a former Crystal Palace player. It's a tactical move by Watford manager Javier Gracia who sacrifices a midfielder to send an extra attacker onto the pitch which is the footballing equivalent of blinking first. It's a bold decision as Watford may leave themselves open to attack as they now have less personnel in the area of the pitch where the game is controlled. But it pays off within seconds! Argentine Robert Pereyra crosses a good ball into the opponent's penalty area which is volleyed in superbly by Gray, his first touch of the ball! There's only ten minutes left and now Harry the Hornet gets excited, whipping up the home support into a frenzy. That's nothing compared to Gomez in the Watford goal though as he is running around his area and screaming at his team-mates like a wild man. Vicarage Road is now full of the familiar sight of yellow and black scarves, shirts and streamers lighting up bleak conditions. Tickertape is caught in the stadium roof eaves flying dramatically in the wind.

Palace boss Roy Hodgson then makes the same tactical change as his opposite number with striker Christian Benteke replacing midfielder James McArthur but there's only six minutes left and surely this is too late to blink second. Watford then nearly make it 3-1 but Deeney's shot is saved. The home fans around me are desperate to hear the final whistle and a woman in front of me is near to tears. Man of the match Deulofeu doesn't help matters when he misses an easy chance from a few yards out as Watford fans go through agony. I've felt their pain in the past, watching Plymouth Argyle at Home Park or England on TV. I know what they're going through and I'm just glad I'm here today as a neutral. Gracia then swaps invention for industry as Deulofeu is replaced by Tom Cleverly, in an attempt to shut up shop.

The fourth official holds up a board indicating there will be an extra five minutes to play. FIVE MINUTES! Where did that come from?!!! Watford fans are going nuts. Those around me are scared stiff. All their hopes and dreams of glory resting on eleven footballers who let's face it, are just like you and I, human. And when you don't support a top team fear is a constant companion. Absolute fear, sometimes lifted by shafts of sheer relief and even unbridled joy which more than makes up for the long suffering.

Palace get a chance to equalise right at the death but a brilliantly timed tackle by a Watford defender brings as many sighs of relief as it does cheers of joy. And then it's all over. I can't remember the last time I saw such emotion at the end of a football match. Goalkeeper Gomez is crying, hugging everything in a black and yellow top. A lovely way to say goodbye to his home fans. The fans themselves are going wild with joy and as happy as I am for them, it's tinged with a little sadness for Crystal Palace's departure from the Cup, the team I've followed for four rounds. Their fans are brilliant, the pride of south London. They're what the game is all about; exciting, colourful, dramatic, noisy, humorous and passionate. Even in defeat there lies a sense of glory sometimes. Thank you Eagles, it was a pleasant flight.

Time to fly, I've got a press conference to attend on the other side of the ground. Grabbing my match programme from the Horizons Suite nothing now is going to stop me now with my date of destiny with the former England manager. No time for Watford hospitality right now,

- "Sir would you like …"

– "No thanks! I've got a gig with Roy."

Swiftly past the walls on the first floor which are adorned with giant size images of the Hornets at Wembley in 1984, down the steps, weaving in and out of hundreds of people with swerves that Paul Gascoigne would be proud of, and quickly around the perimeter of the stands.

A security guard stands between me and a small door simply labelled 'Press'. He puts his hand up to stop me, but I skilfully flash my press pass and circumnavigate the big guy without checking my stride. I feel like a reporter, I could get used to this! Inside there's a small reception desk where two ladies are discussing 'Britain's Got Talent'. I'm stood at the top of a place that resembles a university lecture room with rows of long benches overlooking a small desk at the front. More images of Elton John and Graham Taylor surround me. Their proud smiles capture the achievement of what once was a small football club which they built into something much bigger.

One of the ladies looks up at me and I start... "Hi, this is my first press conference and ..."

she puts her hand up (is this the first thing an employee learns at Watford FC?) and says, "No problem, walk this way".

I decline that advice however because if I did walk that way I might get in trouble, so, instead I follow her down the room and through another door, and there it is! This room is smaller with rows of seats and an elevated desk at the far end with sponsorship logos behind it, just like you see on TV. We're the only ones in the room and she points at a door on the far right-hand side and explains

"Unfortunately you can't go through there. It's for live TV and radio.". I ask if there's any etiquette in a press conference and apparently there's a pecking order of who asks the first questions when the two managers appear through the forbidden door separately. They'll give about twenty minutes each to the waiting media answering questions which are asked by organisations in the following order ... Sky Sports, BT Sports, terrestrial TV, national newspapers, the London Evening Standard, Capital Radio, and finally, little old me!

I take the seat most central and nearest the main desk so I'll be directly in the manager's eyeline and just a few yards away. Behind me a few more filter in. Cameramen and technicians set up their equipment. I then recognise a face from Sky Sports News but can't remember his name. It doesn't matter, I'll ask him later and maybe get an interview. A guy sits on my left and is being informally interviewed by somebody representing a football magazine. All I see is the back of his head but by the nature of the conversation I gather he's a Premiership footballer with Everton connections. On my right is a bloke who like me is armed only with a notebook and pen. Thankfully, that's all he's armed with as I see that he's scribbling madly from right to left on a page, it looks Arabic. Everyone else coming into the conference have laptops and leave mobile phones on the desk in front, ready to record any gems the two managers may impart. Sadly, there won't be any.

The forbidden door opens and out steps Watford's Spanish manager Javier Gracia who can't stop smiling. He's not been in the job long having recently been appointed from Russian side Rubin Kazan, and the home fans have already taken him to their hearts. Most of the journalists run to the desk and switch on their phones which will record his broken English. He's instantly reminded by Sky Sports News of the song Watford fans sing to him to the tune of 'You Are My Sunshine, my only sunshine ...'

- "I am focussed on the next game"
'JAVI GRACIA ...'

- "I am not a master tactician"
'HE DRINKS SANGRIA ...'

- "Substitution was a difficult decision to make"
'HE CAME FROM RUSSIA ...'

- "I am focussed on the next game against Manchester United"
'TO HERTFORDSHIRE ...'

- "Gomez is a very important player"
'HE'S FORTY-SEVEN ...'

- "Our strength and solidarity are hard work"
'HE'S WATFORDS HEAVEN ...'

- "We will need same mentality for semi-final"
'SO PLEASE DON'T TAKE MY JAVI AWAY ...'

Unfortunately, a few months later they did take Javi away shortly after turning forty-eight, as owners of football clubs do with 95% of managers, due to a bad run of results. It begs the question, how can they have a long-term target for the respective clubs they own, when they only think short-term. Too many press the panic button, bring in the next manager to work with players who aren't his own, not give him enough time, sack him and do it all over again.

A lot of emotion can be lost in translation but Senor Gracia did manage to make the room laugh when answering a question on how he felt about the upcoming domestic break, due to international fixtures. "I too need a break!" he stated with an even bigger smile.

But throughout this press conference I couldn't believe the obvious and daft closed end questions being asked to the two managers by qualified journalists. Both Gracia and Hodgson answered them with more detail than the questions warranted but they would have been well within their rights just to answer 'yes' or 'no' to the bleeding obvious. Open ended questions would surely make them give us more and a better insight into how the two managers were thinking during the game. For example, Gracia was asked, "In 1984 Graham Taylor took Watford to the FA Cup final but lost. Would you like to go one better?" I mean come on! Surely you can do better than that guys! How is he supposed to answer that other than 'yes'? Should he respond with 'Nah! This Watford team wants to lose every game it plays!'

He disappears through the forbidden door and minutes later in walks Roy Hodgson accompanied by a female assistant who takes charge of the proceedings. When asked about his thoughts on the game, he basically gives us a match report on which approximately eighteen thousand of us have just witnessed. Everyone is tapping away at their keyboards but I'm just looking at him, waiting for his actual views and not something I know already. And then it's his turn to answer the bleeding obvious.

- Is this a missed opportunity? (nah I like losing!)

- Are you disappointed? (nah, can't wait for the abuse!)

- Is Premiership survival now a priority? (are you a real journalist?!!!)

What a stupid question that last one was! Premiership survival is the ONLY thing left as his team has just been knocked out of the Cup! As the questions get dafter, you can see that Roy clearly doesn't want to be there, mirroring his last press conference as England manager after he resigned.

The longer this waste of time went on, the more confident I felt about asking him a question of my own. Being well down the pecking order I waited patiently, waiting my turn before pointing my pen in the air. The lady behind the desks addresses me. "Yes, the gentleman at the front with the spiky hair." I hesitate and give her a funny look. Hey lady, it's bloody windy out there! But that's not important right now. What is important is that I've got one chance to ask a meaningful question. Meaningful not just to me, but my mates, the vast majority of football fans in England and for that matter, most professionals as well. This is it Kindon! I feel absolutely calm, even when a fluffy red and blue boom with Sky Sports written on it appears out of the corner of my eye ...

"Roy ..." I start as I confidently make eye contact, "although you're not going to be there, how do you feel in general about semi-finals being played at Wembley?" (Well done Kindon!).

His words throw me a bit, "I don't understand the question." (What, am I speaking Swahili or something?).

"What I mean is Roy, surely the whole point of reaching the Cup final is the glory of playing at Wembley and staging semi-finals there diminishes the special occasion?"

"Well, I don't want to open that particular can of worms," he replies as his eyes dart all over the room, "it's a bit late in the day to open that debate. Even Conference play-offs these days are played at Wembley." He's now wearing a little smirk.

But I'm a dog with a bone and I'm not letting it go.

"But Roy surely if you're a traditionalist like me then you believe …"

The lady cuts me off mid-sentence and raises her voice. "Next question please!"

I felt fobbed off. This is an ex-England manager and former employee of the Football Association. He has to have an opinion on something that has bugged football fans for the last ten years or is he that much out of touch? Strangely, when answering a couple of remaining questions, he stares directly at me and not at the journalist who asked.

He finishes his press conference by saying that Palace missed Wilfred Zaha today although the other players did their best. These days, he says, are the days of game management and he knew the ball wouldn't be on the field of play for long periods. I took this as a dig, accusing Watford of time wasting which I didn't notice. But it's his final comment which leaves me baffled. He's now saying that he would have liked to have stayed in the Cup and that reaching the final would be a brilliant day out for the supporters! Apart from an empty answer to the only question I'll ever ask in the only press conference I'll ever attend, hasn't he stated in the previous rounds that the League is more important and fielded weakened teams in this Cup campaign?

The press conference was a real eye opener. But what qualifications do you need exactly to become a sports reporter when most questions asked are banal?

I walk out and into the bleak weather for the short walk back to my hired car, but not before asking Sky Sports reporter Gary Cotterill for an interview for a book I'm writing. He's happy with that but is busy right now so he gives me his email address. My mood lifts. Walking around the front of the stadium, I take a couple of minutes to stop at the statue of Watford's best manager Graham Taylor. Like Roy Hodgson, Taylor was a decent man who was appointed England manager. And like Hodgson, he unfortunately failed as a result of over complicating the game and confusing his teams.

Overall, I'm happy with the day and feel I've accomplished quite a bit. It's not even 3pm as I walk up the friendly neighbour's driveway which he kindly let me use. He's waiting for me in his living room window, wearing a Watford beanie and a massive grin. He reminds me of the score by holding up two fingers on one hand and one finger on the other (the polite way around I hasten to add), and I respond visually with one of those hand gestures which suggests it was a little too close for comfort. I pull away and my smile lasts for miles until that is, I merge with that horrible M25 motorway.

The Journalist

I've met some genuinely friendly people on this journey and Gary Cotterill of Sky Sports is no exception. True to his word, he responded to my request for an interview. The following transcript is word for word our Q&A via email. Gary's responses are in capital letters …

How did you get into reporting?

I AM OLD SCHOOL. I ALWAYS WANTED TO BE A TV REPORTER, BUT BACK IN THE EARLY EIGHTIES THE BEST WAY WAS TO GET A 'CADET/TRAINEE' ROLE AT A LOCAL PAPER. THEY PAID YOU A MINIMUM WAGE, BUT SPONSORED YOUR NCTJ (National Council for the Training of Journalists) TRAINING. I STARTED AS A COPYBOY AT THE ADELAIDE NEWS IN SOUTH AUSTRALIA. THEN ON

MY RETURN TO THE UK I GOT A JOB AS A TRAINEE REPORTER ON THE WEEKLY PAPER 'THE RUGBY ADVERTISER', THE TOWN NOT THE SPORT. THAT WAS 1980-83. THEN IN 1983 I GOT INTO RADIO. BBC RADIO STOKE, INDEPENDENT RADIO IN LIVERPOOL AND RADIO CITY WHERE CLIVE TYLDESLEY (current ITV football television commentator) WAS SPORTS EDITOR. THEN I MOVED TO TV AS A NEWS REPORTER, ENDING UP AT SKY NEWS IN 1991. IN 2004 I MOVED TO SKY SPORTS NEWS.

Who or what is your inspiration?

MY INSPIRATION WAS ITN NEWS AT TEN. IT WAS GREAT BACK THEN. JOHN SNOW WAS A FRONTLINE REPORTER. (wasn't he in Game Of Thrones?)

What is the highlight of your career?

BLIMEY! HARD TO SAY. SO MANY AND LOVED MOST OF IT. BUT MAYBE IN NEWS, I'M THE ONLY JOURNALIST EVER TO INTERVIEW (serial killer) HAROLD SHIPMAN. IT WAS VERY BRIEF. I GUESS SPORTSWISE IT WOULD BE 1999 WHEN I WAS SKY'S NORTH OF ENGLAND CORRESPONDENT AT THE TIME. I WENT TO BARCELONA AS A FAN, THEN FLEW BACK TO MANCHESTER TO FRONT THE HOMECOMING 'TREBLE' PARADE. (Manchester United made history by becoming the first English club to win the League title, FA Cup and European Cup in the same season). THE STREETS WERE PACKED. GREAT ATMOSPHERE.

Describe your typical match day routine and duties.

MATCHDAY USUALLY INVOLVES ARRIVING THREE OR FOUR HOURS BEFORE KICK OFF. DOING A FEW

PITCHSIDE SET UP LIVE INTERVIEWS. THEN AFTER THE GAME INTERVIEWING PLAYERS IN THE 'MIX ZONE'. MAYBE ALSO THE MANAGERS IN THE PRESS CONFERENCE. (I know, I was there!).

Do you believe that television runs football? (yes, I know it's a closed end question!).

I DON'T BELIEVE THAT. OF COURSE, IT HAS INFLUENCE AND PUTS IN LOTS OF MONEY. BUT ATTENDANCES IN STADIUMS ARE UP (this season, overall attendances have been the largest in sixty years), AND I HAVE BEEN AROUND LONG ENOUGH TO SEE THAT ON THE PITCH, AND IN THE DRESSING ROOMS, BEHIND THE SCENES THE OLD TRADITIONS AND ROUTINES AND WAYS OF DOING THINGS REMAIN. TO BE HONEST, WITH ALL THE MONEY TV PUTS IN, I'M SURPRISED IT DOESN'T HAVE EVEN MORE INFLUENCE.

How do you feel about semi-finals being played at Wembley?

I DON'T THINK THEY SHOULD BE. THE FINAL SHOULD BE SPECIAL (Mr Hodgson take note). ALSO, THE SEMIS SOMEHOW FELT SPECIAL WHEN THEY WERE PLAYED AT ANOTHER CLUB'S NEUTRAL STADIUM (Villa Park 1984). IN THE OLD DAYS FANS HAD THE EXCITEMENT OF WHO THEY WOULD GET IN THE SEMI FINAL DRAW, AND THEN A DEBATE ABOUT WHERE IT WOULD BE PLAYED. WATFORD VERSUS WOLVES (my next game as it turned out) COULD BE ANYWHERE. VILLA PARK MAYBE? (maybe a bit close to Wolverhampton to be neutral, but there are more than enough big stadia capable of staging the game).

What is your opinion on journalism/reporting in both football and general news?

I THINK SPORTS JOURNALISM IS STRONGER THAN EVER. THERE ARE EXCEPTIONS OF COURSE. I WONDER, IF YOU TOTTED UP ALL THE TRANSFER WINDOW HEADLINES AT THE END OF THAT PARTICULAR MONTH, WHAT PERCENTAGE WOULD BE TRUE? SOCIAL MEDIA IS A BIG THREAT TO PROPER JOURNALISM. TOO MANY PEOPLE REPEATING PURE SPECULATION.

Are press conferences non-challenging for managers? (as I felt about the one at Watford).

I THINK PRESS CONFERENCES CAN BE CHALLENGING IF THE QUESTIONS ARE RIGHT. PRESS CONFERENCES REGULARLY PRODUCE THE BEST NEWS LINES.

Do you believe people involved in the game should be punished for impartial comments on social media? (I know, I know! Another closed end question. Cut me some slack will ya!)

NO. (I deserved that!)

Finally, your feelings on the current England team compared to previous ones?

I THINK THE ENGLAND TEAM IS BETTER THAN EVER. IT WILL WIN A BIG TROPHY WITHIN TEN YEARS. JUST LOOK AT THE PREMIERSHIP PLAYERS IN THE UNDER 21'S.

Thank you Gary.

"When the seagulls follow the trawler, it is because they know sardines will be thrown into the sea."
ERIC CANTONA

When 'Eric The King' finished an infamous press conference with this quote, the press didn't quite get who he was having a dig at. I'll give you a clue, it was the press themselves. I asked Gary Cotterill about the standard of journalism because my experience of reading tabloid newspapers is that the reporter isn't too bright. Or maybe in Eric's case they DID know what he was talking about but … a) they were in self-denial or b) they wanted their readers to believe something other than the truth.

I got it straight away as the only thing Eric and myself have in common is our contempt for the 'gutter press'. Basically it's a metaphor. The seagulls are the press, Eric is the trawler and the sardines are the insignificant small things he's done that no one cares about apart from the seagulls.

George Best has to be the greatest player seen in our domestic game but Eric Cantona for me has been the best player of the premiership era simply because of the amazing impact he had on the premiership title. Arriving at Leeds in 1992, Cantona played for a team desperately chasing Manchester United who were heading for their first League title in a quarter of a century. In this two-horse race with just a couple of fences left to jump, the 'Red Devils' were a street ahead but began to falter. Cantona slipped into the Leeds saddle, cracked his inspirational whip a couple of times, and the team from Yorkshire sped like a seasoned thoroughbred and became the last side to win what was then known as the First Division Championship.

Months later he joined the team he had just vanquished to runners up and his influence was massive; as the Reds then lifted the first ever premiership title, their first League winning side since George Best himself played for them in 1967.

The following season Manchester United retained the title and added the FA Cup for good measure to secure their first ever double; only the fourth club in the twentieth century to achieve this feat. Again Cantona was the main reason for this. The catalyst was now the talisman; the King of Old Trafford and possibly a bigger influence than manager Alex Ferguson who admitted that when he signed the Frenchman, it wasn't a case of whether he was big enough for Manchester United, but a case of whether Manchester United was big enough for him!

In January 1995, Cantona is sent off at Crystal Palace and takes his frustration and anger out on an abusive Eagles fan with a chest high kung fu kick. He's banned for eight months by the Football Association and Manchester United are resorted to second best in both the Premiership League and the FA Cup.

He returns the following season now as captain to lift both trophies which means Manchester United become the first team in history to win the coveted double twice. The country looks forward to hosting the 1996 European Championship and inevitably takes a nostalgic look back at the only other time England held a tournament, the triumphant 1966 World Cup. Posters and billboards are sprouting up all over the land pronouncing '1966 was a great year for English football … Eric was born'. And there he is, his face appearing on a familiar white flag with a red cross. Not since St George has someone from overseas shaped our flag so much. And no one complained.

Finally in 1997, Manchester United win their fourth title in five years, smashing more records in the process. Eric once more is the leader. And then he retired, just shy of his thirty-first birthday.

The Reds didn't win anything the following season without this maverick, this man of poetry. But hell, didn't they make up for it in 1999 when winning an unprecedented treble, the League title, the FA Cup and the European Champions League. They were now Kings of Europe. A team that included David Beckham, Gary Neville and Ryan Giggs had now come of age. The pupils no longer needed the teacher, but cited him as their biggest influence.

The ninetiess also witnessed the explosion of Britpop which went hand in hand with football. The game had now reached a cultural standard which hadn't been seen since the sixties when George Best unofficially became 'the fifth Beatle'. The Beatles didn't mean to do it, but they shaped that whole decade. And now three decades later a band called Oasis were doing the same, fronted by a sneering, audacious yet intelligent singer named Liam

Gallagher whose older brother Noel penned the hits. As sibling rivalry goes, they made Kane and Abel look like the Nolan Sisters.

Ironic then that these two periods in English musical and foot-balling history both featured charismatic and brilliant Manchester United players who were compared to artists associated with teams that their supporters despised. The Beatles were from Liverpool and the Gallagher brothers supported Manchester City.

The two magicians wouldn't mind though.

Yep! If George Best personified The Beatles then Eric Cantona was definitely Oasis.

Chapter Thirteen

THE RETURN OF MAGIC MIKE

Walking home from work one night, a builder's transit van pulls over in a Tesco car park, the horn beeps and a familiar voice shouts out my name. It's Barry Hawkings, the only Crystal Palace fan I've ever known of (apart from Nookie Bear). We have a quick catch up and I tell him all about my Cup trail and in particular, following the Eagles. Like everyone I know from my generation, he too is fed up with the current fashion of Premiership teams disrespecting and sacrificing the most famous trophy on the planet, just to survive in the top-flight.

He has an idea. How about any team that makes wholesale changes or plays a weakened side in the FA Cup faces the punishment of two extra games? What Bazza means is that they should join the following season in the first round rather than the third; therefore adding to their fixture list which the managers unbelievably believe is congested already. Food for thought mate I tell him. Mind you, this is the same guy who would argue the toss with football referees over the most trivial of decisions when he played, and dishing out instant justice whenever an opponent fouled him. One of the worst disciplinary records I've ever known in our local leagues belied the fact that he was a bloody good player, sometimes brilliant.

As for this season's FA Cup we've reached the semi-final stage but my growing excitement with every round is now diminishing somewhat because I know I'm going to Wembley Stadium to watch Watford no matter who they get drawn against. It will be a false occasion. Semi-finals at our national stadium which was built originally to host the final itself whilst becoming a fortress for the England side is the most cynical exercise commercially imposed on us by the modern thinking of the Football

Association. The game isn't about glory in April; nor is it good for the supporter in general since this daft idea grew into reality round about the millennium, ensuring that the very people funding it's lifeblood would have to blow a full month's budget on just one football match. Gone are the days when the excitement of finding out who you would play was then followed up by the announcement of a neutral venue far easier and cheaper to get to. Going to a ground steeped in history such as Arsenal, Aston Villa, Manchester United or Sheffield Wednesday has now been replaced by a bank balance busting punishment for the football fan and a mean money-making machine masquerading as the fathers of football.

As ideas go in the most romantic Cup competition on the planet this is the worst decision since President Kennedy turned to his wife and said, "What a beautiful day here in Dallas. Let's have the roof down!"

There is more madness when the draw is made. To suit television, Manchester City will play Brighton on the Saturday and Watford will take on Wolves the following day. This means that City have just three days to prepare for their game, since their last League match, yet Wolves will have five days to prepare for theirs! Listening to Talksport Radio an incensed City fan phones up a live show and demands that the FA should be brought to book; but by whom? Who do they answer to? His rant continues (just like mine) and he tells the presenters that attending the League Cup final against Chelsea a couple of months ago was a far cheaper experience than the semi-final of the FA Cup is going to be. "I'm paying through the nose for myself and my son!" And that's the whole point. He works for a living and his spare cash will now be swallowed up by travelling expenses, match tickets and the overnight stay he's now being forced into, due to TV dictating the later kick-off time.

The first domestic silverware of the season has gone to Manchester City in the shape of the League Cup (so called as it's run by the Football League and excludes teams below level four). Not only have City already won a competition which ninety-two teams entered, but they currently sit at the top of the twenty-team Premiership and are hot favourites to achieve a history making treble by winning all three domestic trophies. Only a bizarre video assisted refereeing verdict has denied them of European glory in a quarter-final against Tottenham; not bizarre in the decision itself, but bizarre as in celebrating a winning goal while three men sat in a room miles away disallowed it.

I decide to take the train from Plymouth station on a four-hour journey to Paddington the afternoon before the game, where I'll be meeting my Wembley wife Mike Vallis for a few pints. He's driven up before me in order to visit and spend time with his daughter Jen, who works in London. Before I travel I'm messaged by my cousin Jeff Nurse who has come up from west Cornwall to visit his immediate family and suggests we meet for a few drinks. Being the cheapskate he is, we end up in a Wetherspoons pub on Plymouth's historic Barbican.

Jeff's great company as long as you can live with his non-stop, mostly unfunny one liners, and I make it worse by telling him what I'm doing and more importantly in his eyes, that I'm writing a book about it. In a vain attempt to get me to mention him in this chapter, his jokes are cutting me down like a machine gun and unbelievably, they're getting worse. Crude as well, such as saying that having a 'semi' experience isn't as 'hard' as the real thing. At least he agrees with me on the Wembley principle! When I ask him what neutral venue he would like to see semi-finals played at, he replies 'Switzerland'. And so the liquid lunchtime went in the same manner; jokes getting crummier but at least the lager numbed most of it. It didn't stop there. More jokes followed by text messages as I boarded the train. Anyway, Jeff my dear cousin, you achieved it. I've mentioned you in my book you unfunny cheapskate! LOL.

I feel mellow during the journey and have a little snooze before reaching Paddington at 5.30pm. Mike texts me and says he's waiting in a bar not two hundred yards from the station where we watch Manchester City beat Brighton 1-0 in an absolutely dire game. City look jaded and Brighton hardly come out of their seashells.

After the game we walk for about ten minutes so I can check into my hotel. The foreign girl behind the reception desk doesn't seem to be able to grasp basic English and I virtually have to point to my name in the register in front of her. My room is on the top floor of a very old building which resembles more of a kennel than a bedroom, but that doesn't bother me. It's only somewhere I want to put my head down after a few more drinks. I literally throw my rucksack onto the small bed and meet Mike downstairs, wasting no time. Beers await us. We like London. It's got a great vibe in the evening and every bar is different. In fact, we like the capital so much that between us we are veterans of no less than eight London marathons (he's ran seven).

Mike gets the first round in at the first bar we find, where an older bloke with a Scandinavian accent invites us to join him. Invitation politely declined. He then turns his attention to a couple of guys on the next table and comments on the length of one of their beards.

"Excuse me," he asks, "what do you call that beard?"

"Derek!" is my too quick and not too clever quip, thankfully ignored by both big guys who look more than capable of bouncing The Incredible Hulk off every wall in the room.

The Scandinavian either can't seem to take a hint or he has a death wish. The hint comes in the form of two icy stares but still he goes on and enquires about the facial hair until a member of staff asks/advises him in a professional manner, to wind his neck in. But still he goes on, stupidly and unnecessarily. It's the pub equivalent to placing your head into a lion's mouth and flicking it's testicles with a wet towel.

The atmosphere as well as the faces are getting ugly so we decide to move on after this pint. The two guys have left the bar but wait outside for a while to see if the drunken viking fancies his chances. He clearly doesn't. It's the first thing he's done right this evening.

Mike had a good idea about getting cheap accommodation in London, or rather outside it. He drove to Slough and booked a much cheaper room there than the attic space I've been screwed for, and then got a short cheap train journey into Paddington. But that meant he had to leave early to get back to the station, so we arranged to meet the next day in the afternoon on a main road about thirty minutes' walk from Wembley Stadium. Two more pints and a portion of chicken and chips later, I crash out in Kindon's kennel dreaming about chasing cats before an early walk in the morning.

A grey chilly morning in Paddington and I've got a few hours to kill. I buy an all-day tube ticket at the station and think about how to use it over a McDonald's breakfast. In walks Jack McDermott from Plymouth, son of my friend and former team-mate Paul. Jack was our Sunday morning football team mascot in his younger years for two different pub sides in a place called Plympton, namely The Unicorn and The George. Sometimes, I'd lift him onto my shoulders and run about making him laugh but wouldn't even attempt it nowadays seeing as he's a heavyweight six-foot-two giant. He's a helluva character and always made us laugh as a kid with that brutal childlike honesty and his forthright opinions. Always asking questions about anything and about as inquisitive as you're ever likely to get, he was one of the team. So much so that he was allowed to vote for 'Player of the Year' after every season. He never once voted for his dad though!

Fans of TV reality show Big Brother might remember him as 'Pieface' from a few series ago when he finished third. "What a time to be alive!" was his catchphrase and he soon became a local celebrity back home, switching on the Christmas lights in Plymouth city centre and even co-commentating on an Argyle game, working for Radio Devon, which is something I'd love to do (he wrote dropping a heavy hint). Jack is Plymouth Argyle through and through, following them up and down the country; although his sometimes shall we say 'over-enthusiastic' support can get him in trouble from time to time. He still has that chat.

We catch up over an egg and bacon McMuffin and the memories come flooding back. Like the time we played a game in a remote field somewhere in Cornwall. I was playing in defence and father Paul behind me in goal. Jack stood by one of the goalposts and told his dad he wanted to go for a pee. Paul pointed to a bush about twenty yards away and said to answer his call of nature over there. A minute later Jack is back and says he's scared to do it there as he's just spotted a spider in the bush. Paul, or 'Wormy' as he was known (never found out why and never wanted to), is frustrated as half of his attention is on his own flesh and blood telling him off, whilst trying to concentrate on the game.

This debate is going on behind us as one of our opponents spots it and tries his luck with a thirty-yard shot which on any given day would be no problem for a goalkeeper. Any given day but today that is! The seemingly harmless effort sails over our heads and as we turn expecting Wormy to catch it, we realise with horror that he's not even seen it. The ball nestles into the back of our net and we berate our man between the sticks as he in turn berates his tearful son. Spider 1 Unicorn 0.

Jack boards the train back to the city of Pilgrims while I decide to make my own pilgrimage to Abbey Road just to recreate THAT walk from the last Beatle's recorded album of the same name. I google the nearest tube station to it, which is St John's Wood, a couple of stops away.

Obviously, I won't be the only one making this nostalgic trip today. There are dozens of tourists from all corners of the globe already outside the recording studios wanting to pay homage to probably the most iconic album cover of all time, portraying the band that musically changed everything. But here are a few words of caution. If you ever want to visit this musical mecca then do not, and I mean DO NOT attempt to set foot on that zebra crossing unless you are absolutely, positively, one hundred per cent sure that no traffic whatsoever is in sight! The problem being that the local motorists either take it for granted that you'll be there just to take pictures or they're just plain fed up with Beatles' fans and don't bother to stop. I nearly found out the fatal way. After assuming that a car fifty yards away would slow down as I made my first step onto the most famous road on the planet, the bastard actually accelerated out of spite and my big moment never nearly happened. Instead of hearing 'Here Comes The Sun' as I crossed, I could have easily heard ambulance sirens.

Walking towards Abbey Road it had occurred to me that it was fifty years ago when John, Paul, George and Ringo took that walk from the recording studio to the zebra crossing outside of it and had no idea how iconic it would become as it was the last time they recorded together as The Beatles. Something else that happened in the summer of '69 was Man first setting foot on the Moon, or not, depending on whether you're a conspiracy theorist. You know the type, they believe the moon landings were faked, JFK was shot by somebody behind a grassy knoll, the Earth is flat, all world leaders are actually lizards inside human skin and that Katie Price has talent.

Eventually, I managed to cross the road. 'One small step for man, one giant leap for a Beatle's fan,' I tell myself. The studio itself is a fortress behind iron gates and walls covered by graffiti from Fab Four worshippers from all over the World. Next door is a souvenir shop complete with a small zebra crossing painted on the pathway leading up to it's entrance. Inside, memorabilia and gifts are everywhere not just for The Beatles but also other bands who have recorded there such as Nirvana and Oasis. I buy Mike a book on the Fab Four as an early birthday present because just like me, he's been a massive fan since school.

Next stop on the tube is Wembley Stadium itself. Even though we're still four hours from kick-off, Wolves fans are there in numbers. They've made the trip down from the west midlands but Watford fans only have to arrive via a few tube stops. Surely this is too far south to be neutral. Supporters wearing gold replica and retro shirts don't seem to mind though as they sit around fast-food stalls and walk around the nearby shopping centre. This is the first time I'm on my own at the national stadium and I slowly walk up Wembley Way watched by the statue of Bobby Moore. I was just two months old when he lifted the World Cup here in front of a hundred thousand people and a billion television viewers.

Before walking around the empty arena, I take a look around underneath the walkways where security teams are being briefed. I email Gary Cotterill of Sky Sports on my iPhone to see if he'll be here today. He won't be as he's not working today and messages me saying 'enjoy the game'. And I would!

Killing further time, I enjoy an English breakfast in a nearby café before taking a slow walk towards Wembley High Road to meet Mike. He's been here a few times and always parks on a major road just off the A40, the idea being that it's a quick getaway towards the M25 and M4 motorways, and we're fit enough to jog back from the stadium. It's a very strange experience walking to the stadium however as you feel you're in a different country. Cutting through playing fields there are no football goalposts in sight, just Asian kids playing their national game of cricket. Into a cul-de-sac with houses boarded up and souped up cars on driveways. The locals are looking at us strangely because in this part of the capital it's actually us who are the ethnic minority. But that's nothing compared to Ealing Road. The pavements are wall to wall with stalls selling middle eastern food and traditional garb. More stares accompany us and we don't feel that comfortable until we see football shirts on Wembley High Road.

Pubs are a plenty here and are segregated for the two sets of supporters. This is where the organisation starts and we're still a twenty-minute walk away. We circumvent the stadium at the north end glimpsing the towering Triumphant Arch between well-kept houses and the only pub in the area called 'The Green Man' where appropriately, Argyle fans have visited on their only two visits to Wembley. Reaching the bottom of Wembley Way which joins the stadium to Wembley Park Tube Station, the excitement builds because the atmosphere does. There are Wolves fans everywhere making all the noise. For the second time today, I head up Wembley Way, keeping to the right, as it splits into two, surrounded by quiet Watford fans. I look across at the Wolverhampton contingent and wish I was walking up to their end of the stadium as gold shirts, modern and retro, swamp the place, singing all the way.

Mike then asks me at which end did Keith Houchen score a diving header for Coventry in the '87 Cup final against Spurs. I tell him it's the end we are walking towards, as the cameras are on the opposite side of the ground from us. Mike has always said that he reckons there can't be a single day go by when Houchen doesn't stop and think about that goal.

1987 WINNERS – COVENTRY CITY

Keith Houchen isn't what you call a household name, in fact most football fans either would have never heard of him or maybe forgotten him, but he is woven into the fabric of FA Cup glory as much as Stanley Matthews. As an avid football fan, I first saw him on TV scoring the winning goal for York City against Arsenal from the penalty spot in the last minute of a 1985 FA Cup third round game. I never forgot his name after that.

He then moved to Scunthorpe United virtually disappearing into obscurity; and only entering my thoughts once more when Plymouth Argyle nearly signed him. But at about the same time, he was tempted by a once in a lifetime opportunity to play for a top-level side, and so turned out in sky blue and white striped shirts for Coventry City. Little did the midlands side realise they'd just signed a Cup specialist because although Houchen's League goalscoring record didn't stand up to much, his Cup exploits were astonishing as he scored against Leeds, Sheffield Wednesday and even Manchester United who all succumbed to the Sky Blues on a fun filled and thrilling run that took them all the way to Wembley for the first time in their 104 year history; and the best was yet to come against Tottenham Hotspur in a final which to this day has remained my favourite one.

The 1987 final was the most appealing to me even before a ball was kicked because of the amazing magnetism of both teams who offered differing styles, but at the same time showed everything that was good about the way the game should be played. For Tottenham versus Coventry, read pedigree versus mongrels, stars versus journeymen, class versus spirit, the boxer versus the fighter.

On the morning of the game, I still had no idea who I wanted to win. It was a real dilemma for me. On one side, my favourite player Glenn Hoddle was making his farewell appearance for Spurs and in England (so we thought at the time) before moving abroad to Monaco, where his genius would be more appreciated under a young French manager named Arsene Wenger. Spurs also had Ossie Ardiles back playing for them, veteran goalkeeper Ray Clemence making his fifth Cup final appearance that spanned sixteen years, hot shot goalscorer Clive Allen who had hit nearly fifty goals that season and Chris Waddle, who had emerged as a top-class winger. Tottenham Hotspur had finished third in the League that year, which was a travesty of the attacking and creative play which had entertained English football that year. They simply were irresistible to watch, scoring more goals than anyone else in the country.

And what of their understated opponents? Coventry had gone through a transformation the previous summer when the board of directors appointed the management duo of ex-players John Sillett and George Curtis. The Odd Couple! Chalk and cheese but both determined to bring the spirit of the sixties back to Highfield Road, the name of their home ground back then. Sillett or 'Schnoz' as he was known, was a fantastic character, brilliant TV viewing. His comment after beating Leeds in the semi-final for example was … "Well me and George have always been lucky in the game, and I feel wonderful right now until I get home and look at the wife!" You can imagine the fun his players were having under him, allied to hard work. As for Curtis, he was quiet in comparison, well spoken, but in his day one of the hardest players in the country.

John Sillett had also played for Plymouth in the 1960's and the Argyle connection didn't stop there. Welsh international Dave

Phillips was a veteran of our memorable 1984 Cup run and that's what finally convinced me I should support Coventry on the day. This was bound to be a one off for them, but Spurs had the resource and the pulling power to sign exceptional players to ensure more Cup finals in the future. The whole Coventry team were made up of players who had either seen better days or had been signed from teams further down the pyramid for a pittance, by comparison. They had no chance claimed the Press. 'It'll be a doddle with Hoddle and Waddle' the headlines predicted. The two players had even got into the charts with a non-Cup final pop song entitled Diamond Lights.

A quick head count just before the kick off revealed fifteen of us watching the game in Lee Cameron's living room, accompanied by the obligatory lager. Lee himself was a Tottenham fan and was in raptures after only two minutes of the game when Chris Waddle twisted and turned before firing a perfect cross into the penalty area where Clive Allen scored his forty-ninth goal of the season with a bullet header. This was going to be a walkover surely. Even the most ardent Coventry fan would be forgiven for thinking so, but everyone reckoned without the incredible characters wearing striped shirts that day. Within ten minutes, Houchen headed on a pass that caused semi-panic in the Tottenham area which was taken advantage by David Bennett who levelled the scores. What a sweet moment for Bennett after losing for Manchester City in the 1981 final against …Tottenham! Like a few of his team mates, he must have thought his chances of glory and silverware were behind him as he now played for a decent but mid-table team. Striker Cyrille Regis was another. Built like a heavyweight boxer, Regis had scared defences for years whilst exciting his supporters, he'd played for England a few times but had never won anything playing for West Bromwich Albion. On two occasions he had just missed out on a Cup final appearance, losing semi-finals in 1978 and 1982. His emotion at the end of this 1987 final almost brought tears to my eyes. He almost scored on two occasions in this game, but one attempt was foiled by Tottenham goalkeeper Ray Clemence who as I mentioned was making his fifth Cup final appearance, and a goal was disallowed after it was ruled there was a foul on a Tottenham defender.

Clemence himself had left Wembley in 1974 with a winner's medal for the mighty Liverpool, a victory that was symmetrically sandwiched between two defeats in 1971 and 1977. After moving to Tottenham in 1981, he gained another winner's medal the following year and now in 1987 approaching forty years of age, would never have dared to dream he would be performing at Wembley Stadium again.

Tottenham regained the lead shortly before half-time with a goal credited to defender Gary Mabbutt but to this day I'm absolutely convinced he didn't touch the ball. Instead, a Glenn Hoddle delivery resulted in an unfortunate own goal by Coventry captain Brian Kilcline after the ball deflected off his knee and into his own net. What gives away the fact that Mabbutt didn't get the vital touch for me was his reaction when the ball hits the net. He's obviously happy to see that his team has scored but doesn't celebrate himself, just looks over to his team mates as if to say, 'what happened there?'. Doesn't matter who scores it anyway, the fact is that Spurs are leading 2-1 at the interval. Coventry have to come back yet again against their star-studded opponents.

And that's exactly what they did with the goal that Mike and I reminisce about from time to time.

Cyrille Regis and Keith Houchen combined before the ball was played out to David Bennett on the right wing. Bennett delivered a beautiful curling cross into the Tottenham area where Houchen sprinted into. In his words, someone shouted "Fly!" which prompted him to throw himself at the ball sending a brilliant diving header into the Tottenham net; two goals each and this game became even more enthralling. On two occasions Coventry had been floored by Tottenham punches, and both times got up before the count of ten to knock the favourites out of their stride.

One of the main reasons this final was such a good game was down to referee Neil Midgeley who I mentioned in chapter three. Quite simply he let the game flow, only blowing the whistle when absolutely necessary after a late physical challenge by Kilcline on Mabbutt. However, this game was so perfect it was the Coventry skipper who came off worse and had to be replaced. Mabbutt sportingly shook his hand as he left the arena. Kilcline's defensive partner Trevor Peake took over the captain's armband and soon was tussling with hotshot striker Clive Allen somehow picking him up and holding him suspended in mid-air. Allen put his arms out as if he was flying and ninety-six thousand football fans laughed, along with the players before applauding the brilliant spirit in which this game was played. It was that sort of final. The player's attitude determined the referee's. Neil Midgeley had it spot on regarding the policing of the game. You didn't notice him and that's the way it should be. He was a man of football and not the star of it.

The game ended in a draw after ninety minutes which meant a further half-hour of extra time. Any follower of the beautiful game didn't mind one bit, but for both sets of supporters, nerves were shredded. The game was then decided cruelly by the second (unofficial) own goal of the game. Coventry's workhorse Lloyd McGrath who had been detailed to snub out Glenn Hoddle's brilliant creativity found himself in space with the ball at his feet. Homing in on Tottenham's penalty area he crossed the ball more in the general direction of his team mates rather than accurately, and watched in delight as it struck Gary Mabbutt on the knee and flew high into the net. I'd seen the image before years earlier. Mabbutt on his haunches with his head in his hands, mirrored the unfortunate Tommy Hutchison in 1981 on virtually the same spot of the hallowed turf. This time though, fate had conspired against Tottenham Hotspur.

And then it was over. The mongrel had won at Crufts. It was moving, exciting and even a little romantic; the stuff that inspires poetry and a generation of football folk. Months later Coventry manager John Sillett was asked to describe the ingredients that make a great footballer. He answered "passion, skill and flair". He could have been describing the 1987 FA Cup final when his team took on and beat a brilliant Tottenham team.

His captain Brian Kilcline sporting long hair and a beard limped up the thirty-nine steps to the Royal Box before triumphantly roaring as he lifted the most famous trophy on the planet, resembling more of an invading viking holding up treasures audaciously snatched from kings.

The next day an estimated quarter of a million people swamped the streets of Coventry to welcome home the unlikely heroes in Sky Blue on their victory parade. The magic of the Cup had now touched this midlands city which had wallowed in lethargy for far too long, it's only place in history it had occupied prior to this being the victims of the German Luftwaffe forty-five years earlier. The sun was out and the odd white cloud appeared. Even the sky paid homage to Coventry City Football Club on this momentous day, replicating the colours of their striped shirts.

If anyone of a younger age ever asked me about the great appeal of the FA Cup final and what it means to my generation, I'll tell them to just YouTube 1987 Coventry 3 Tottenham 2. It shows everything that's good about football in England. The passion and the glory. Wembley Stadium standing proud, the mecca of football showcasing an event which is envied the world over. To all the players who took part in that memorable game, our generation salutes you.

There is one bizarre detail from this game that almost went unnoticed on the day but was highlighted the next day in every newspaper. Tottenham, as some clubs do on Cup Final Day, took to the pitch wearing a brand-new strip which officially belonged to the following season. It was basically an all-white kit with their sponsors names 'Holsten' emblazoned across the chest in black print, but something had gone wrong. Somehow the name of the famous pilsner beer only found its way onto some of the shirts while most of the others were plain apart from the club badge. This was too good an opportunity for one of their rival breweries to ignore, so in most of the Sunday papers appeared a full-page advert picturing those blank shirts in action with the famous slogan of the day proclaiming. 'I bet he drinks Carling Black Label!'

FA CUP SEMI FINAL
SUNDAY 7TH APRIL
WEMBLEY STADIUM
ATTENDANCE – 80092

WATFORD 3 WOLVERHAMPTON WANDERERS 2

The Wolves may be howling their heads off out on Wembley Way, but the Hornets are buzzing inside Wembley Stadium. Half of the arena is vibrant with red, yellow and black; shimmering flags easily upstaging the placards held up by the west midlanders at the other end. There are no favourites to win today. It's 7th versus 8th in Premiership terms and both clubs have exceeded all expectations this season. Just as importantly, both have been safe from relegation for a few months hence their Cup runs (with strong selections).

Once again Gomez is in goal for Watford. Is this a sentimental decision by Gracia to select him or does he think the thirty-eight-year-old is a lucky omen in the Cup? Or maybe he's sensing the veteran goalkeeper wants to retire on a high. The brilliant Spaniard Gerard Deulofeu is on the substitute's bench today and is replaced by quarter-final hero Andre Gray who will partner captain Troy Deeney in attack. The atmosphere around us when both teams walk out is electrifying and colourful.

Wolves immediately attack and after only twenty seconds come close to scoring but it's the only chance carved out early on in a game which would eventually grow ever more dramatic. Yellow cards flourish in the opening sparring as challenges are ill-timed. After half an hour of exchanging a few tame jabs there is no indication of what is to follow, when suddenly the Wolves get their snouts in front. I've never understood 'zonal marking' in the modern game which coaches instil into their teams when defending set pieces. What I mean is, I understand the theory but I don't understand why teams are made to play that way. As far as I can see, it's easier to score against compared to 'man marking'.

If a defender is instructed to mark a certain opponent from a corner or free kick, then surely it's easier to stop them because you're in a position where you can see both opponent and the ball. You stay with them and basically stop them heading or shooting towards goal, but when you're marking a certain zone, you are virtually statuesque, hardly moving and can't get enough elevation to jump with your opponent as they have an aerial advantage after running several yards towards the ball. Players score goals. I've never seen a zone score a goal. Therefore, marking players makes sense doesn't it?

Wolves have a corner kick against Watford's zonal marking. But instead of the ball being delivered at height into the penalty area, the corner taker simply passes it a few yards to a teammate who launches a cross from a different angle. Watford's defensive training hasn't accounted for this and Wolves have done their homework on them. I nudge Mike and shout above the noise, "they've lost him!" as Matt Doherty scores an easy header from close range, his run on the far side of the pitch undetected by Watford players more pre-occupied with their respective zones. All Doherty had to do was make that run between two opponents, neither one accepting responsibility.

The Hornets have been stung and first blood has been drawn by a pack of wolves who attack sensing their prey are disorientated. The pride of Hertfordshire are relieved to hear the half-time whistle and they can now use the next twenty minutes regaining their composure. The second half though starts the way the first ended and Gomez is called into action as the Wolves with their tails up dominate. Mike comments on Conor Coady, a big central defender and reckons he should be in attack for the team currently leading 1-0. Another Watford player is booked and after an hour of the game gone Raul Jimenez doubles the scoreline, and it comes from another corner kick. Zonal marking again is the culprit as the Mexican showing great composure chests the ball at height and coolly smashes in a volley. Wolves are on their way to Wembley … I mean, Wolves are already at Wembley and coming back for the final! Watford don't look one bit like scoring, let alone winning.

Twenty-five minutes left and it's shit or bust for Javier Gracia. He takes off Will Hughes for the second Cup game running and replaces him with Deulofeu, a more attack minded player. The game is losing momentum and descends into a scrappy affair as more players get booked. Gracia's tactical change is so far making no impact, unlike in the quarter-final and time is running out.

Then all of a sudden it's 2-1. The goal is pure quality. Deulofeu, entices opposing defenders and just stands over the ball, then deliberately and delightfully chips it over everyone's head from an acute angle. Wolves' goalkeeper John Ruddy is just like us, a mere spectator as the ball drops behind him and into the net. But as I've put a fiver on Wolves to win 2-1 it's inevitable that won't be the final score!

The Wolves' manager Nuno Santos from Portugal then makes a tactical substitution himself, but a defensive one. This just encourages Watford to attack with more pace and vigour, desperately trying to beat the clock. And then get this! Watford fans are actually starting to leave! Why?!!! There's still time for this game to be saved and as legendary manager Brian Clough once said, "it only takes a second to score a goal." And it's not as if they have to travel two hundred miles to get home is it? Unlike Mike and I.

In the ninetieth minute, the fourth official holds up the illuminated board that shows there will be an extra six minutes to play due to numerous hold ups in the game including substitutions and a full referee's notebook detailing player's cautions.

Drama! The Watford 'fans' who have left early miss their leader Troy Deeney get tripped inside Wolves' area and much to the horror of the west midlanders, points to the penalty spot. There's only two minutes left. Two minutes for Deeney to save the game and send it into a further half-hour with impetus driving his team forward. Two minutes left to become an even bigger hero with his supporters than he already is ...... two minutes to screw my bet up which would have paid for the petrol on the way back to Plymouth. Bloody Watford again!

And Deeney scores. Ice cold blood wins the moment in the hottest of situations. For the second time today, John Ruddy is powerless to stop the ball hitting his net. Now it's Wolves turn to become disorientated. They've let a two-goal lead slip and the whole shape of their team is top heavy on the defensive side. It's something that managers often do when trying to protect a slender advantage. Believing that they are making their team defensively stronger by adding a player to their rearguard, all they are doing in fact is giving their opponents the encouragement to attack even more. And now the Wolves have to play another thirty minutes with less attacking options.

The joy around us in the more colourful half of the stadium is a complete contrast to the silence that has struck over forty thousand supporters to our left. Extra time starts, and the Hornets fly in for the kill, every challenge wounding two-legged wolves. It's no surprise whatsoever when they go 3-2 up. The once more brilliant Deulofeu links with Andre Gray and strokes the ball agonisingly for Ruddy low into the net. The comeback is complete.

'Yellow Army! Yellow Army!'

This is the chant beneath the Triumphant Arch and then it suddenly hits me that my Wembley wife Mike has brought the magic of the FA Cup with him. The first time he accompanied me on this journey was sheer quality and the best game so far when Taunton beat St Albans 5-2. This second game is just as exciting, not through quality but through absolute drama. It can't be just coincidence that he's brought something to both parties and right on cue, he then gets a text message from his friend within the FA, guaranteeing us tickets for the final itself!

Later that evening, I re-christen Mike on my iPhone to Magic Mike. I already have a Jihadi John in my contacts as well as a Shallow Sean, and now Mr Vallis has joined my own honours list. Arise Sir Michael of Magicshire!

In the remainder of extra-time Wolves get just one chance to send the tie to a penalty shoot-out but like a fairy-tale in waiting, Gomez saves the effort and the day. He's not even the first-choice goalkeeper at Watford but now will play in an FA Cup final for them at the end of his career, and this half of Wembley love him.

The final whistle brings astonishing scenes of both despair and delight. Watford players are delirious, running around wildly, joining in the fan's celebrations. The Wolves players are broken figures, on their knees, devastated, some visibly in tears. Try telling all these players on the pitch that the FA Cup isn't important! The Watford team were heading toward emptiness a short while ago. For the likes of Gomez and Deeney, the dreams will become reality over the next six weeks. Wolves can't believe what's just happened to them. They've managed to snatch defeat from the jaws of victory. They've been jilted at the altar.

Watford will face Manchester City in only their second Cup final; a chance to atone for a disappointing performance in the 1984 showpiece. They'll celebrate long into the Hertfordshire night. Wolves will leave Wembley with their tails between their legs. That 125-mile journey by road will seem like a thousand. The famous gold shirts won't even get silver on May 18th. Like the rest of the nation, they'll just be watching it on TV. And I, with thousands of other Argyle fans, know that feeling only too well. Bloody Watford!

The Agent

'The only agent back in the seventies was 007- and he just shagged women, not entire football clubs.'
BRIAN CLOUGH

So how much do footballers care about the teams they play for then? Judging by the agony/ecstasy I'd just witnessed at Wembley, I'd say the whole lot of them, until their agent gets involved with new contract talks or a transfer. Agents, just like referees, are perceived to be the villains of the game; greedy bastards sucking the blood out of it whilst pretending to represent their clients, but in reality just boosting their bank balances and wrecking player's careers.

"It's total media crap" Barry Silkman tells me. "The maximum you can earn from a client is 10%. If you work on behalf of the club it can be more but compared to a Premier League player's salary it's tiny."

'Silk' as he's known, graced the football pitch with a stylish and visionary approach for three different clubs at the top level, Crystal Palace, Manchester City and Queens Park Rangers. The way he comes across convinces me that he, like a number of referees, is involved in the professional game for the right reasons.

He goes on, "I never hear the same said about estate agents or financial advisors or any other form of agent, only football agents. People read what an agent has got in a deal and believe everyone gets it. A vast majority of agents are only part time and have other jobs. What's incredible is that your contract with a player only allows you to 5%, but in acting, music and all other forms of entertainment it's 20% percent. But I don't hear the media scream 'look at Tom Cruise's agent. He's just earned six million dollars; he's bleeding the film industry dry! It's a joke. Also, all salaries paid by football clubs stay in football. The media needs to stop what they say."

Barry Silkman speaks with an enlightment and passion which mirrored the way he played the game in a career that spanned sixteen years. So how did he become an agent?

"It was more luck than judgement," he admits. Apparently, one of his ex-team-mates asked him if he could get a Cambridge United player called Alan Kimble a move away as Barry knew so many people in football. He convinced Wimbledon to sign him, and after that his late wife Ally drove him mad by insisting that he should become an agent.

This was in the nineties and by 2013, he was in the top ten most influential agents on Planet Football whose clients included World Cup winners Roberto Carlos of Brazil and David Villa of Spain. Sometimes, he has too many names on his books and other times not enough, but none of them are managers or coaches. He's adamant when I ask when we'll see the first million pound a week footballer in this country. "Won't happen", is his blunt reply.

What qualifications does an agent need? After all, they're dealing with contracts and analysing finances. 'Silk' did actually study contractual law but it's not needed in an agent's make up as every footballer's contract is identical as a result of the Football Association's standard issue. It's only the financial detail that differs from player to player.

He still enjoys the game and has even dipped his toe into non-league management waters but was forced to stand down as it could have created a conflict of interest given his role of agent. The greatest satisfaction in his job is watching one of his clients do really well at a club where he's convinced them to sign him.

As a player himself, it was the brash but brilliant Malcolm Allison who signed him for a few clubs and the midfield maestro describes him as: "the second-best coach I worked with, but he was a very complex person." Shades of Graham Taylor and Roy Hodgson methinks. So, who was the best coach then? "Terry Venables (Allison's apprentice) by a long way. I told him that as well."

Barry then ends our chat with a true story about the charismatic England manager who was within a whisker of taking the national team to glory in Euro '96. "When Terry had his first manager's job at Crystal Palace (1976) I was his first signing. His next job was Queens Park Rangers (1980) and again I was his first signing. His next job (1984) was the massive Barcelona … didn't hear from him!"

Then Silk gives me a bit of advice about writing this book, "make sure any literary agent doesn't charge you more than 5%"

Amen to that.

Chapter Fourteen

BLACK DOG AND A BLUE MOON

'I have a black dog and its name is Depression.'

So starts an educational film made by the World Health Organisation on mental health issues. Through work, I volunteered to attend a first aid course aimed at not only to fully understand my psychological state and how to deal with another relapse, but how to help others going through the same illness; and there are a lot of people going through it; many more than we would be led to believe.

The video itself is only four minutes long but goes into some detail and so did the course after which I left with a standard first aid certificate but with a willingness to help others. For the first time in my life, I understood why retired footballers stayed in the game stating that they 'wanted to give something back to the game.' I never got that statement in the past. I mean, why should they give something back? They've worked hard, dedicated themselves to the job (often with no reward), been injured, and those talented enough to play at the top of the pyramid have been exposed to abuse, ridicule and slander. But now I understand why they stay in football. It's their passion! Just as an agent such as Barry Silkman finds it rewarding when one of his clients makes the grade, so I would be happy about making a difference in someone's life.

There are ten steps to living happy and one of them is doing things for others. I've always had pleasure in giving so that's one box already ticked. Out of the other nine I've also conquered most of them including exercising, being self-aware, accepting and being comfortable with my illness, setting myself targets, trying new things and most importantly, developing a resilience which is key to survival, and when you survive, the meaning of life gets bigger. This explains why people who have suffered from depression can have incredible highs and be the life and soul of the party whilst also disappearing for long periods as they endure sadness more than others. The trick is embracing this anxiety and beating it.

Apparently suicide is illegal. Try telling that to a corpse! But for me the crime isn't taking your own life, it's missing out on life. As I got older, the black dog got bigger and bit harder until I learned how to control it. It now lives outside of my home and jumps to my every command. Through regular exercise and challenging myself on ventures such as travelling on a Cup journey and writing a book about it, I keep focussed and I keep living. My mental and physical state has never been stronger. But the black dog is still outside my contented sanctuary waiting for that opportunity to bite the hand that refuses to feed him. If it ever happened again, I know exactly how to protect myself.

Everyone goes through sad times and when I see someone going through those periods it can get to me, but I'm always thinking that they're going to get through it. They may be at a low ebb but they're not in a state of depression. Once you're experienced through having had your own illness, you can see it in others. One customer in work went through depression a couple of years ago and took medication to combat it but to no avail. I encouraged him to get fitter and to set himself a mental target. Eventually he visited the gym most mornings before going to work. He took it one day at a time and started to feel better physically. He'd look in the mirror, see a difference and start to feel good about himself. The low esteem disappeared and his confidence flooded back. When I saw he was in a relationship with a lovely woman I felt delighted for him. He can't keep the smile off his face these days.

My heart though went out to Vinnie Jones when I saw him interviewed on a news programme a few months after losing his wife at too young an age. To see a big hard man like that in tears and admit his mental weakness which he'd carried for years was as surprising as it was tragic. Luckily Vinnie sought professional help and even though his sadness never left him, he was on the road to recovery. He couldn't praise the medical team enough and mentioned that with their support he could now look after himself and became disciplined into doing the small things that he never used to; making the bed for example. A daily routine that made him face the day and reminded him not to go back to bed until nightfall; a small job which someone in the services had recommended he do.

My own disciplines as well as exercising were keeping a daily record of my finances, keeping the place tidy, keeping my own company and sticking to my writing targets as best as I could. And when this book is written, then I'll think of something else. And when you can think this way, life is so much better.

And back to the book. There's a Cup final to look forward to and a final chapter to write. I'm lucky as well that I don't have the worry of getting a ticket as that part has been done for me. I just have to pay on the day but even still, £115 to watch a football match is a helluva lot to ask the normal working-class person to pay. And that's one of the cheapest for a big Wembley game! Watford and Manchester City fans are being made to pay up to £145 for theirs, and those wishing to return north that evening may not be able to due to the late final whistle therefore forcing them to stay in the capital overnight. For following their teams all the way to the FA Cup final, it seems loyal supporters are being punished financially. Here's an idea, Manchester City have billions so why not pay for their season ticket holder's tickets. A fitting gesture for the support they've given their obscenely paid team this season.

Magic Mike picks me up in the morning for the two-hundred-mile trek to the Venue Of Legends. We're armed with a tank full of fuel, two bottles of water and various CD's chosen by yours truly which includes '101 Indie Classics'. Feeling nostalgic for the first time we made a road trip together in the summer of 1985, the first sounds I put in his stereo are the greatest hits of Squeeze, the soundtrack of speeding through southern England when we drove his brother Graham up to Romsey in

Hampshire in a mark III Ford Cortina. One of the best songs on there is 'This Summer' but as the opening bars kick in, it starts to rain. As we pull in two hours later for the obligatory coffee there's an appropriate and poignant scene in the service's car park. Beautiful poppies, so beautiful that Mike feels compelled to take a picture. Why appropriate? Because just as we drive by them the Indie album is belting out 'All Together Now' by The Farm, a song adopted by England football fans which tells the story of a senseless sacrifice made by First World War generals when sending the foot soldiers out of the trenches and inevitable slaughter. Tales of tragedy only interrupted briefly by an impromptu football match between the British and the Germans on Christmas Day.

'All together now, all together now, all together now …
in no man's land, together!'

I swear Costa Coffee are taking over Planet Earth! They have shops everywhere and virtually in every services on the motorway. As we sip a hot skinny latte, Mike tells me a true story about his experience in one of their outlets somewhere in Plymouth. A story I liked so much I asked him to put it in words for me. And here it is …

'COSTA' by MAGIC MIKE

'As you drift through life you realise change is bad, and comfort lies in routine. So, one Saturday morning as with all Saturday mornings, I found myself in the queue at the COSTA, adjacent to the local retail park. As I stood there eagerly anticipating the caffeine fix I was about to have, I casually gazed out of the window and watched a large BMW pull up outside with four men sat inside it. Two of the men got out and as soon as I saw their uniforms, I realised that all four were policemen, travelling in an unmarked car. The two police officers took up their position next to me at the end of the queue, and I couldn't help but notice the technology and equipment that adorned their bodies. Both were wearing baseball cap type helmets with a video camera on top, independent headphones in each ear and a microphone over which I'm certain were bullet proof vests. This was just the start however. Each had handcuffs, a truncheon, a tazer, pepper spray and a hand gun carefully stowed in a black leather holster. Various pouches on their uniforms bulged with other stuff I couldn't see, but I felt sure it would have been equally devastating and important. as we waited, I struck up a conversation.

- "Do you have to sign that lot back in at the end of each shift? It must take ages!"

The policeman laughed replying,

- "No, only the weapons. The rest we take home each day, thankfully."

The dialogue continued and they explained that they were all part of an armed response unit that had (quite worryingly) already dealt with one incident that morning even though it was only half past nine! We talked some more on topics ranging from from drug dealers to illegal immigrants, to boy racers, to funding cuts and more.

I started to ask a question about the car they were driving when all of a sudden one officer put his arm across me gesturing to me to stop talking. With his other hand he carefully positioned a finger on one of his ear pieces, gently pushing it to make sure he could hear. I stood there in awe, imagining he was getting instruction on their next operation, probably to sweep some low-life scumbag off the streets. He stared right through me concentrating intensely on the voice in his ear. His voice dropped as he muttered a number of `yeah' and `OK' responses.

His eyes briefly made contact with mine and he blinked sheepishly as his chin dropped closer to his chest. After a brief pause he breathed into his microphone ...

- "Do you want marshmallows with that?"

THE END

Clint Eastwood is my favourite actor, and probably best known for playing vigilante San Francisco cop 'Dirty' Harry Callahan. This character struck a chord with cinema audiences so much that the film spawned four sequels. The first of these was 'Magnum Force' of which I saw the trailer when my mum took myself and a mate to watch Roger Moore's first James Bond adventure 'Live And Let Die'. Just a kid at the time, I'd never even heard of Clint Eastwood but the image of him spreadeagled over a runaway car's bonnet and shooting the bad guys stuck with me. My mum explained that I was too young to watch it when released as it carried an 'X' certificate.

I've watched that film a million times on TV and virtually know the script from beginning to end but there's one scene and in particular one line that runs through my head from time to time. In an underground garage, three vigilante motorcycle cops confront our Clint as he gets out of his car. They've been executing the bad guys themselves and Dirty Harry at one point asks them … "Is that what you're all about? Being heroes?" The reply has stuck with me …

"All our heroes are dead."

And I'm now at the age when my childhood heroes are passing away one by one. The latest is Freddie Starr, the 'Gazza' of comedy. Just like Gazza, Freddie was a tortured genius. Unpredictable, often outrageous but ultimately someone who made you laugh so much, that you remember them with fondness. There were highs and lows in his personal life and like anyone of us who have carried demons, his main joy was to make others happy. Like a judge in a Magistrates Court for example after Freddie was caught speeding and pleaded guilty. Being the comedian he was, the scene was re-enacted in front of the courtroom which left everyone in fits of laughter including the judge. He just wanted to be loved and in order to feel that love, he felt the need to make even total strangers laugh. This form of self-preservation kept the Black Dog away.

There's a story about a member of the public who had an encounter with Freddie Starr. which I don't know whether is true
or not. I really hope it is, even though it shows how lonely a life
he lived at the time. It took place early one freezing morning
somewhere out in the country. A motorist was driving to work
negotiating slippery lanes when he saw a man stood in the distance
waving his arms about in an attempt to flag the motorist down.
The driver wound the window down and to his astonishment
saw that it was Freddie Starr. He looked hurried and exasperated.

"Can you give me a push?" he asked.

The driver asked him. "Are you Freddie Starr?"

"Yes I am. Look, I'm sorry to be blunt but I really need a push!"

With that, the motorist quickly got out and followed Freddie
around the side of his house and strangely past a parked car. He
carried on until he stood in his back garden where he saw Freddie
sat on a swing.

The County Rep

*"The people in the cheaper seats clap your hands.
And the rest of you just rattle your jewellery."*
JOHN LENNON

The man who sits in the 'jewellery' seats at Wembley Stadium is
the same man that Magic Mike and I buy our tickets from. Tom
Sampson is the Rep for the Devon County Football Association
(DCFA) which was founded in Plymouth way back in 1888 and
therefore gets to sit in one of the best seats in the house. We're
just happy to sit in the expensive cheaper seats and clap along.

I arrange to meet Tom in Costa Coffee (where else?) on an industrial estate near my place of work. Trouble is, there's so many
Costa shops on this estate that we both end up in separate ones
thinking that the other isn't going to turn up. Eventually Tom

rings and realises which one I'm in. Now in his late 60's, to say he's old school is an understatement. Retired from working in Devonport Royal Dockyard, the largest naval base in Europe and once upon a time the heartbeat in the city of Plymouth, he now has 'pensioners rights', which basically means he can say what he bloody well wants to. A Leeds United fan, he also has one helluva sense of humour, depending on whether you're easily offended in this age of the 'snowflake'. We're soul mates in the making as he loves music as much as football, and in his spare time plays guitar in a duet named 'Highway Revisited' after a Bob Dylan album, a songwriter who'd influenced John Lennon.

In the 1970's Tom played football at a senior level for local side City Engineers before taking up refereeing in the East Cornwall League (possibly a case of poacher turned gamekeeper) and therefore has a balanced view of the game having performed on both sides of the law; similar to Sean Rothwell in chapter three. Small world as it is, he coached Sean through his refereeing course. Back in the sixties, he tells me, hundreds of spectators would watch amateur games in and around the city. But what is his role inside the DCFA and as county representative for Devon?

Based in Newton Abbot these days, the DCFA covers all aspects of the game encompassing north, south, east and west Devon and is responsible for the administration of all affiliated football clubs as well as promoting development amongst referees. If you looked at the 1992-93 DCFA handbook which lists all registered Devon clubs in alphabetical order, you would see the team I founded 'Pilgrim Sportswear' and my name as manager just above Plymouth Argyle, then managed by the most capped player for England, Peter Shilton. Not exactly my fifteen minutes of fame, but fifteen centimetres of indulgence.

The DCFA also oversees approximately fifteen per cent of all adult teams in England, but numbers are diminishing due to the growth of youth football, ironically encouraged and promoted by the same organisation. Tom agrees with the theory that the reason for this is that dads now give up their spare time at weekends to watch their kids instead of playing themselves but says there remains a commitment to see a resurgence in the adult game. "Sunday football is dying," he says, "in fact it's already dead in the north and south of the county. The east has just one division left; the west has two." Historically, east and west Devon have dominated the countywide Cup competitions largely down to the population and size of the two main cities, Exeter and Plymouth (people from Exeter will always say that their home city is the capital of Devon, but they're wrong! The capital of Devon is the letter 'D').

Another reason for such a huge loss in the number of amateur teams is lack of sponsorship; no surprise when you consider that the majority of teams were funded by pubs which are closing down at a rapid rate. And in the Sunday game, beer and football go hand in hand.

What is Tom's role inside the actual national FA? Regularly he'll travel to Wembley Stadium as he's part of the 'Adult Participation and Development' committee and has been since 2013. This focus includes walking football, pioneered by Chesterfield director John Croot who I interviewed in chapter eight. The committee has jurisdiction within our national game, starting at the bottom of the pyramid all the way up to level four where the professional game starts.

He also plays a part in a referee's committee which meets up four times a year, a set up where no club official is allowed as it may be construed as a conflict of interests. Part of their agenda is nominating seven referees from England to take control of matches all around the globe and one of those may be lucky enough to be selected to officiate at a World Cup tournament.

Every March possible law changes in the game are discussed which leaves enough time for them to be implemented for the following season. The day any particular law becomes set in stone is always June 1st as this allows all clubs the time to prepare for pre-season training in July. The changes affect the whole of world football and are always passed in this country for two reasons. Firstly, England have good representation on the committee and secondly, we invented the game by giving it the original rules.

As Tom used to referee, I ask him about the newest change in the game called VAR and also about the grey area of 'Foul and Abusive Language'. How did he handle the latter? What would he do if one of his assistants was verbally abused? "There is a tolerance level for assistants," he answers, "they don't normally wave their flag for such incidents but if they do, you just go over for a chat before deciding whether to take further action." It's all down to that unwritten law of the game called man-management. "By nature, players don't like referees, so a little bit of humour should come into it. If a player misses an easy chance to score I would tell them that my missus could have scored that one!"

So, what about VAR then? Apparently this present complicated and confusing set up was devised by ex-referee David Ellery (mentioned in chapter three), as he is president of the technical committee; a system that as far as I can see just puts the referee under a more pressurised scrutiny because he's being judged by three other officials, all armed with TV monitors, miles away from the ground where the decision's being made. The offside law for example is a contentious one. Is a player offside simply because their chest is sticking out over a graphic white line on a TV replay? (Obviously the chest is more prominent in women's football). Tom believes that if it's a borderline case, then the attacking team should get the benefit of the doubt in the name of entertainment. That is actually a FIFA directive but hasn't been communicated well from the rulers of world football, which brings us on to FIFA President Gianni Infantino who was amazed on a recent visit to England when told that match referees weren't using the TV monitors at the side of the pitch, in order to either uphold or overturn an appeal. Why have we made a simple idea so complicated? Over to you Mr Ellery and your technical committee.

Going back to the offside law, Tom tells me that back in the day, it was black and white. Tottenham legend and Northern Ireland captain Danny Blanchflower who was a very intelligent and successful player simply said, "if you're on the pitch you're offside," referring to the questions that pop up every time an offside decision is debated … 'was that player active?'… 'was that player interfering with play?'… 'was that player seeking to gain an advantage from an offside position?'…

"The offside law is the most contentious one as it's basically based on opinion," Tom states.

There is unrest presently in the Premier League regarding VAR, primarily as it's not actually a law stated in the rule book. It was voted in by club officials which means it could just as easily get voted out. When it was introduced at the top of the pyramid, it was believed that a big problem in the game had been solved but instead has been proved divisive.

Tom is genuinely concerned about the welfare of football clubs, claiming that so many are on the brink financially, and points the finger at the English Football League (levels two to four) who he believes are acting against their own rules and have failed to safeguard clubs in financial difficulty. The clubs often sell their grounds in an attempt to sidestep the 'Financial Fair Play Regulations' which was brought in to prevent clubs spending more than they earn, meaning that they can go out and buy success. These clubs are unsustainable and now more now than ever before, are receiving winding up orders from the HMRC over outstanding tax bills and various creditors. What if something unprecedented happened to our national game which saw all matches suspended and in turn meant that football clubs didn't receive any revenue? For example, a pandemic.

1972 WINNERS – LEEDS UNITED

"Clarke… ONE-NIL!"

The only goal of the game punctuated in his own inimitable way by BBC TV Cup final commentator David Coleman. No one else could describe a big goal like him and it remains Tom Sampson's favourite memory as a Leeds fan. He also recalls this winning goal against Arsenal, as it was set up by Allan Clarke's strike partner Mick Jones who Tom claims "wore his boots up to his ankles."

"Every player was hard," he adds, but I already knew that. Everyone who remembers the Leeds side in that era will either smile or wince, all depending on whether you were a fan or not. Nobody liked playing against them.

Tom also admits a fondness for Liverpool as a young lad but pledged his allegiance to the Yorkshire Peacocks after seeing them play at Plymouth Argyle in the early 1960's and after a few years changed their traditional blue and gold strip to all-white, as a tribute to the great Real Madrid.

The goalscorer on the day, Allan Clarke, was a hard player like all of his team-mates but unlike some of them he didn't possess a nasty streak on the pitch. He has always been verbally forthright however; and reckons he scored the most important Cup final goal in history, as this was the only goal in the centenary final. The very first was in 1872 which saw a team called Wanderers beat the Royal Engineers by the same scoreline. That final took place at the Oval cricket ground in Surrey on a Saturday morning, enabling the players to watch the University Boat Race in the afternoon. One hundred years later, the FA Cup final had reached such heights and was held in such high esteem worldwide, that anyone connected to Leeds and Arsenal either physically or emotionally, had reached fever pitch.

It may have been a landmark final but unless you wanted Leeds to win, it wasn't a memorable one. In fact, those a few years older than I remember only two things from it. The goal itself and Mick Jones dislocating his shoulder in the last minute and receiving a winners medal with his arm in a sling.

Two years later, Leeds lost their revered manager Don Revie to the England job and the country then witnessed a bizarre forty-four days when a young Brian Clough took over the reins; but his abrasive and critical style of management rubbed proven internationals up the wrong way, and his slating of the team in previous years could never be forgotten or forgiven. Admirably, it was Allan Clarke who approached the board of directors and pleaded with them to back "the best in the business" but to no avail. After just six weeks in charge of the current League champions, Clough was dismissed and English domestic football had to wait for it's new king to come of age.

Jimmy Armfield was then appointed manager sailing the ship into calmer waters and then steering it towards the 1975 European Cup final in Paris to face the holders and West German champions Bayern Munich. If Danny Blanchflower or Tom Sampson had been referee then Leeds wouldn't have won that final anyway, as a contentious offside decision went against them when Peter Lorimer's 'goal' was disallowed. Add to that a blatant penalty kick which wasn't awarded when Kaiser Franz Beckenbauer tripped Allan Clarke and the fuse was lit on the terraces. Leeds supporters rioted after a two-goal defeat and were promptly banned from European competition for five years by UEFA, the European governing body. It took a few seasons but the once mighty Leeds were then relegated from the top level, simply because a team that weren't allowed to compete in Europe couldn't attract the top players to sign for them, and their brilliant team retired one by one. Then salt was rubbed into their wounds as Brian Clough took over at Nottingham Forest and instead led them to European glory in 1979 & 1980. 'What if …' is a huge phrase in football.

Forty-seven years after Leeds won their only FA Cup at the 'old' Wembley, Magic Mike and myself I are walking up to the 'new' stadium. It's overcast as it always is when I walk up the famous Wembley Way but the whole place is given colour by the hordes of Watford fans surrounding us. It's a good atmosphere as Bobby Moore's statue looks down approvingly at both yellow and sky-blue mingling near Wembley Park Tube Station.

The match programme costs a tenner and encourages us to become tenors as the words to Cup final hymn 'Abide With Me' are printed within. It's the one tradition this special day has kept since Wembley Stadium was erected almost a century ago. Sadly, other traditions have fallen by the wayside in recent years which are lamented by the two of us. So, what would we bring back if we ran the FA? What if we picked up the famous trophy, rubbed it and out popped the FA Cup genie granting us three wishes each?

There is a train of thought from a few football fans: for example that the FA Cup winners should be allowed to enter the following season's European Champions League, thus giving Premiership managers an incentive to field their strongest teams.

Magic Mike's three wishes:
No other games to be played on Cup final weekend making this a special 'stand-alone' fixture; a Royal Marine band to perform at half time; Prince William to present the Cup at the end of the game (he is the president of the FA after all!).

Kindon's three wishes:
Revert back to a 3pm kick off on both BBC and ITV with a day-long build up to it, (not this daft 5.30 start as dictated by TV as part of their 'Saturday night entertainment'); no more semi-finals or even League play-offs to be played here to make the Cup final more special; entrance onto the pitch should be from behind one of the goals and not near the halfway line, so that this unique walk can be savoured by both players and supporters (they managed to change the tunnel entrance at Old Trafford).

Then we think of just one more each. I want cheaper beer inside the stadium as I've just spent £6 on a pint of Budweiser, and Magic Mike reckons both teams should release a 'shit' Cup final song like they all did back in the day.

Whilst drinking my overpriced beer and reading my overpriced programme, a very strange feeling comes over me. It's as though I've travelled back in time and have ended up in a parallel universe. A sort of twist in a 'Planet Of The Apes' ending. I'm surrounded by Watford fans and a load of them are wearing retro 1984 shirts. Yellow with a red v-neck and cuffs and the sponsors name 'IVECO' emblazoned across the chest, just below a red hornet badge.

It seems like Cup Final Day in 1984, but I shouldn't be there. I should be back in Plymouth watching it with by my then best mate Phil Marshall, his older brother Steve and his dad Gerald. And just to amplify this strange feeling the match programme is full of 1984 Watford memories. Interviews with ex-players John Barnes, Steve Sherwood and several members of Graham Taylor's backroom staff. But the one that really jumps out of the pages at me stinging just as painfully is an article by chairman Elton John headlined in huge yellow and red graphics which simply screams '1984'. And in every single article the defeat of Plymouth Argyle in the semi-final at Villa Park is mentioned. Get me back to the future! Or at least the present.

Magic Mike and I find our seats in this awesome arena. We're behind one one of the goals in the middle tier with an amazing view and an even more amazing atmosphere. A wall of yellow and red noise is available in Sensurround and the sky-blue of Manchester City, sing their hearts out on the opposite side of the ground. Wonderful colour illuminates a grey day; the Wembley hallowed turf resembling the green baize of a snooker table. Stadium music then blasts away the tribal songs as we're 'treated' to a set by DJ Annie Mac from Radio One filling our eardrums instead of filling dance floors. The energy is tangible. The power of music and the promise of football combine and NOW it really starts to feel and look like a big game. Almost eighty-six thousand of us wait patiently for our Annie to finish spinning her 'wheels of steel' before paying tribute to Hollywood legend Doris Day. Flags on all four sides of the stadium flutter and wave.

'Que sera sera, whatever will be will be,
we're going to Wemb-er-ley, que sera sera ...'

The impromptu version of one of Doris' better-known musicals is then followed by the formal and official hymn of the day.

'Abide with me, fast falls the eventide,
the darkness deepens, Lord with me abide ...'

It's hard to sing when feeling emotional.

I'm almost at the end of a nine-month journey which has taken me over five and a half thousand miles. Saltash versus Odd Down at Kimberley Stadium last August, and now we're just ten minutes from Man City versus Watford at Wembley Stadium, the Mecca of football. So who's going to win the Cup then? Which team from the 736 who entered the oldest Cup competition in the world will be joyfully hoisting this famous trophy towards the imposing Triumphant Arch? My heart says Watford, my head says their deadly opponents.

Then I remember a conversation I had with my mum on the phone last night. She's deposited her usual weekly tenner into my account but it's the end of the League season so I rang to tell her there's no need to do so for a few months, but as the money is there already, I'll stick my tenner with it and our collective £20 is placed on an accumulator consisting of half a dozen Cup finals taking place around Europe in the next couple of weeks. For us to win about £500 each, first of all we need Watford to win the Cup.

"I couldn't resist the odds," I tell her, "Watford are 6/1 against lifting the Cup."

"Six to one?" she responds, "that's not going to happen!" I try to explain that 6/1 are brilliant odds considering this is a two-horse race. "Six to one?" she goes on, "that just won't happen!"

Hang on, who's supposed to be the football expert in the family, I'm thinking. "Why can't it happen? Shocks and surprises have happened in Cup finals before. It was only six years ago that Wigan beat Man City here. Why not Watford? They're no mugs are they?" I tell her.

She carries on though, "but six to one is a far-fetched scoreline!"

Ah! My mum thinks my bet includes predicting the result that Watford would win the game by six GOALS to one! No wonder she sounds confused. "No Mum," I explain, "the odds are six to one AGAINST Watford winning by any scoreline, not for them to win 6-1".

I mean, no one scores six goals in an FA Cup final do they?

FA CUP FINAL
SATURDAY 18TH MAY
WEMBLEY STADIUM
ATTENDANCE – 85854

MANCHESTER CITY 6 WATFORD 0

Well, what I meant was that no one has scored six goals in an FA Cup final since 1903! And never at Wembley. Yeah, that's what I meant. Think I might have slightly lost that little bet!

Every one of us in the stadium that day are about to witness a special team breaking and equalling all sorts of records. The first team to hit six Cup final goals in over a century, and the first English club side to win all three major domestic competitions in one season. The League title, The FA Cup, and The League Cup. Watford are swept aside by a majestic masterclass as the absolute brilliance that fill sky-blue shirts engineered by Pep Guardiola who once again has proved his doubters wrong, of which I was one. Okay, he did it at Barcelona where he learnt his trade as both player and coach. Then he did it at Bayern Munich when his arrival at the German champions brought the cynicism out of us as we claimed that his style of football wouldn't work in the more physical climate of the 'Bundesliga'.

But now he's done it in England! A domestic game renowned not only for it's physicality, but also it's energy and high-speed tempo. No way could he make the same impact playing HIS type of football. A game based on patient possession of the ball. Pass … pass … pass … pass …pass …, allied with the minimum of movement. Never before has the mantra of 'let the ball do the work' been more proven. Opposing players fly in at speed from all angles but they look hopeless against a team accomplished in caressing the tool of their trade, keeping it on the green carpet, trusting each other with it, like matadors enticing bulls, tormenting them, demoralising them before killing off the shattered beasts. Today the Wembley pitch is a bullring and the chief matador is a likeable Spaniard, absolutely brimming with self-belief.

The encouraging thing about this technical and intelligent side of the game is that Guardiola believes in English talent. He recruits them or nurtures them from his youth team. He coaches them and improves them to such an extent that England's manager has no choice but to select them. I hear that Gareth Southgate and Pep are good friends and frequently talk to each other. When you consider this, then at long last there may be grounds for optimism regarding our national side.

It's cruel for Watford though. By the end of the game, they are resembling yellow and black striped traffic cones as City's pace, imagination and ruthlessness in front of goal turns this game of football into a glorified game of 'piggy in the middle'. Months after this, Tom Sampson would say to me that from his viewpoint up in the 'jewellery' seating Pep Guardiola looked uncomfortable and embarrassed for Watford, even suggesting that Man City should have taken it easier on them. But putting myself in Watford's shoes (or boots) I think THAT would be embarrassing and an insult for any professional footballer on the receiving end. At least Watford reached the final and can say they were beaten by one of the best sides the country has ever seen, or Europe for that matter.

At the beginning of this game though a massacre didn't look on the cards given the feeling of the brilliant support in our half of the stadium. About half a dozen seats to my right is an absolute tosser who's either drunk or drugged up to the eyeballs or even both. He's sweating profusely and screaming at us all to sing, sing and keep singing. His wild-eyed mug appears on terrestrial TV and the big stadium screens as he screams out the national anthem. He carries on like a demented madman for the first ten minutes of the game before being given two choices by Watford fans around him. Either leave on your own two feet or on a stretcher. He's just sober enough to choose the former and starts to behave like a human being.

If Roberto Pereyra had scored for Watford in the first few minutes, would that have changed the outcome of this game or would it have woken a sleeping giant and just delay the inevitable? We'll never know. Put in possession by the brilliant Gerard Deulofeu, the Argentine has a golden chance but is thwarted by goalkeeper Ederson. Manager Javi Gracia screams in anguish as if he knows this may be the best chance his team have of taking the lead. Minutes later the Watford players are screaming for a penalty but referee Kevin Friend correctly waves away their claims. It's not handball according to the rules of the game when the ball strikes an arm which is held tightly into the chest. Players kitted out in yellow and black are adamant but for me this smacks of desperation. Is the writing on the wall even at this early stage?

The first goal of this year's Cup final is scored in the twenty-sixth minute when Spanish magician David Silva gets a second bite of the Hornet's cherry. Goalkeeper Gomez playing his last game has no chance as the left foot strike is hit into the ground from close range and finds the net via a deflection from defender Kiko Ferrera's boot when he throws himself in front of the goalscorer.

Manchester City already have too much time and space and nonchalantly pass the ball between them which is second nature for a Guardiola side. Another Silva, Bernardo, sets up the second goal in the thirty-eighth minute when he finds striker Gabriel Jesus who taps the ball into the net from an acute angle. How will the papers describe that goal tomorrow? Jesus getting onto the end of a cross and nailing it?

Half time arrives and its 2-0. The majority of us go for a burger or a beer, and the majority watching at home get to see a celebrity such as actor Ray Winstone advertise reckless gambling ...

'What will be the correct score?'... 'Who will score the next goal?'... 'How many corner kicks will be given?'... 'How many bookings for players?'... 'Penalty kick'... 'Sending off?'... 'Winning margin?'... 'Total goals?...'

'How cool is that?' Ray asks us. Then a small sentence pops up at the end of the advert without any narration …

'Please bet responsibly.'

Manchester City have made a substitution at the break. Brilliant (they're all brilliant in this team) Belgian Kevin De Bruyne is now on the pitch and amazingly will win the Man Of The Match award for only taking part in half the game. Watford defenders to a man are probably thinking. 'I don't believe it! We're already knackered and now we've got to stop this world class genius!!!'

A moment of irony happens at the start of this half. Gomez makes a save from Jesus. I thought it was Jesus who saved!

In the sixty-first minute, it's 3-0. Jesus is walking on Wembley water and sets up De Bruyne who teases a few Watford players and scores with his eyes shut. Manchester City fans show their unusual way of celebrating a goal by turning their backs on the action whilst bouncing up and down with arms around each other's shoulders. Mind you, Manchester United fans will tell you that the sky-blue half of the city always turned their backs on their team between 1976 and 2011 in those silverless wilderness years. But these days the 'noisy neighbours' as Sir Alex Ferguson once called them are now the dominant force in the city of Manchester. I don't know how many loaves and fishes it takes, but players such as Jesus are feeding literally thousands of them. Turning water into wine, and the Manchester City faithful who were starved of success in those barren years are loving every delicious sip.

Sixty-eight minutes pass and it's 4-0. Christ…Jesus scores again!

In the last ten minutes, a further two goals are scored but they're merely of statistical interest as the football match was virtually decided at half-time. A singing contest is now taking place. Watford fans are fantastic and lay down the gauntlet. The yellow half of the stadium sing their hearts out in defiance of a shattering scoreline and the sky-blue and white half respond with their anthem …

'Blue Moon, you saw me standing alone, without a dream in my heart, without a love of my own ...'

No doubt this song was adopted in those 'lost' years as the red side of Manchester swept away all before them. A sorrowful song which then turns to true love ...

'And then there suddenly appeared before me, the only one my arms will ever hold. I heard somebody whisper, "Please adore me", and when I looked, the moon had turned to gold ...'

Or in this case, their blue moon has turned to silver.

Meanwhile on the pitch, Bernardo Silva (no relation to David) sets up Raheem Sterling and it's 5-0. There's no emotion on Pep Guardiola's face, he's been expecting this performance. History is then equalled when Sterling scores the sixth, finishing off a millionth passing sequence seen today involving Bernardo Silva and Kevin De Bruyne. John Stones almost gets a seventh which would have broken a goalscoring record but Gomez finishes his colourful career saving well and keeping the headlines down to 'Six Of The Best'.

So, Manchester City raise the FA Cup and with it the standard of football itself. A wonderful creative team. Beautiful football played by brilliant footballers. Physical when the situation demands, but poetry in motion, as demanded by the purists. There is however an indignant twist as the Cup is lifted. The FA Cup competition is currently sponsored by Emirates Airlines of the United Arab Emirates, the largest airline in the middle east. Manchester City are sponsored by Etihad, the second biggest. It was only noticed at the time but when the Manchester City players held the Emirates FA Cup up high beneath the Triumphant Arch, the front of their shirts had been changed to 'choose Etihad'. Those hilarious mischievous Sheiks!

The skies are still grey as Magic Mike and I depart the stadium and walk down Wembley Way. He's driving back to Plymouth tonight due to a commitment of running the Plymouth half-marathon with his son Paul and so heads back toward Wembley High Road. I head towards Wembley Park Tube Station surrounded by sad Hertfordshire Hornets and very happy Manchester Citizens. There's a bit of bother at the entrance of the station but it is quickly quelled by the police, Her Majesty's finest. It takes over an hour to board a train heading for Watford as thousands of us are funnelled through various staircases. Nobody's talking to each other. In fact they can't even look at each other.

I follow the hordes as we disembark at Watford Station and head towards the town centre. The streets are pretty and quiet, apart from the slow plodding of despondent feet. Still, no one talks. There's hardly any traffic on this funeral procession, just yellow football shirts flanked by a stream of green trees in this leafy suburb. The houses are big and worth a few million each. It's a million miles from inner London. Everything around here is well kept and tidy. It even smells cleaner. The climate is also different from London and is now a pleasant evening but that isn't noticed or appreciated by Watford fans walking with heads sadly bowed. And that's lucky for them, because if those heads lifted and looked up at the sky directly in front of them, they would be staring at a cruel reminder of what they've had to endure today.

It's not so much a blue moon but get this! Although still light, the moon is visible in all it's glory. And it's silver! Shining down on Watford folk symbolising the FA Cup itself. A silver gleaming football against a sky-blue background. It's the most amazing sight I've seen on this adventure and comes virtually at the end of my journey. Poignant for me but so bloody cruel for those around me. As cruel as a 6-0 final scoreline. Is this the FA Cup trying to give me closure on the Watford game in '84?

The town centre is absolutely buzzing with human hornets. Yellow and red bunting lining a pedestrianised busy pub scene. The police are out in force but they're in for a quiet shift even though the place is crawling with hundreds of disappointed football fans filling bars and beer gardens. The Saturday night scene here in Watford could be described as a game of two halves. The first half bellows out club tunes for the younger clientele, and the second half which is a ten-minute interval away is designed for my generation belting out rock, indie, 80's hits and classic rock 'n' roll tracks from jukeboxes. I resist the temptation to put on Blue Moon.

In a crowded bar I spot a few blokes (not 'geezers' as I'm not in London) wearing the unmistakeable 1984 retro shirts. They look about my age, so I approach them and speak to one. He's four years younger than me but I think the last few hours have aged him. Yes, he says looking down at his iconic top, he remembers Villa Park that year and also attended the final at Wembley against Everton. I ask him how he would compare that day to this one. His answer is philosophical. They may have only lost by two goals to Everton back then, but this Manchester City side are 'special'.

"I was only fourteen years old at the 1984 final," he tells me, "and therefore sober. The old Wembley was a shithole! The seats were horrible and there were pillars in the way."

And that's a stark difference between then and now; the difference being that the stadium being owned by the local (Brent) council back then is now owned by the Football Association these days, even though there's been talk of a possible sell. I guess our fondest memories of Cup Final Day are watching it at home, but nowadays it's the opposite. The memories since 2007 are carried only by those who have been in the actual place.

I've had an enjoyable night out in Watford. Hundreds of friendly people, different music in different pubs, no sign of trouble and easy enough to get back to my hotel which is situated a mile from Wembley. Through my window I can see the stadium's dominant Triumphant Arch now lit up in sky blue, paying tribute to the team which has just triumphed beneath it. Most of London can see it. Driving me from the tube station to the hotel is a taxi driver of Asian persuasion who claims to be a Manchester City fan. His cockney accent leads me to believe he probably started 'supporting' them a few hours ago when the full-time whistle was blown.

I'm having a restless night in my room thanks to some idiot banging on my door. There's no peephole in this kennel so I'm reluctant to open it. It happens again and this time I tentatively open it but there's no one there. I wait for the third time and they don't disappoint. As soon as it happens I leap from the foot of the bed and fling the door open just as I hear a bloke shout "Oh shit!" and the door next to mine slams shut. I put my ear to the door and can hear two voices. After a few seconds I decide to reason calmly with them.

Both my fists smash into the door as I scream, "FUCKING GROW UP YOU FUCKING TWATS!!!" They don't come back a fourth time.

Next morning and an English full breakfast is part of the package. The small hotel adjoins a bigger cafe and the place is full of police officers tucking into their fry-ups. I ask two of them on the table next to mine if there's been any trouble. "No", one of them replies, "we usually meet here on a Sunday morning. In fact this place is so popular with us, a few of us stay over on a Saturday night. At our own expense of course." I ask them if any of these fine law-abiding officers were staying in one of the two rooms on the top floor last night. The pair of them just look at each other and say nothing. Guilty as charged! Her Majesty's bloody finest.

Rucksack and coat on, I google the nearest tube station and within thirty minutes of checking out I'm at Paddington Station. I'll be back in Plymouth by early afternoon so the rest of the day is mine. Strangely, even though I've enjoyed the last nine months I feel as if a huge weight has been lifted from my shoulders. Mission accomplished! So, I celebrate on the train with a few glasses of prosecco, the nearest thing they've got to champagne. It's a good feeling as I reflect on where I've been and more importantly, the people I've met. When I reach Plymouth Train Station, one helluva pub crawl will be waiting for this first-time author.

As well as reflecting about this quest I'm also pondering the future of English football. Basically, my conclusion is that despite the obscene money overloading the top of the silver pyramid, despite the neglect of the oldest footballing competition in the world and despite our national team only winning one tournament in its history, the future actually does look bright. It's just that the the game itself needs tweaking in regards to the odd rule clarification, a fairer financial structure for both supporters and lower levels of the pyramid, and giving the big occasions the respect they deserve.

This season has seen the highest total attendances in League football since 1959 which is remarkable when you consider that in this digital age, all teams at levels three and four of the pyramid often play games on the same midweek evenings as the glamorous European Champions League on TV, which boasts the best players on the planet. These supporters are the salt of the earth. Venturing out in all weathers watching a lower standard of football whilst spending a chunk of their income and often returning home disappointed at what they've just witnessed; but they follow their hearts.

At international level, as recently as 2017, England were crowned world champions in the only two age groups available to enter, the under-17's and the under-20's; the first time this has happened in our national game. There's a conveyor belt of young talent coming through, thanks to the FA's investment in the St George's Park National Football Centre that opened in 2012 at Burton upon Trent. The development of coaches and players is coming to fruition and the current manager of the England senior team, Gareth Southgate, has an embarrassment of riches from whom to select allied to his ethos which states that every kid in youth football must be technically accomplished in possession of the ball.

We have the best structure in the world. It's called a pyramid, but as I've mentioned it's top heavy with money. The top of the pyramid has to look after the bottom because putting it simply, you can't have a top without a bottom. The game is generally healthy but teams and the individuals in those teams, need to be safeguarded. Steps are being put in place for this to be the case.

I truly believe in a world order and in football we all live under the same big umbrella. It doesn't matter if you play in the World Cup final, an FA Cup final or a Sunday League match at your local park. The rules are the same. The game isn't fragmented. There is always one definitive world champion, currently it's France. FIFA, who run the world game, have been found unofficially corrupt in the past but have now cleaned their act up and have dealt with the offenders; another reason to be optimistic.

Well that's the end of my story, and if you've enjoyed it just half as much as I have, then that means I've enjoyed it twice as much as you. So, what do I do next? I'll think of something. Another footballing adventure perhaps? Or maybe a road trip in the United States? How about Route 66, the 'mother road'? The Rock 'n Roll Road! Thousands of miles driving from Chicago to Los Angeles finishing at Santa Monica.

Hang on, I feel another book coming on …

THE AUTHOR

Born on Saturday 21st May 1966, David Kindon was only two months old when the England football team achieved its finest victory to date and so obviously he wouldn't remember it, but apparently threw his teddy out of the pram when the Germans equalised!

A modest footballer at school and in minor Leagues preceded a few hundred senior appearances in both the Plymouth & District League on Saturday afternoons and in the Plymouth Sunday League. A week after his twenty-eighth birthday, a local shock occurred on a Bank Holiday weekend when as a player/manager he led a team of pub players to victory over a side dotted with semi-professional footballers in a Sunday Cup final.

Deciding to step down and walk away to another pub side, he then enjoyed five years of playing without the hassles of management and gained a League winners medal to fulfil his own personal double.

Plymothian born bred and buttered, he still has a fondness for his local team Plymouth Argyle even though he stopped watching them as a regular supporter in 1990 and is a passionate fan of the England side.

Having worked in the construction industry his entire adult life, he has found the time to raise money for his local hospice and his preferred charity, the PDSA, by finishing the London marathon and Plymouth half-marathon respectively, and is a great believer in raising awareness for the mental health charity MIND which is close to his heart.

Living a quiet life in an even quieter street, he loves to spend his time beating the bookies, keeping fit, socialising with friends and annoying people on social media.

The publisher

*He who stops
getting better
stops being good.*

This is the motto of novum publishing, and our focus
is on finding new manuscripts, publishing them and
offering long-term support to the authors.
Our publishing house was founded in 1997, and since
then it has become THE expert for new authors and
has won numerous awards.

**Our editorial team will peruse each manuscript
within a few weeks free of charge and without
obligation.**

You will find more information about
novum publishing and our books on the internet:

w w w . n o v u m - p u b l i s h i n g . c o . u k

Printed in Great Britain
by Amazon